ALKALI TRAILS

OR

Social and Economic Movements
of the Texas Frontier
1846-1900

BY

WILLIAM CURRY HOLDEN, Ph.D.

Professor of History, Texas Technological College

Foreword by Lawrence L. Graves

VILLA JULIE COLLEGE LIBRARY
STEVENSON MD 21153

D1158960

TEXAS TECH UNIVERSITY PRESS

To My Wife

Alkali Trails is reproduced from a first edition copy by the Southwest Press and is published as part of the special series Double Mountain Books—Classic Reissues of the American West

© Copyright 1930 by The Southwest Press

Foreword © copyright 1998 Texas Tech University Press

All rights reserved. No portion of this book may be reproduced in any form or by any means, including electronic storage and retrieval systems, except by explicit, prior written permission of the publisher except for brief passages excerpted for review and critical purposes.

The paper used in this book meets the minimum requirements of ANSI/NISO Z39.48-1992 (R1997). ∞

Cover design by Melissa Bartz

Printed in the United States of America

Library of Congress Cataloging-in-Publication Data
Holden, William Curry, 1896-1993.
    Alkali trails, or, Social and economic movements of the Texas
frontier, 1846-1900 / by William Curry Holden.
        p. cm. (Double mountain books—classic reissues of the
American West)
        Originally published: Dallas : Southwest Press, c 1930.
        Includes bibliographical references and index.
        ISBN 0-89672-394-1 (alk. paper)
        1. Texas—History—1846-1950. 2. Frontier and pioneer life—Texas.
3. Texas—Social conditions. 4. Texas—Economic conditions. I. Title.
II. Series.
F391.H78   1998
976.4'06—dc21   98-26111
                                                    CIP

98 99 00 01 02 03 04 05 06 / 9 8 7 6 5 4 3 2 1

Texas Tech University Press
Box 41037
Lubbock, Texas 79409-1037 USA

800-832-4042
ttup@ttu.edu
Http://www.ttup.ttu.edu

FOREWORD

Curry Holden was born before the turn of the twentieth century and spent his entire life in West Texas. By the time *Alkali Trails*, his first book, appeared in 1930, he had already taught in a one-room country school, served in the army during World War I, taught at three colleges, earned his doctorate in history at the University of Texas, and become professor of history at Texas Technological College. He possessed unending vision and determination that led him throughout his career to a series of undertakings for West Texas. He visualized the need for a museum at Texas Tech and worked through the years until it was done. He realized the importance of an ancient Indian arrowhead and publicized it until the site where it was found became the Lubbock Lakesite Memorial State Park. He led in the creation of the complex of historic buildings at Texas Tech University that is now the Ranching Heritage Center. It was Curry who conceived the Project that became the two volumes of *A History of Lubbock* and to which he contributed an article on the archaeology of the region.

In Holden Hall at Texas Tech the Peter Hurd mural, which he persuaded the artist to paint, has a segment showing Hurd, J. Evetts Haley, Holden, Tom Lea and John A. Lomax drinking coffee around a campfire. One can almost hear them reminiscing about the lives and times of pioneers. In this vein he wrote *Alkali Trails* about Texas west of present-day I-35. He used as his main source country newspapers, commenting that "On the frontier this period (1846-1900) is one of adventure, of action, and of change, and nowhere can a more authentic picture of it be found than in the columns of these frontier newspapers."

It was a picture he painted, impressionistic perhaps, of how this part of the West was won. He writes as though he were talking to a friend about the land he loved and knew so well—the slaughter of the great southern herd of buffalo, the empire of the cattlemen and their trail drives to markets in Kansas, the anticipation and excitement of the pushing through of railroads, the fruitless search for gold and silver—mirages he calls them—the coming of the farmer. He tells of the growing alienation of West Texans and their demands for a division into a state of West Texas.

Through it all there runs a stream of hardships and challenges in a none-too-friendly environment for the farmer, the terror of drouths that broke many a family, and the chronic lack of money. The lighter side is here too: their three-day dances, weddings, horse races, frontier religion, and of course the editors who reported and wrote about it all. But there are no outlaws here, no John Wesley Hardins, no Dallas Stoudenmires, no King Fishers or Ben Thompsons. That he left for another day.

Curry had no intent to make a minutely detailed examination of West Texas, but for the reader of today the book is as fresh and entertaining as when he lived and wrote it. And informing as well.

Lawrence L. Graves
Lubbock, Texas, 1998

PREFACE

THE purpose of this work is to present some of the economic and social problems and movements of West Texas between 1846 and 1900. The chapters really constitute more or less isolated, descriptive studies bound together by a sort of geographic unity. It would be difficult to tie them together in any kind of organized order or sequence.

The movements for the most part are parallel to, or contemporary with, each other. Sometimes they criss-cross, and at other times they influence each other. The railroad and mineral movements were going on at the same time; they both reached their peak in 1886 and were intensified by the drouth of 1886. The mineral movement had considerable effect upon the railroad movement, but the railroad movement had little influence upon the mineral movement. The people had their amusements* from the time of the earliest settlements, but the building of railroads and the introduction of a large influx of immigrants caused the nature of the amusements to undergo a radical change.

The author wishes to call attention to the fact that the chapters on immigration and settlement, the railroad movement and the mineral movement do not pretend to be comprehensive or exhaustive. In each of these chapters he has undertaken to give the point of view of the people. In regard to the railroad movement, he makes no attempt to set forth a factual history of the roads, but he does try to show the feverish desire of the people for railroads, what they thought the railroads would do for the country, and the way they acted in order to get the railroads. The same may be said of the mineral movement. The chapter on the cattle kingdom is nothing more than a survey of the development of the cattle industry. The author realizes that the treatment of cattle trails is, at best, inadequate.

The term "West Texas" is frequently used by the author, and the reader will naturally desire to know what geographic area is included in the term. The eastern boundary is somewhat vague. It has been considered at different places at different times, and is generally considered farther west in more recent years than formerly. For the purpose of this work it has been taken as passing roughly through the tier of counties composed of Nueces, San Patricio, Live Oak, Atascosa, Medina, Kendall, Blanco, Burnet, Coryell, Bosque, Johnson, Tarrant, Denton, and Cooke counties. In a general way this line represents the western boundary of the old Spanish Province of Texas, although it is not so far west in places. It also represents the extreme western settlement in 1846, the year Texas became a state.

The Civil War and Reconstruction caused the people along this tier of counties and those who settled west of the line prior to 1861 to be exposed to Indian depredations for twenty years longer than would have been the case had it not been for those unfortunate episodes; for the frontier fell back in 1866 and 1867 to where it was in 1846. The long period, almost a generation, of common danger caused a feeling of common interest and unity among the people, which was the beginning of a distinctive West Texas spirit.

The limits of West Texas have been set off by several contributing factors of historic, economic, climatic and geographic importance. For the first thirty or forty years after the first settlements began, West Texas was regarded as a cattle and sheep country. The grazing interests constituted a different problem from, and were at variance with, the agricultural interests of the east. It was not until the penetration of railroads into West Texas, beginning about 1880, that agriculture had any appreciable part in the economic life of the region. Climatic conditions set West Texas apart. The rainfall east of the tier of counties named above is usually abundant for the needs of vegetation; to the west it is more uncertain, spasmodic and more likely to swing from one extreme to another. West Texas is more subject to periodic drouths, which tend to exert a leveling and unifying influence upon the people. The topography and flora furnish a distinctive environment for most of the region, though not for all of it. The grass-covered rolling hills of the central west and of the Staked Plains, or Llano Estacado, the mesquite trees, common to all the region except the upper Llano Estacado, the occasional patches of chaparral and cacti, the hazy blue horizons in the distance, and the shifting mirages, all tend to create a distinctive local color. West Texas, too, has its sandstorms to differentiate it from the remainder of the state.

The author is aware of the shortcomings of this volume. The treatment of none of the topics is exhaustive, although he has endeavored to approach them from a somewhat new angle. He wishes to express his appreciation to Professor Eugene C. Barker of the University of Texas for advice and suggestions in the formative period of the work and to Professor John C. Granbery and Mrs. Mary Dale Buckner of Texas Technological College for reading the manuscript and giving suggestions for its revision. The author is especially indebted to his wife for her constant aid and encouragement.

W. C. H.

Lubbock, Texas.
July 1, 1930.

CONTENTS

ALKALI TRAILS

CHAPTER I

THE NORDICS COME

WEST TEXAS is a new country so far as Anglo-American settlement is concerned, but according to recent archaeological discoveries it has been inhabited longer than any other part of the state. Pleistocene Man lived there, fashioned his exquisitely shaped arrow points, and hunted the gigantic bison whose species has now been extinct for 10,000 years. Another race of men lived in the Canadian valley of the Panhandle, built substantial houses of stone, and cultivated fields several centuries before the coming of Columbus. The civilized Pueblo Indians of the Southwest made summer camps and hunted buffalo on the Llano Estacado before the advent of the Spaniards. A few years after he was cast ashore on the Texas coast, Cabeza de Vaca, foot-sore, naked, and bronzed, trudged across the western part of the state. A few years later, in 1541, Coronado, at the head of a bedraggled army of grandees, looking for a country whose "ruler was lulled to sleep each day by the tinkling of innumerable golden bells which hung in the boughs of a giant apple tree," traveled for weeks across the Llano Estacado, a country as "level as a sea." During the remainder of the sixteenth century a series of Spanish explorers,—Espejo, Sosa, Humaña, and Oñate,—tramped across long stretches of West Texas plains. For more than a century after Cabeza de Vaca's time, Spanish activity in Texas was confined almost entirely to West Texas.

Coronado found the plains Indians, especially the Apaches

and Comanches, friendly and peaceful. These Indians hunted the buffalo on foot and moved their scanty belongings from place to place by means of dog sleds. At some time between the coming of the Spaniards and the advent of the Anglo-Americans from the east into Texas the plains Indians domesticated the horse which had migrated northward from Mexico. The horse revolutionized the Indian's manner of living, as well as his disposition. Henceforth he was a wiry, stealthy, dreaded, hostile individual, doggedly resisting all encroachments into his range.

For twenty years after Texas became a state, frontier defense against the Indians was the most vital domestic problem before the people. By the annexation agreement with the United States, Texas ceded to the general government all her material means of defense. The United States assumed full responsibility for protection against foreign foes from without and Indians from within. For the first two years after annexation, the war with Mexico occupied the center of attention. Little time or force was left to attend the needs of more than a thousand miles of newly acquired Indian frontier. Although Texas had relinquished the responsibility of defending her frontier settlements, she soon realized that if there was to be any defense she must provide it herself. Accordingly in June, 1846, the acting Governor stationed five companies of state troops at Castroville, San Antonio, Benjamin Bryant's place on Little River, Torrey's trading house on the Brazos, and on the west fork of the Trinity,— all of which constituted the first line of defense after Texas became a state.

When the United States began to withdraw forces of the regular army from Mexico in 1848, state troops on the Texas frontier were replaced by federal troops. In 1849, a more permanent line of defense was established. Beginning in the north, the new military posts consisted of Fort Worth on the Trinity, Fort Graham on the Brazos, Fort Gates on the Leon, Fort Croghan on Hamilton Creek just east of the Colorado, Fort Martin Scott near Federicksburg, Fort Lincoln on the Seco, Fort Inge on the Leona, and Fort Duncan at Eagle Pass.

By 1853, a new line of posts was established 150 miles in advance of the old one. Beginning on the north, the posts were Fort Belknap in Young County, Camp Cooper in Shackelford County, Fort Phantom Hill in Jones County, Fort Chadbourne in Coke County, Fort Mason in Mason County, Fort McKavett in Menard County, Fort Territt in Sutton County, Fort Clark in Val Verde County, and Fort Duncan at Eagle Pass. This line of posts with the addition of Camp Lancaster, Fort Bliss, and Fort Davis in 1854, and Fort Stockton in 1858 remained the line of defense until 1861.

During the Civil War frontier defense again became a state function. The Frontier Regiment, stationed in eighteen camps extending from the Trinity River in Archer County to Eagle Pass, furnished the settlements what protection it could during the first two years of the war. A system of "home defense" by the frontier counties replaced the Frontier Regiment the last two years of the war. During 1866 there was practically no frontier defense. Indians swarmed into the settlements, raiding and plundering. During that year the line of settlements fell back more than a hundred miles.

Federal troops tardily reoccupied the frontier posts in November, 1866. The post-war line of defense was practically the same as the pre-war line. Forts Concho, Griffin, and Richardson were added and Forts Chadbourne, Phantom Hill and Belnap were abandoned.

From 1848 to 1874, the frontier posts, for the most part, were inadequately manned. Throughout the period Indians frequently raided with impunity in spite of the presence of the federal troops. State troops were called out time and again to assist in stopping depredations. Until 1874 the policy of the United States government towards the Indians seemed to be a negative one. The idea was to let the Indians run at large and simply prevent them from breaking into the settlements. In the summer of 1874 the federal government changed its policy because of the aggressiveness of the Comanches and Kiowas. In a vigorous campaign in the fall of 1874 and the winter of

1874-75, the plains tribes were conquered and sent to reservations in the Indian Territory.

The removal of the Indian menace eliminated the most serious obstacle to the settlement of West Texas. A lesser obstacle remained,—the buffalo. Everywhere in the great plains area the grazing industry has preceded the small settler. Cattle raising, in turn, could not exist in West Texas until the buffalo was removed from the range.

CHAPTER II

THE BUFFALO SLAUGHTER

THE buffalo has been a considerable historic factor in Texas. The area he frequented in the state was greater than that of New England. The Indian followed him with all the diligence that the Eskimo follows the seal. When the value of the buffalo's hide was discovered, his slaughter became one of those national episodes, comparable to the "gold rush of '49," railroad building of the 80's, or the Florida real estate boom of the 1920's. The cattle industry could not extend across the Middle West until he was removed. With his extermination, the matter of frontier defense against the Indian was almost automatically settled. The buffalo was not confined to Texas, neither was the hide industry, and so it is necessary to consider that part of it which took place in Texas in connection with the movement as a whole.

The buffalo, or bison,[1] was indigenous to the area of the United States and Canada known as the Great Plains. The eastern limit of the buffalo land followed roughly from the north along the 90th meridian to the northeast corner of Iowa; then it bore slightly to the southwest, crossing the Red River about the 98th meridian, ran south in Texas to about the 31st degree of latitude, entered the southern part of New Mexico about the 104th meridian, and roughly followed the eastern slope of the Rocky Mountains to the north.

The shaggy, stupid animal was a picturesque companion to the plains Indian; but to the Indian he was more than a bit of local color. He was life itself. He was almost the Indian's only source of food, shelter, and fuel.

[1] The word "buffalo" is technically incorrect, but common usage has caused it to be almost universally used.

The number of buffalo which inhabited the plains before the advent of the white man is almost unthinkable.[2] Colonel Inman of the United States Army estimated the number slaughtered for their hides in the State of Kansas alone between 1868 and 1881. Basing his estimate upon statistics gathered from the freight departments of the railroads of Kansas, he found $2,500,000 was paid for bones gathered from the prairies to be utilized by various carbon works of the country. It required 100 carcasses to make a ton of bones, and the price averaged $8.00 per ton. This represents 31,000,000 buffalo which had died before the slaughter or were killed, in Kansas alone.[3] Colonel Inman rode with Generals Sheridan, Custer, and Sully three days through an enormous herd which must have numbered millions. In 1869, a train on the Kansas Pacific Railroad was delayed from 9 a.m. to 5 p.m. while waiting for a herd to cross the track.

Colonel Dodge of the United States Army, long stationed on the frontier, characterized the buffalo as the most unwieldy, sluggish, and stupid of all plains animals.[4] The buffalo, he says, was endowed with the smallest amount of instinct; the little he had seemed to be adapted to getting him into trouble rather than for getting him out of it. If he was not alarmed at the sight or smell of a foe, he would stand stupidly gazing at his companions in their death throes until the whole herd was shot down. He would walk unconcernedly into quicksand or a quagmire already choked with struggling, dying victims. When he made up his mind to go a certain way, it was almost impossible to divert him from his purpose. He would stampede upon the slightest pretext; the bark of a prairie dog, his own shadow, or a passing cloud would sometimes cause him to run for miles as if a real enemy were at his heels.

It was only in the organization of the herd that the buffalo showed any degree of intelligence. If one could have approached a herd unobserved and watched its movements and the apparent

[2] *Albany News,* February 20, 1891.
[3] Inman, H., *The Old Santa Fe Trail,* Macmillan (N. Y. 1897), p. 203.
[4] Dodge, R. I., *The Plains of the Great West,* Putnam (N. Y. 1877), p. 119.

discipline its leaders exerted, he would have been surprised at the uniformity with which everything moved. Frequently, a large herd would break up into many smaller ones, which would travel relatively close together, each under an independent master. Perhaps only a few rods marked the dividing line between them, but it was unmistakably plain; and each group would move systematically in one direction. This separation seemed an instinctive act. Some have said that each group was the harem of some powerful bull who kept his family in subjection; but this was not true. There was a constant shifting from one group to others. The animals in one group might be in a dozen different groups at other times. The cows and calves were always to be found in the center of the herd with the bulls on the outside. When the herds would consolidate (or divide) this relative position would always be kept. The leadership of a herd was won by hard struggle. When a bull had vanquished all rivals, he was recognized as the victor and kept his authority until some new aspirant overcame him, or he was superannuated and driven out of the herd. The old bulls would leave the herd and wander off in rear guards and flankers. It is not unlikely that this was voluntary on their part, instead of their being driven out by the younger bulls. No doubt, female companionship no longer had any charms for them. Sometimes they would leave the herd entirely and spend the last of their lives in solitude near a creek or river. An old bull wandering aimlessly about with a pack of wolves at his heels waiting for him to become too weak to resist them was certainly a picture of forlorn desolation. Like an army, a buffalo herd would keep out sentinels to give alarms. These were groups of four or five bulls which would graze at some distance from the main herd. To give the alarm they would run toward the herd; whereupon a stampede would usually follow.

As a rule, the buffalo went to water once a day, usually in the late afternoon. They would amble along, one following another in single file. This accounts for the many buffalo trails found on the plains, all of which ended at some stream or lake. As they frequently traveled 20 or 30 miles for water, the trails often became worn over a foot deep. In a somewhat similar way the buffalo wallows of the plains were made. The buffalo would paw and lick the salty alkaline earth, and when the sod was once broken the dust would be carried away by the constant action of the wind. Year after year, after more pawing, licking, rolling and wallowing a considerable hole would be made on the prairie.[5] Many a trapper's or hunter's life has been saved by finding a buffalo trail or wallow. The wallows often held great quantities of water, sufficient to save a whole company of cavalry, both men and horses.

The Indians had a number of ways of hunting the bison. The usual method was called "buffalo running," and was, next to war, their favorite sport. The Indians on horse back ran down the buffalo and killed them with bows and arrows. This method was hard on the ponies and dangerous to the riders.[6] Another method of killing the bison was by means of the "surround." James Stuart, who went to the northwest in 1857, describes this sort of hunting. The Indians ran their ponies around the herd, forming it into a compact mass. The bulls would force the cows and calves within the pack, and would then run round and round the margin, presenting themselves broadside to the Indians. Stuart says from 300 to 1000 buffalo were often killed in each of these "surrounds."

The whites, on the other hand, preferred a method of slaughter called the "still hunt."[7] The hunter would conceal himself upon a hill or in the brush and shoot the unwary victims at will. A large number could be killed in this manner in a short time.[8] The white hunters, who were mostly professionals, found this method both safe and efficient. But the Indians preferred a more sportsmanlike and active manner of hunting.

[5] *Taylor County News,* January 30, 1891.

[6] Hornaday, W. T., "Extermination of the American Bison" in Board of Regents of the Smithsonian Institution *Annual Report,* 1887, pt. 2, pp. 478–480.

[7] "Adventures on the Upper Missouri," in *Contributions to the Historical Society of Montana,* pp. 1–74.

[8] Hornaday, Smithsonian Institution *Annual Report,* 1887, pt. 2, pp. 465–470.

By 1870, the original great buffalo range had become permanently divided into two ranges. The southern buffalo ranged from North Texas to about 41 degrees 30 minutes north latitude. The northern herd ranged from about 43 degrees north latitude through the Powder River country to the British possessions.

In the winter of 1844-45 there occurred a four-foot snow in what was later known as the Laramie Plains. There was no wind, and the snow covered the surface of the earth evenly everywhere. The warm sun melted the top of the snow and that night a freeze crusted it over. Countless buffalo were caught here and perished. Since that time the buffalo have not gone there. Colonel Dodge crossed the plain in 1868 and found it covered with buffalo skulls—all apparently of the same age.

At a later date the Sioux Indians were driven by the oncoming settlers across the Missouri River. They thrust themselves between the Pawnees on the south and the Crows on the north. Long wars had taught them mutual respect, and an immense area including the Black Hills, became a no-man's-land where none of the war parties ever went. The buffalo flocked there for security. When the Pawnees were finally overthrown and forced on to their reservation, the Sioux poured into the country, found the buffalo very plentiful, discovered a ready market for their robes, and made such a furious onslaught on the animals that in a few years scarcely a buffalo could be found in all the wide area south of the Cheyenne and east and north of the Platte. This area, in which the buffalo had become practically extinct, joined the Laramie Plains country on the southwest; and there resulted a broad east and west belt from the Missouri to the Rocky Mountains which contained no buffalo.[9]

In the fall of 1870 W. C. Lobenstein was engaged in the fur trading business at Ft. Leavenworth, Kansas. Charlie Rath and Charlie Myer, buffalo hunters and adventurers, acting as agents, delivered the furs of the Indians, trappers, and hunters to Lobenstein, and were busily engaged in building up a vast fur trade.

[9] Dodge, *The Plains of the Great West*, p. 130.

In the winter of 1870-1871 Lobenstein apprised Rath of the fact that an English firm had asked for 500 buffalo hides which it wanted to use in an experiment for making leather; and if the experiment were successful, it would take an unlimited number. This would open up a new kind of trade in a leather new to the markets of the world.

Among others, J. Wright Mooar, who at that time had a contract with the government to cut timber on Smoky River, Kansas, became interested in the enterprise.[10] He gave up his timber-cutting project to enter actively into the work of killing buffalo and, thus furnished his pro rata of the first 500 hides. When Mooar had supplied his quota of the English order he had 57 hides left over. He packed these for shipment and consigned them to his brother, John W. Mooar, and brother-in-law, J. W. Combs of New York City, suggesting that they undertake to sell them to the tanners of that city, just as Lobenstein was doing to the tanners of England. When the hides arrived in New York they created a mild sensation. The hides were sold to the tanners; the experiment was made, and proved successful.

Even before the English firm had reported its success in the treatment of the buffalo hides and asked for a large number of them, Mooar was informed that the American tanners were ready to open negotiations for all the hides he could deliver. The moment it became known that a new industry was beginning which promised great returns, Charlie Myer opened a business at Ft. Dodge, dealing in hides and furnishing supplies to the Indians, trappers, and hunters over a vast section of the country. Charlie Rath started a similar business in the territory south of Ft. Dodge. The Mooar Brothers operated one of the largest buffalo outfits during the entire period of the buffalo extermination, 1871 to 1878.

By 1872, it became generally known that buffalo hides were marketable. The price at that time was about $3.75 per hide. The Union Pacific, Kansas Pacific, and Atchison, Topeka and Santa Fe soon swarmed with "would-be hunters" from the east,

[10] Hunt to Holden, July 25, 1925.

excited by the prospect of having a buffalo hunt that would pay. By rail, wagon, horseback, and afoot, the pot-hunters poured in, and the slaughter was on.

A typical buffalo hunting outfit consisted of about three men; that is, one killer and two skinners. Their equipment consisted of a wagon and a span of mules or a yoke of oxen, one or more powerful buffalo rifles, a supply of ammunition, and a goodly number of butcher knives and whet-rocks. The outfit usually had one or more saddle horses which were used for scouting, selecting new camp sites, *et cetera*, but seldom used in the hunt itself. The outfit would establish a camp at some convenient place where the buffalo were plentiful and, using this site as a base, operate daily in different directions. The killer would go out early in the morning and kill as many buffalo as the skinners could attend to that day. If the buffalo were plentiful it would take only a few hours for one man to kill more animals than two men could skin in one day.[11]

The hunters devised various methods for skinning the buffalo, but, perhaps, the most common is described by John R. Cook, an experienced buffalo hunter.

"We fastened a forked stick to the center of the hind axle-tree of a wagon, letting the end drag on the ground on an incline to say 20 degrees; fastened a chain or rope to the same axle, then we would drive up, quartering to carcass and hook the loose end of the chain over a front leg. After skinning the upper side down, then start the team up and pull the dead animal up a little, and stop. The stick prevented the wagon from backing up. Then we would skin the belly down mid-sides; start the team again and pull the carcass over, having rolled the first side of the hide to the backbone. Then we would skin down to the backbone, and the hide was separated from the carcass. We would then throw the hide in the wagon, and proceed as before until all the hides were skinned from the dead carcasses."[12] An experienced

11 *Albany News*, February 20, 1891.

12 Cook, John R., *The Border and the Buffalo*, Crane and Coe (Topeka, 1907), p. 116.

skinner would average from 20 to 40 hides a day. They were usually paid 25 cents per hide.

The hides were hauled to the camp where they were pegged to the ground with the flesh side up. After three, four, or five days, they were turned over with the flesh side down. Then, every other day they were turned over again until they were dried. After they were dried, they were stacked one on top of the other until the pile was about eight feet high. Strings would be cut from a green hide, fastened in a peg hole at the corner of the bottom hide, run through the peg hole of the top hide, pulled as tight as possible and knotted. The pile was then ready for market. In stacking, bull hides, cow hides, and calf hides were piled separately, as each type of hide had a different price in the market.[13]

The professional buffalo hunter first entered Texas from the north. In the fall of 1873, a number of hunting outfits operating from Dodge City as a base, crossed into the northern Panhandle of Texas in violation of the Medicine Lodge Treaty. The treaty, made in 1867 between the Federal Government and the Indians, reserved the region between the Arkansas and Canadian Rivers for an Indian hunting ground. White men could build trading posts in it and railroads across it, but they were not to hunt there. The buffalo hunters cared naught for a treaty. So brisk was the killing during the fall of 1873, that Charlie Myer established a supply store on the Canadian River about four miles east of some abandoned ruins. The new trading post was called Adobe Walls, a term which had been previously applied to the ruins. Charlie Rath, a competitor of Myer for the hunters' trade, soon followed with a stock of supplies. A saloon and blacksmith shop shortly made their appearance; and before June, 1874, a typical buffalo town was doing business. On June 28, several hundred Indians attacked the place. Twenty-eight men and one woman made a successful defense. The battle caused a cessation of hunting activities for a time. Some hunting was done in the Panhandle that winter, but the ugly mood of the Indians made the hunters

[13] *Ibid.*

very uneasy. Some of them decided to shift their operations to the southern part of the buffalo range.

The action of the Mooar Brothers may be regarded as typical of the change of location. In the spring of 1875, they took a long, circuitous route around the Indian country through the eastern part of Indian Territory, by Denison, Decatur, and Jacksboro to Fort Griffin. They had in their outfit twelve wagons which they loaded with supplies at Denison. At Fort Griffin, the commanding officer warned them not to go over twenty miles west of that place. In fact, he threatened to arrest them if they did so. But, once beyond the Fort, the hunters showed as fine a contempt for a Federal officer's command as for Federal treaties. They went a hundred miles instead of twenty.[14]

Other outfits, large and small, were already operating on the southern range. Some professional hunting had been done in 1874.[15] By the fall of 1875, the slaughter was definitely under way in an organized and systematic manner. Fort Griffin was the principal supply base. Several immediate supply camps soon sprang up on the range itself, such as Buffalo Gap in Taylor County, Hide Town, afterwards Snyder, in Scurry County, and Rath City in Stonewall County.

The destruction of the herds went on at an increasing rate throughout 1876 and 1877. Operations were temporarily suspended during the hot weather of the summer months. As soon as the northers of early winter began, the herds started southward and the booming of the hunters' "Sharp's 44's" or "Big 50's" was heard anew.[16] As time passed, the number of hunters increased. The *Frontier Echo* estimated there were 1500 outfits on the range west of Fort Griffin in February, 1877. The greatest slaughter came in the winter of 1877-1878. More than 100,000 hides were taken in the months of December and January on the Texas range. No large herds were left east of the Staked

[14] Mooar, J. W., "Frontier Experiences," *West Texas Historical Association Yearbook*, IV, 89.

[15] Webb, W. P., "A Texas Buffalo Hunt," *Holland's Magazine*, October, 1927.

[16] *Fort Griffin Echo*, January 4, 1879.

Plains. Many of the hunters began to leave the range during the spring and summer of 1878. Some went to the mines of Colorado and Mexico, some went to the Black Hills to help exterminate the northern herd, others went back to "the states," while a number remained to take up ranching on sites already selected.

In the winter of 1878-79, several small herds were found in the Yellowhouse, Blanco, and Palo Duro Canyons, in the valley of the Canadian River, and along other water courses traversing the Staked Plains.[17] The hunters still in the country gave the animals no rest. A few of the animals escaped the hunters, and propagated the rapidly vanishing species for another season.[18] A few stragglers were seen on the Staked Plains in December, 1880. After the winter of 1880-81, practically the only buffalo to be found in Texas were in the tame herds of a few cattlemen.

Along with the buffalo hunter came another character peculiar to the plains area, the freighter. It was his mission to transport the hides to some shipping point. A freighter usually had two wagons, a lead wagon and a trail wagon, drawn by six yoke of oxen. Two hundred hides were considered a load for the lead wagon and a hundred and fifty for the trail wagon. When crossing bad places the wagons were uncoupled and pulled over one at a time. It was not an uncommon sight to see as many as twenty-five outfits crossing the range at one time.

Every hunting outfit had at least one freight wagon which was used to haul hides to some supply post where they could be sold to the buyers. The larger outfits operated several freight wagons and often hauled their pelts to Fort Griffin or to the railroad towns of Fort Worth, Dallas or Denison. The professional freighter hauled for the hide buyer. He loaded his wagons at Fort Griffin or the range supply posts and transported the hides to the railroad points. In March, 1876, the agent of W. C. Lobenstein was advertising for freighters to haul a half million pounds of buffalo hides from Fort Griffin to Dallas or Denison. The rates were $1.25 per hundred pounds to Dallas and $1.50 to

17 *Frontier Echo*, December 6, 1878.
18 *Fort Griffin Echo*, November 4, 1879.

Denison.[19] The great bulk of the hides went to Dallas. The busiest time for the freighter came between April and July. Often during that time more than a hundred wagons a day passed Weatherford en route to Dallas.[20]

Some of the hides were utilized at Fort Griffin. A tannery was established there in the spring of 1880. The buffalo was becoming exceedingly scarce by that time. The tannery, therefore, operated but one season.[21]

The sale of buffalo meat was a rather important item throughout the decade of the slaughter. Compared to the hide industry, the meat business was negligible; yet, all the frontier newspapers and many over the state at large made frequent mention of the price of buffalo steaks, showing that its use was rather widespread.

The hunters who undertook to traffic in meat took the cuts from the animal at the same time the hide was removed. From the cows and yearlings they took the hump, tongue, backstrip, tenderloin, and the hind quarters. From the bulls they usually took nothing except the tongue. The fresh meat was hauled to camp where a long ditch was dug and lined with hides. In this they salted down the meat, using large quantities of salt. The meat remained in the salt pit five or six days to draw out the blood. Then it was taken up and placed on scaffolds built of mesquite or willow poles. A slow, smoke fire was kept going under the scaffold for two weeks. Green mesquite or willow with dry brush or buffalo "chips" were used as fuel. In time, a crust would form outside the chunks of meat. When treated in this fashion the meat would keep fresh and sweet. After it was "cured," it could be handled like stove wood.[22] Wagon load after wagon load passed from the buffalo range into the settlements.

The sequel to the hide industry was the bone hauling business.

[19] *Frontier Echo*, March 24, 1876.
[20] *Galveston News*, June 6, 1876.
[21] *Fort Griffin Echo*, May 22, 1880.
[22] Webb, W. P., "A Texas Buffalo Hunt."

After the hides were taken from the bodies, a part of the flesh was devoured by the carnivorous animals of the range, but the most of it rotted. In the course of a few years nothing was left of the buffalo but their bones bleaching whiter and whiter in the sun. Carcasses were scattered over the entire buffalo range. On killing grounds where the hunters had got good "stands," many acres were literally covered with bones.

Fertilizer and carbon companies were utilizing bones in the manufacture of their commodities. As soon as the railroads reached the old buffalo range, buyers began to offer six dollars per ton for bleached bones. Before the bone era closed they were selling for twice that amount. The first Texas shipment was made from Abilene to New Orleans early in 1881. As soon as the news of the shipment was broadcasted through the country bone haulers hurried to all parts of the old buffalo range. Soon thousands of tons of bones were being shipped from all the nearby railroad stations. Colorado, Sweetwater, Abilene, Baird, and Albany were the principal shipping points.[23]

Thousands of people went bone gathering. A man never thought of traveling through the country with an empty wagon. Freighters carrying cargoes of supplies to ranches and inland towns always returned to the railroad points with their wagons loaded with bones. One freighter hauling wire to the Quitaque Ranch in the Panhandle realized $1500 in one season from bones alone by bringing back a load each trip. The "bone boom" proper lasted over a year, but the hauling went on in ever decreasing degree for ten years.

The prairies presented a unique sight during the "bone boom." Great piles of white bones could be seen scattered at irregular intervals in various directions. Many of them were as large as a two-story house. Probably all the bones within a mile had been collected and put in one of these piles. A person with some degree of sentimentality might observe that these white mounds were temporary monuments in memory of the slaughtered buffalo. Perhaps, they were.

[23] *Fort Griffin Echo*, January 21, 1882.

The bone gatherers soon developed a code of procedure. They recognized the same system of individual rights which the buffalo hunters observed. Each man had a sort of "right of discovery" to a particular locality. He would stack the bones on his "pre-empted" area, and then put up some kind of sign on which he wrote his name. This action denoted ownership. The unwritten law demanded that all persons respect owner's rights, or take the consequences.

The scenes about the towns during the bone-hauling days were something like those today in a cotton growing region during the gathering season. The roads coming into town were filled with wagons loaded with bones.[24] On the streets the bone wagons could be seen standing, with buyers going from one to another bidding on the contents. Those who had sold their bones were unloading beside the railroad switch tracks. They pitched the bones into long piles. The heaps were often several hundred yards long and six to eight feet high.[25] Every freight train going east carried a few cars of bones. Occasionally, an entire train load would be sent out.[26]

As long as bones were easy to get and the hauls were short, everybody was anxious to make the easy money hauling afforded. When bones became scarce and the hauler had to look in the most out-of-the-way places to find them, fewer and fewer people engaged in the occupation. In all, more than a half million tons of bones were shipped over the Texas Central and the Texas and Pacific railroads. Estimating an average price of six dollars a ton, the total shipments aggregated over $3,000,000.

The events taking place in Texas had their counterpart in the buffalo region to the north. The northern herd lasted two or three years longer than the Texas herd. It is estimated that between 1870 and 1875, after the completion of the Union Pacific Railroad, the average destruction on the entire buffalo range was about 2,500,000. The last Dakota buffalo were destroyed by the

24 *Haskell Free Press,* August 28, 1886.
25 *Taylor County News,* February 24, 1893.
26 *Fort Griffin Echo,* January 21, 1882.

Indians in 1883, leaving less than 1000 individuals in the United States. A count in 1903 put captive buffalo at 1119, of which 969 were in the United States, 41 in Canada, and 109 in Europe. At the same time it was estimated that there were 34 wild buffalo in the United States and 600 in Canada.

The extermination of the buffalo has been considered by many people as wanton wastefulness. The *Weatherford Times* vigorously agitated for a state law in Texas to prohibit the slaughter of buffalo for their hides alone. That newspaper would have made it unlawful to leave buffalo meat to rot on the range.[27] Some writers lament the butchery as a national calamity.[28] Others have insisted that the buffalo hunters were directly responsible for the outbreak of the Indian wars of 1874-75, and those during the next several years.

On the other hand, the buffalo hunters, themselves, insist they have rendered a great service in removing the buffalo from the plains. Their attitude was expressed by General Phil Sheridan before the Texas Legislature in 1875. At that time the Legislature was considering a bill to protect the buffalo. General Sheridan, in command of the Southwestern Department and stationed at San Antonio, appeared before a joint meeting of the Senate and House of Representatives and told them they were making a sentimental mistake. Instead of stopping the hunters, he said, the Legislature should give them a hearty, unanimous vote of thanks and appropriate money to present to each hunter a medal of bronze with a dead buffalo on one side and a discouraged Indian on the other. He said:

"Those men have done more in the last two years and will do more in the next year to settle the vexed Indian question than the entire regular army has done in the last 30 years. They are destroying the Indian's commissary; and it is a well known fact that an army losing its base of supplies is placed at a great disadvantage. Send them powder and lead, if you will, and for the sake of a lasting peace, let

[27] *Frontier Echo*, December 14, 1877.
[28] Biggers, Don H., "Buffalo Butchery in Texas," in *The Cattleman*, January, 1926.

them kill, skin, and sell until they have exterminated the buffalo. Then your prairies will be covered with speckled cattle and the festive cowboy, who follows the hunter as a second forerunner of civilization."[29]

The question of the justice and expediency of exterminating the buffalo, then, is a moot one which will never be settled. However that may be, one thing is clear: the buffalo has had a place in the history of Texas and the great plains region generally. The plains Indian depended upon it for food and clothing. Because of this fact the Indian developed certain nomadic traits. He learned to live and fight in the open country. When the white man came in contact with the Plains Indian, he had to modify his way of living and methods of warfare in order to compete with the Indian. Frontier influences tend to leave a permanent imprint on the locality where they operated. So, it may be argued that the buffalo has left a stamp, indirectly at least, upon later-day plains culture. With vast herds exterminated, the way was cleared for the rapid expansion of the cattle kingdom across the old buffalo range.

[29] Cook, *The Border and the Buffalo*, p. 113.

CHAPTER III

THE CATTLE KINGDOM

OUT of the ruin, desolation and despair of the same war which laid prostrate in the Southland the cotton kingdom, there arose conditions which were shortly to call forth a new kingdom, one that was more romantic, more arduous, more adventurous and more far-flung than the old. The cattle baron was a more lordly person in many respects than the ante-bellum cotton planter. More medieval, to be sure, not so polished, not so elegant in dress or manner, he exercised within his domain a power all but absolute. His brand was his "coat of arms." The loyalty of his cowboys to his interest was like that of vassals in a feudal army. The everyday equipment of one of these leathery knights of the cattle industry was far more deadly than that of his prototype in the days of chivalry. The area of the cattle kingdom within a decade after its beginning was more than twice that of the cotton kingdom during the '50's.

There was nothing new about the cattle business. As Badger Clark puts it, "since the days when Abraham and Lot split the Jordan range in two, just to fix it so their punchers wouldn't fight," grazing has had a more or less important place in the vocational life of all peoples. It was especially true in the expansion and development of the Latin-Americans and the Anglo-Americans in the New World. The Spaniard with his long-horned cattle and hard riding *vaqueros* moved northward from the interior of Mexico. The American with his domestic cattle moved westward from the Atlantic seaboard. The two movements met in southern Texas. From their fusion resulted the cattle kingdom.

Columbus was scarcely in his grave when cattle from Andalusia were transported to stock the *haciendas* of the *conquista-dores* in Mexico.[1] Cortez, before his death, entered the cattle business and introduced the use of the branding iron. This happened just 400 years ago.[2]

As the industry expanded and extended northward, the *vaquero,* the forerunner of the American cowboy, came into being. These fellows, hard riders and as tough as the wiry ponies they rode, acquired a skill which was uncanny in the use of their lassos, the training of their mounts, and the management of the cattle. The last named job was no easy one. The cattle were long-legged, active, and vicious.

Almost two centuries passed before the cattle business crossed the Rio Grande. When the Ramon expedition, under the leadership of that shrewd Frenchman, Saint Denis, came into Texas in 1716, it brought "one thousand head of livestock," consisting of "cattle, sheep, and goats." Gil Ybarbo, who founded Nacogdoches, was a considerable cowman himself. It is known that there were a number of Spanish ranches between the Nueces and the Rio Grande, even before Mexico freed herself from Spain.[3] When Mexico inaugurated the empresario system, after 1821, among others obtaining colonization contracts was Martin De Leon, a Mexican stockman. He founded Victoria, and the "hundred and fifty families" he brought consisted, for the most part, of his *vaqueros.*

At the same time, the Anglo-American colonists were coming and bringing along their milch cows. The Kuykendalls drove several head of cows to the Colorado River from Natchitoches in 1821. Soon afterwards, William Morton brought milch cows into the region now known as Fort Bend County. Randal Jones went to Louisiana and purchased sixty head of cattle and drove them to the banks of the Brazos. So it went. Almonte reported to the Mexican Government in 1833 that there were 25,000 cattle

---

[1] *Taylor County News,* July 2, 1886.
[2] Youngblood, B., "The History of Ranching in Texas," *The Cattleman,* February, 1925.
[3] *Ibid.*

in the department of the Brazos and 50,000 in the department of
Nacogdoches. At the time, the market for Texas cattle was
Natchitoches on Red River in northwest Louisiana.[4]

The Texas Revolution came. As long as there were armies
marching and counter-marching about the state the local demand
for beef exceeded the supply. Peace came. Santa Anna
promised to send his army "beyond the Rio Grande." As Filisola
led the returning Mexican army southward, he made a hurried
and unsuccessful attempt to drive into Mexico all the cattle owned
by Mexican cattlemen between the Nueces and the Rio Grande.
For several years this region became a practically uninhabited
"no man's land." The cattle left unattended there by the
Mexicans in their pell-mell exit became "wild" cattle. Climatic
and range conditions were extremely favorable for their rapid
increase. It became quite a common practice for certain adventurous stockmen to go on round-up expeditions into the "wild"
cattle region, gather as many of the animals as possible, and drive
them back to the settlements east and southeast of San Antonio
where they were sold for "stocker" purposes. Goliad became the
first "stocker" market in Texas. The blood of the "wild"
Spanish cattle became mixed with that of the Anglo-American
domestic breed and the cattle industry, later destined to expand
across the Great Plains region to Canada, was born in the southeastern part of southern Texas in the vicinity of Victoria, Goliad,
Cuero and Gonzales.[5]

Grass was free and plentiful. The mild climate made little
tending necessary. The handling of cattle has a certain lure and
fascination. The nucleus of a herd was easy to start, for cattle
were reasonably cheap, and "wild" ones were to be had for the
taking. Consequently, many Americans soon found in cattle
raising an attraction not to be resisted. With a limited market
and an ever increasing supply the price of cattle went lower and

---

[4] A fair account of the beginning of the cattle industry in Texas is
found in Wortham, L. P., *A History of Texas*, Vol. V, ch. LXV.

[5] For a description of the capturing of "wild" cattle see Cook, James M.,
Fifty Years on the Old Frontier, Yale University Press, 1923.

lower. Cattle became so cheap that by 1845 some cattlemen were hardly taking the trouble to round-up and brand their new crop of calves each year.[6] Taxes were paid in 1846 in Texas on 382,873 head of cattle. This did not include the "wild" cattle, the unbranded cattle, and, perhaps, a great many cattle that were branded. Although the price remained low, the number of cattle increased at a phenomenal rate. In 1855, 1,363,688 head were assessed for taxes; five years later, the number had grown to 3,786,443. There were more than six times as many cattle as there were people in Texas. The normal ratio in the United States at the time was eighty head of cattle to one hundred persons. There was a shortage in New England. The market was a long way off, but indications were that a better day was ahead for the Texas cattleman. In fact, prices had already begun to take a slight rise, but the Civil War began, and all was changed.

War, as a rule, has a tendency to increase the demand for beef. Not so the Civil War, so far as Texas cattle were concerned. The Union fleet blockaded the coast; Vicksburg fell and the Mississippi was being patrolled by Federal gunboats before the close of the second year of the war. Little opportunity was left for sending beef to the Confederate armies east of the Mississippi. The Confederate and state troops located in Texas and Arkansas used some beef, but the amount was negligible compared to the millions of calves born each year on the Texas prairies. Texas, by virtue of her location, suffered less than any other Southern State during the struggle. While the armies of Sherman were "marching through Georgia" and back again through the Carolinas, and while "bushwhackers" and "jayhawkers" were devastating the border states, the cattle herds of Texas were for the most part unmolested save for an occasional Indian raid. Southern and Central Texas had become a vast reservoir of cattle.[7] Hundreds of thousands were unbranded. The state was "cattle-poor."

[6] It was in this connection that the term "maverick" originated; for an account, see Wortham, *History of Texas*, V, 152–153.

[7] Dale, E. E., "The Ranchman's Last Frontier," *Mississippi Valley Historical Review*, Vol. X, No. 1, p. 37.

At the close of the Civil War, when the paroled Texas soldier returned home, he found affairs in hard straits. There was privation on every hand. There was no money in circulation; even the taxes had been paid in kind during the last years of the war. But there were plenty of cattle.

At this same time there was a scarcity of beef in the North. The Union armies had been larger and better fed than the Confederate armies. The main source of meat supply had been the Northwest. The price of corn and wheat had been good. The farmers had found it more profitable to sell the grain than to feed it to cattle; at least, there was a quicker turn-over. With a shortage of beef in the Northwest and an ever increasing surplus in the Southwest there remained but one problem: how to get the southern beef to the northern market. The solution was found in the "northern drives."

There was nothing new about trail-driving in 1866. Cattle had been driven to Natchitoches before the Texas Revolution. During the period of the Republic, they had been driven to New Orleans and other points on the Mississippi River.[8] Numerous herds, during the late 40's and 50's, had gone from Texas to Missouri, Kansas, Nebraska, and California.[9] Saint Louis, before the Civil War, had become a considerable "stocker market." Herds from the Southwest were driven there and sold to cattle feeders from the corn belt.[10] With United States currency badly needed in Texas, it is most natural that cattlemen should have begun exercising their wits in devising ways to get their herds to a market. The Union Stock Yards at Chicago were opened Christmas Day, 1865. Railroads had been built into Missouri. Herds had previously tramped across southwestern Oklahoma and Arkansas into Missouri. Why not try that route again? So cattlemen reasoned; so they did.

The early summer of 1866 found more than 200,000 cattle

[8] Youngblood, B., "History of Ranching in Texas," *The Cattleman*, February, 1925, p. 15.

[9] *Clarksville Standard*, May 8, 1858. Allen, *Early Pioneer Days in Texas*.

[10] *Albany News*, February 29, 1884.

concentrated in northwestern Texas ready to trudge across the country to the Missouri railroad stations.[11] Visions of great profits shimmered before the imagination of the owners as they nerved themselves for greater hardships. Their rosy dreams were soon blasted by the unexpected reception given them in southeastern Kansas and southern Missouri by bands of organized, armed, and determined farmers. These fellows had a horror of "Texas fever"; it might play havoc among their milch cows. Besides, they did not relish the idea of having herds of reckless long-horn Texas cattle in the vicinity of their farms. The brutes would eat their grass, mangle their fences, and ravage their growing crops. There was "blood in the eyes" of the rustics. The drovers could only turn back or go entirely around one state and part of another. A few of the more persevering headed their herds west, and drove them along the southern Kansas line for more than two hundred miles. When beyond the settlements, they turned north to a point due west of Saint Jo. Then, turning east, they drove to Saint Jo, and from there shipped their cattle to Chicago over the Hannibal and Saint Jo Railroad. The route was long and circuitous, but Texas cattle had found their way to the new stock yards at Chicago; and the drovers with real money, perhaps the first they had seen in years, jingling in their pockets were ready to go back to Texas and spread their joyous report among their less fortunate neighbors. The northern market had been tapped.

It still remained, however, to make the shipping facilities more accessible to the Texas cattleman. Joseph G. McCoy, a stock raiser in Illinois, had an idea. The Kansas Pacific Railroad was building west through the north central part of Kansas and in the spring of 1867 was already past the outskirts of the settlements. McCoy made a trade with the Kansas Pacific for a percentage of the revenues derived from cattle shipments he might solicit for the road, built cattle pens at Abilene, and sent a drummer south in the spring of 1867 to intercept the herds going north and tell the drovers of the new shipping point. The scheme

[11] *Amarillo News-Globe,* June 13, 1926.

worked; McCoy congratulated himself for having rendered humanity a great service, and, afterwards, wrote a book to prove it.[12]

The drives of 1867 were extremely disappointing. Fate seems to have had all the cards stacked against the drover that year. Heavy rains during the spring and summer had caused the grass to become coarse and sappy, with little nutritive value. Stampedes were frequent. Rainstorms flooded the rivers, causing delays. An epidemic of cholera left thousands of dead cattle along the trail. There was constant danger of Spanish fever. When the herds reached Abilene, they were poor, jaded, and scarcely worth marketing.

The drover's troubles were not yet ended. Fate held two more high cards. In the first place, the corn crop had partially failed in the Northwest. Because of the shortage, there was no demand for feeders. Obviously there was nothing left to do but to offer the cattle, with their raw bones and huge stomachs, for immediate slaughter.

In the second place, the ready market was hard to find. Northern people had heard weird tales about the long horns of Texas. Their meat was considered by many persons to be about as "palatable as that of prairie wolves." It would require time for them to find that Texas beef recently fattened was as good as native beef. But the cattle forced on the market in the summer and fall of 1867 were not fat. The first shipment from Abilene was sent to Chicago, but it returned no profit. The second was sent to Albany, New York. This shipment of 900 head sold for $300 less than the freight bill. The New Yorkers saw no more Texas cattle on the hoof that year. From first to last 35,000 were driven to Abilene and disposed of during the year.[13]

More than 75,000 cattle arrived in Abilene in 1868. About a fourth of the number was taken by Illinois grazers and shipped

[12] McCoy, J. G., *Historic Sketches of the Cattle Trade of the West and Southwest* (Kansas City, Mo., 1874).

[13] Emerson Hough has commemorated one of the initial drives of 1867 in his book, *North of '36.*

to pastures in the early summer. Something else happened that season, a thing of far-reaching consequences for the future development of the cattle kingdom. A few cattlemen had just begun to push out beyond the settlements in the Northwest territories. By accident two years before it had been discovered that cattle could winter without shelter on the northern plains.[14] "Stocker" cattle were still scarce in the Northwest. A few of the operators of the new region went to Abilene in the summer of 1868 and bought several thousand of the Texas cattle. It was more or less of an experiment. When the buyers from Illinois and the territories had purchased what they wanted, all demand ceased, with more than half the year's drive still herded on the prairies about the town.

To add to the depression of the owners, new cases of Spanish fever were developing each day among the cattle. The raisers of the native cattle in Illinois became alarmed and appealed to the state legislature for quarantine protection. The solons responded with the Anti-Texas Cattle Act. The original bill was an unconditional embargo against Texas cattle. They could not be brought into the state or even shipped across the state. Things were looking rather bad for the drovers. The cattlemen, a rather clever lot on the whole, found they could do some lobbying themselves. Unable to prevent the passage of the bill, they secured an amendment which would permit the introduction of Texas cattle into the state, provided they had been "wintered" in Kansas. Therein lay a joker. It was astonishing how many "wintered" cattle arrived in Abilene during the seasons following. A cattleman could arrive with a herd fresh from Texas in the afternoon, visit a disreputable notary public in the evening, and the next morning send out a shipment of "wintered" cattle.

Something had to be done to dispose of the unsold cattle still being herded around Abilene in mid-summer of 1868. Those who were promoting that town as a shipping point took counsel among themselves and decided that an advertising campaign was

[14] The incident is related by F. L. Paxson in "The Cow Country," *American Historical Review*, Vol. XXII, No. 1.

needed. Handbills and posters were printed, and agents sent to
distribute them throughout the Northwest. The result was dis-
heartening. The promoters were desperate, and the drovers were
becoming glum. At last, someone had a brilliant idea. Why not
capture a car load of wild buffalo, and send them through the
North and East? Great crowds would gather everywhere to see
the animals; the newspapers would give the project more publicity than the same amount of money could possibly buy; and
the whole affair could be used to advertise Texas cattle, and
Abilene as a market. The plan worked. Buyers began to arrive
in the fall; and before the year was over, all cattle on hand were
disposed of. Abilene's future was assured; the price of cattle was
between $25 and $30 a head; the Texas cowman was jubilant.

It seemed too good to be true. All the cattle country in Texas
was astir in early spring, 1869. Men were planning bigger drives
than ever. In the midst of the big preparations, many prospective drovers did not particularly care whose cattle they rounded
into their herds. Along the edge of the settlements, many a
farmer's milch cow wandered away and never came back. Cattle
stealing became so widespread that the commanding general of
the Fifth Military District—reconstruction was at its zenith,—
was forced to issue a general order directing all post commanders
in the state to furnish military aid upon the request of any responsible person for the purpose of inspecting trail herds for stolen
cattle. In case the search revealed no stolen animals, the drover
was to be reimbursed for his delay by the party requesting the
inspection.[15] Honestly or otherwise, more than 150,000 head
arrived at Abilene during the season. The price remained good,
and the drovers brought more than $3,000,000 back to Texas, a
sum badly needed in the carpet-bagger ridden state.

Cattlemen could hardly have hoped for better conditions than
the season of 1869 had brought, but had they known beforehand
what 1870 had in store for them, they would have been beside
themselves with joy. The season was dry, the grass fine, and
driving conditions were ideal. Furthermore, the railroads east

[15] *Flakes Daily Bulletin*, July 23, 1869.

of the Mississippi River were engaged in a rate war. Each company was trying to strangle its competitor. They had not yet learned the value of agreements. Trainloads of cattle were carried from Kansas to Chicago and New York at rates as low as $1.60 per car. The result was to bring eastern beef prices to Texas cattlemen. Professional drovers sold steers for $50.00 each that they had paid $20.00 for in Texas. Over 300,000 Texas cattle were sold in Kansas during the summer, part of them going afterwards to the northwestern grazing grounds.

This unprecedented prosperity for Texas cattle raisers was not to last. When spring opened in 1871, more than 600,000 cattle were moving northward over the Kansas trail. The season was wet, the grass coarse and spongy; the streams were swollen, the cattle restless, stampedes frequent, the trails crowded. Consequently the herds reached the shipping points in poor condition, and the drovers, with their corps of cowboys, were jaded and in a bad humor. They found the railroads had adjusted their differences, and were raising the rates to compensate for the losses of the year before. Beef prices had slumped; and, as the season advanced, they went lower and lower. Winter found more than half of the year's drive unsold. More than 300,000 head were forced to spend the cold season on the plains of western Kansas and eastern Colorado. The winter was the most severe ever experienced by cattlemen in that region. A piercing blizzard swept across the plains and took its toll of cowboys and horses. It was estimated that more than a quarter million cattle perished. Many Texas cattlemen were left bankrupt.[16]

The season of 1872 was a fairly good one for drovers. The price was not much better than that of the previous year, but the demand was greater. Huge corn crops in the Northwest created a big demand for winter feeders. All the cattle driven up the trail, approximately 350,000 head, were sold before the end of the season. This same year marked the end of Abilene's career as a shipping point. The farming frontier in Kansas had been

---

[16] McCoy, J. G., *Historical Sketches*, p. 220.

moving apace. It had reached Abilene. The land was being fenced, and the farmers were complaining loudly about the proximity of so many trail herds. The Kansas Pacific built new stock pens at Fort Harker, sixty-five miles west of Abilene. Other roads were competing for the cattle trade. In the preceding year, the Atchison, Topeka, and Santa Fe had opened shipping yards at Newton, sixty miles south of Abilene. A branch line, extended from Newton to Wichita in 1872, made the latter place a shipping point. But the restless farmer would not permit any of these places to enjoy the cattle trade for long.[17]

The disasters of 1870 were repeated after a fashion in 1873. With more than half a million cattle on the trail, the outlook was hopeful enough in early spring. But again the grass was coarse and spongy. Few buyers came from the northwest territories. The cattle that had been carried to the corn belt the previous year for winter feeding were now coming on the market. Texas grass-fed cattle could not compete with corn-fed beef. September found most of the year's drive unsold, and the middle of that month brought the memorable "panic of '73." Business was paralyzed everywhere. A short corn crop curtailed the demand for winter feeders. More than 200,000 head were driven into Colorado and western Kansas for the winter. Considering the experience of the winter 1870-71, this undertaking was rather risky. Many cattlemen, not caring to take chances with the blizzards, resorted to "tanking."[18]

As the depression caused by the "panic of '73" passed, the cattle market recovered in 1874. The prices were low, but the demand for grazers in the northwestern territories and feeders in the corn belt was fair. The year's drive, together with the surplus left over from the year before, was sold. Nothing occurred during the next ten years to upset general market conditions. The prices gradually rose. Cows sold for $10 a head in

[17] *Fort Griffin Echo*, June 26, 1880.
[18] "Tanking" means slaughtering the cattle, removing the hides, horns, and hoofs, placing the rest of the carcasses in a huge tank, and cooking them for the tallow.

1875 and ten years later were bringing $25 each.[19] One must not conclude, however, that, because the demand for beef was constant and prices stable, the Texas cattle raiser was not having his ups and downs. He had the drouths, pests, plagues, and other factors to disturb his peace of mind.

The year 1876 was unusual in the history of the range industry. It marks the beginning of a rapid expansion of the cattle kingdom, which, fortunately for prices, was counterbalanced by heavy exportation of beef. It is necessary to pause long enough to survey these new movements.

The advancement of the cattle frontier in Texas, prior to 1876, had been rather slow and halting. Before 1850 the Black Prairie and Grand Prairie,[20] as well as the region south and southeast of San Antonio was given over almost exclusively to cattle raising. As indicative of the movement to the West, in 1851 David S. Files moved the first herd into Hill County; the next year, Robert K. Wylie drove a few cattle into Erath County; and in 1857 Charles Goodnight carried a herd to Palo Pinto County.[21] By 1860 the grazing industry had extended in some places as far west as the hundredth meridian. In a general way, the advance line extended from Grayson County through Wise, Stephens, Shackelford, Brown, San Saba, and Bandera counties to Kennedy County. No advance was made during the Civil War or in the first two years after the war. But beginning in 1869 the herdsmen made slow, steady headway until 1876. Then, within the space of two years, the industry shot out across the plains area, covering more territory than it had covered in the previous quarter of a century. The acceleration of the movement was due to two factors. The Indian menace had been removed by the military campaigns of 1874-75. The wild plains tribes which had so long ravaged the live stock industry of the western part of the state were defeated, rounded up, and sent permanently to the reserva-

[19] Pryor, Ike T., "The Past, Present and Future," *The Cattleman*, December, 1924, p. 13.

[20] See Simonds, F. W., *The Geography of Texas*, p. 16.

[21] McArthur Manuscript, University of Texas.

tions in Oklahoma. Scarcly had the Indians been ousted when the extermination of the buffalo was completed. The grass on an area twice the size of New England, which had previously fed millions of buffalo, was now available for cattle;[22] and, furthermore, it was free. It is not strange, then, that the cattlemen who for several years had been crowded behind the hundredth meridian should literally run over each other in order to get the choicest grazing lands to the west.[23]

A factor which tended to foment the rapid expansion of the cattle industry about 1876 was the discovery of a process of refrigeration which made it possible to send dressed beef across the ocean. Timothy C. Eastman, as a result of some experiments, began shipping beef to England in October, 1875.[24] By December of the following year, his monthly shipments had risen to more than three million pounds. In the meanwhile, other shippers had entered the business. The amount of cold storage beef exported in 1877 amounted to more than 50,000 head of cattle.[25] The traffic steadily increased during the next four years, and in 1881 almost 190,000 head were used. The utilization of refrigeration and the foreign demand for American beef came at a most opportune time for the Texas cattleman.

After 1875, it is more difficult to determine how many cattle were sent to markets outside the state. The Missouri, Kansas and Texas Railroad had just reached Denison, and the Houston

[22] *Frontier Echo,* June 30, 1876; August 4, 1876; September 27, 1878.

[23] Among cattlemen ranching west of the hundredth meridian in 1877 were: "One-armed" Jim Reed on Tonkawa Creek in Stonewall County; J. N. Simpson, running the Hash knife brand in Taylor County and the eastern part of Nolan; E. Harrell, the Ikards, Dan Waggoner, Buck Burnett, and E. P. Davis ranching along the hundredth meridian between Taylor County and Red River; the Lee-Scott Cattle Company, located in the Panhandle on the Canadian River; Adair and Goodnight in the Palo Dura Canyon region; to the south in the Concho vicinity, Ike Mullins, near old Fort Concho; R. K. Wylie in Runnels County; T. L. Odom, near old Fort Chadbourne in Coke County; De Long at Lipan Springs in Tom Green County; R. F. Tankersley, on the South Concho; and A. B. Robertson, on the Horse Head crossing of the Pecos River.

[24] *Report of the Commissioner of Agriculture,* 1876, p. 314.

[25] Nimmo, Joseph, *Range and Ranch Cattle Traffic,* p. 170.

and Texas Central was completed to Waco. Denison became a big shipping point for the next few years, and Waco became one of smaller importance.[26] The number of cattle shipped from these places was not published at the time; but reliable records were kept of the cattle going up the trail. The yearly drives for the next ten years averaged about 400,000 head. Add to this the ever increasing number carried to market by the railroads, and the average total neared the half million mark.

The medieval principality had its roads; the cattle kingdom had its trails. As it expanded, the number of trails became greater and their directions more diverse. As the years have passed numerous legends have grown up concerning them.

The historian faces a hard task today when he starts in to sift the ever-increasing mass of lore and determine those trails which the cattle actually traveled. At the outset, he faces the Chisholm Trail myth everywhere in the Southwest. The writer was once in Gonzales, and the people there explained with much pride that the Chisholm Trail headed north from that vicinity; in fact, it originated there. He was in Fort Worth, and one of the citizens, an official in the Cattleman's Association, took him down to the Trinity River and pointed out the place where the trail crossed the river. In Mason County he found the mythical trail again; this time, it was running north, slightly northwest. On a visit to Lubbock, he found it again, this time running northwest. The Boy Scout District which is comprised of Runnels, Coleman, Taylor, Callahan, Jones, Shackelford and Haskell counties bears the official title of the Chisholm Trail District. If one asks any middle-aged person who has lived more than twenty years in Texas west of a line drawn from Fort Worth to San Antonio if a cattle trail ever ran through his particular vicinity, the chances are that he will ponder a moment, then gravely reply, "Yes, the old Chisholm Trail used to run so many miles over that way," indicating the direction with a motion of his arm. For the last fifteen years a journalistic debate concerning the real route of the Chisholm Trail has been in progress. These news-

[26] *Frontier Echo*, November 26, 1875.

paper discussions usually get nowhere, for each editor upholds his particular section.

The original trail, used by freighters supplying military posts in Indian territory before the Civil War, took its name from Jesse Chisholm. He was bold and eccentric—a scout, a guide, a professional trail-blazer, a Cherokee Indian trader, a freighter, and later on a cattleman. The Chisholm Trail was followed by the first herds going to Kansas when the market was opened after the Civil War. The Indian Territory section of the trail began at the mouth of Mud Creek on Red River, followed Mud Creek to its source, turned north near the 98th meridian, paralleled the 98th meridian to Caldwell, Kansas, and continued thence to the shipping points of Wichita, Newton, Abilene, Fort Harker, *et cetera.* The Chicago, Rock Island and Pacific Railroad afterwards followed roughly the Chisholm route across Oklahoma. South of Red River the trail, fan-like, divided into several branches. These branches led, in the late '60's and '70's, into the grazing region of central and southern Texas. At the time, that part of the trail in Oklahoma was usually referred to as the Chisholm Trail, and the various sectors in Texas were known as the Kansas Trail or the McCoy Trail.

In the late '70's, when the farmer was pushing the cattle interests farther west in both Kansas and Texas, Dodge City replaced the earlier Kansas shipping points as the mecca for Texas cattle. A new trail, known at that time as the Dodge Trail, was opened. With various branches in West Central Texas—the principal one running through Mason, Brady, Coleman, and Fort Griffin to Doan's Store on Red River a few miles north of the present town of Vernon—the route crossed Red River near the mouth of its North Fork, extended across western Oklahoma in a slightly northwesterly direction between the 99th and the 100th meridian, and ran almost due north to Dodge City. Nor did it end there. Dodge City was not so much a railway shipping point, like Abilene, as it was a "stocker" market. The buffalo had scarcely been exterminated when the northwestern range cattle interests had appropriated the grass regions of western Kansas and Nebraska, North and South Dakota, eastern Colorado, Wyoming, and Montana. Since this was not a good breeding region, the operators were forced to stock with Texas cattle. A steer, bred in Texas and driven to the northwestern ranges, would fatten and gain considerably in size, due to the higher altitude, cooler climate, and more nutritive grasses. Dodge City was the meeting place of the Texas drover and the northwestern buyer. The great majority of the Texas herds changed owners as well as trail outfits, at Dodge City, and then continued to the grazing regions.

Popular belief in recent years has had it that the Dodge Trail was the old Kansas or Chisholm Trail "forced to move west." Such a conception is erroneous. The two trails were in use at the same time from 1878 to 1884. Fewer cattle went up the eastern trail each year of the concurrent operation, and more cattle went up the Dodge Trail. Only a few cattle went by Fort Worth in 1884; and, after that, none at all. A heated controversy was carried on by the *Fort Griffin Echo* and the *Fort Worth Democrat* in the spring of 1879 in regard to predictions as to how many cattle would travel by each route. The *Democrat* contended that three-fourths of the cattle from southern Texas would be driven by Fort Worth. The *Echo* disagreed. The interest and indignation of the citizens of each town was greatly aroused. A wager of $2500 was placed. Fort Worth lost; for, at the end of the season, it was found that almost half of the total drive had gone by Fort Griffin.[27]

Opened in 1865 by Charles Goodnight and Oliver Loving, the Pecos Trail was the earliest of the post Civil War period, although only third in importance.[28] The trail proper began at Fort Concho, Tom Green County, extended up the Middle Concho River to its source, proceeded on a three-day "dry drive" southwest to the Horsehead Crossing on the Pecos, and thence up

[27] *Fort Griffin Echo,* April 26, 1879; May 19, 1879; May 31, 1879; August 9, 1879.

[28] For full account of the original drive, see Dobie, J. Frank, "Charles Goodnight, Trail Blazer," *Country Gentlemen,* March, 1927. Also, *Amarillo Sunday News-Globe,* June 13, 1926.

the Pecos River into New Mexico. Some of the cattle driven over this route were sold to the United States Government for use in feeding the Indians on reservations in New Mexico. Others were used for "stocker" purposes on New Mexico ranges.

Eleven years after opening the Pecos Trail Charles Goodnight blazed another trail into Texas in 1876. He had been operating in Southern Colorado, and had decided to move his herds into the southern Panhandle of Texas. Accordingly, he trekked from Trinidad, Colorado, to the Palo Dura Canyon in Armstrong County.[29] The route followed by Goodnight later became a section of what was known as the Goodnight Trail.[30] Cattlemen from central and southern Texas, during the late '70's and '80's, desiring to drive directly to Colorado, would follow the Dodge Trail to the Double Mountain Fork of the Brazos above Fort Griffin, then turn northwest, crossing the Wichita and Pease Rivers, to Palo Duro Canyon, and thence up the route laid out by Goodnight. A later modification of the Goodnight Trail was a branch leading from Tascosa, Oldham County, in a northeasterly direction to Dodge City, Kansas.

It was not long after 1867 before trail-driving became a science, if not an art. The details were worked out by the trial and error method with scientific precision. In time, the drovers discovered the number of cattle making the most manageable, as well as the most economical unit for trail driving, the number of cowboys necessary to manage it, the number of mounts required for each man, the best way to manage the *remuda,* the kind of "chuck-wagon" to use, the type of food to carry, the best routine for the cook, how to direct the daily movements of the herd, how to bed-down and control the herd at night, what to do in time of stampedes and storms, how to swim the herd across swollen streams, and how to treat other trail outfits—the etiquette of the trail.[31]

[29] Burton, H. T., "History of the J. A. Ranch," Southwestern Historical Quarterly, XXXI, No. 3.

[30] *Amarillo Sunday News-Globe,* June 13, 1926.

[31] *Taylor County News,* September 24, 1886.

The technique of the cowboy, or his ability to manage the "critters" under his care, his capacity to tame a wild bunch of rangy longhorns and to reduce them within a few days' time to a "trail-broke," almost gentle, herd; his power to soothe the animals when restless and panicky at night by singing to them; and his skill in controlling a stampede on a dark, blustering, storming night by getting the leaders of a fleeing herd to run in a circle until eventually the whole herd was "milling,"—these phases of trail driving were an art. Space does not permit here a detailed account of a drive. Suffice it to say that life on the trail was hard, fascinating, sometimes monotonous and dreary, but always dangerous.[32] It had its joys, its adventures, its sorrows and tragedies.[33]

It has been estimated, that between 1867 and 1890 approximately 10,000,000 cattle went up the various trails. Each year there were from 150 to 200 herds of about 2500 head each.[34] A herd required about twelve men, at least six saddle horses for each man, and a mess wagon and team. The cattle traveled on an average of fifteen miles or more a day, or 450 to 500 miles a month. Each year the cattle movement up the trail required an army of approximately 2400 cowboys and 14,000 saddle horses. From first to last, between 45,000 and 50,000 cowboys using almost 300,000 saddle horses, took part in the drives. The cost of operating a trail unit was about $500 a month. It cost the drover between fifty and sixty cents to transport a cow from southern Texas to the Kansas railroad stations, and slightly more for transportation to the northwest grazing grounds. Compared with modern freight rates this was rather economical.[35]

Besides such disquieting elements as fluctuating markets and prices, drouths, floods, blizzards and plagues, the drover found

[32] *Fort Griffin Echo*, June 12, 1880.

[33] One of the best accounts of trail life is found in Andy Adam's *Log of a Cowboy*. Also, see Rollins, P. A., *The Cowboy*, ch. XIII.

[34] *Taylor County News*, July 3, 1885.

[35] Pryor, Ike T., "The Past, Present, and Future," *The Cattleman*, December, 1924.

other things to vex his spirit—inspection laws, quarantine laws, lease laws, trail laws, trail blockades by associations of other cattlemen having opposing interests, and boycotts. The drive of 1866 was almost entirely spoiled by the unfriendly attitude of the farmers in southeastern Kansas and southern Missouri. Four years later, in 1870, the commanding officer at Fort Sill ordered that henceforth no cattle should be driven into or across the Kiowa, Apache, and Comanche Reservations except for the use of the agency or the post.[36] This meant that for a time drives must keep east of the 98th meridian.

Various inspection laws were passed. In Texas some of them were enacted by the cattleman; all of them in the states to the north were aimed at him. The solons at Austin in 1874, just at the close of the "reign of E. J. Davis," were sympathetic, even solicitous, towards the cowman. Was he not bringing millions of good hard Yankee dollars into the state? If laws he needed, laws he should have. If he asked for ten, he should have a hundred. If he desired a half dozen inspectors scattered along the trails, he should have one in every western county. Furthermore, the inspector had to be careful what he did, lest he be liable to a $500 fine. Any person driving horses or cattle out of the state without first having them "road-branded" "in accordance with the 14th section" would be fined not more than $100 for each animal so driven. Should the matter of a bill of sale be overlooked in a transfer of animals or hides the purchaser would be fined a like amount. Any minor branding cattle, unless accompanied by his father, mother, or guardian, risked a heavy penalty. The same was applicable to any person altering a brand or mark. Any person selling hides without having them inspected was liable to a penalty of five dollars for each hide sold.[37] The legislative mill ground on. Scarcely three years had passed before the cattleman found himself so engulfed in legislation that the very laws first designed to help him became a maze to enmesh him. Most

[36] Grierson to Oakes, June 18, 1870, Records Adjutant General's Office, Austin.

[37] *Frontier Echo*, June 16, 1876.

of the lobbying done by the cattlemen after 1874 sought the repeal rather than the passage of laws.[38]

The next thing to tantalize the cattleman from central or southern Texas came from his own kind. By 1880 a number of drovers going to Colorado or Montana were taking the Goodnight Trail through the Panhandle country. The passing herds were spreading "Texas Fever" among the native range cattle. The cattlemen of the Panhandle met at Mobeetie, Wheeler County in July, 1880, and solemnly resolved to stop further drives through their territory, designating two trails around their ranges, one to the east to be called the Rath Trail and one to the west to be known as the Western Trail which might be used.[39] The drovers to the south and southeast did not propose to turn aside for the sake of a mere resolution, however, and the spring and summer of 1881 found herds of southern cattle on the Goodnight Trail. More cases of fever broke out. Then cattlemen of the Panhandle sent word to prospective drovers that henceforth no more herds should pass through their ranges if the outfits in charge wished to enjoy "good health."[40]

[38] *Frontier Echo,* February 1, 1879; *Mason News,* January 16, 1879; *Albany Echo,* January 12, 1884.

[39] *Fort Griffin Echo,* August 7, 1880.

[40] The following extract from the *Fort Griffin Echo,* November 8, 1881, tells its own story. Of no person in Northwest Texas, has there been so much written of as of Charles Goodnight. In fact, there is imminent danger of "cherry tree" legends growing around him. The following letter gives an insight into the straightforward character of the man, but the preceding remarks by Mr. Reynolds indicate what some of his contemporaries thought of him.

Editor *Echo:*   Fort Griffin, Oct. 5.

Herewith I hand you a letter which is so plain it requires no explanation. I desire its publication that stock men generally may know how overbearing prosperity can make a man.

Respectfully,

Geo. T. Reynolds.

Que Ti Qua Ranch, Aug. 20.

Geo. T. Reynolds, Esq.,

Dear Sir:

I send Mr. Smith to turn your cattle so they will not pass through our range. He will show you around and guide you until you strike

Before two years had passed some of the same persons against whom the Panhandle herdsmen had acted, were themselves muttering warnings to drovers trailing through their ranges. Their cattle had a way of taking up with the trail herds. The drover, apparently unconscious of the strange brands jostling about among the herd before his eyes day after day, kept serenely on, never taking occasion to cut out the "strays." The cattlemen of Callahan and adjoining counties on the Dodge Trail in solemn conclave assembled, publicly declared that a passing drover found with any of their cattle in his herd "would be prosecuted to the fullest extent of the law."[41] Incidentally, cow stealing was a penitentiary offense.

The next year, 1884, organized opposition to Texas cattle interest shifted northward. Southern Kansas ranchmen's fear of "Texas Fever" had reached a pitch which meant positive action. They had sent forth a manifesto that no southern trail herds should enter Kansas that year. Several drovers from the south with well armed outfits determined to drive as usual to the

the head of this stream and then you will have a road. The way he will show you is nearer and there are shorter drives to water than any route you can take. Should you come by here you will have a drive of 35 miles to make.

I hope you will take this advice as yourselves and I have always been good friends, but even friendship will not protect you in the drive through here, and should you attempt to pass through, be kind enough to tell your men what they will have to face as I do not wish to hurt men that do not understand what they will be very sure to meet.

I hope you will not treat this as idle talk, for I mean every word of this, and if you have any feeling for me as a friend or acquaintance, you will not put me to any desperate actions. I will not perhaps see you myself, but take this advice from one that is and always has been your friend.

My cattle are now dying of the fever contracted from cattle driven from Fort Worth, therefore do not have any hope that you can convince me that your cattle will not give mine the fever, this we will not speak of. I simply say to you that you will never pass through here in good health.

Yours truly,

C. GOODNIGHT.

[41] *Albany Star*, March 9, 1883.

shipping points in Kansas. At Campbell's Ranch in Barber County, Kansas, they met—about one hundred fifty local stockmen, fully armed. For a while war seemed imminent. In a short time, the number of belligerent Kansans increased to more than three hundred. The drovers, seeing the odds against them, backed off, and, continuing along the southern boundary, proceeded to Colorado.[42]

Kansans have always been ready to resort to the statute book for correction of offenses against their interests or piety. A law was quickly framed forbidding the introduction of Texas cattle into the state.[43] This act permanently closed the trails from Texas so far as the Sun Flower State was concerned. At the same time, Colorado passed a law requiring all cattle driven into that state from regions south of the 36th degree of latitude to be held in quarantine for sixty days in Indian territory.[44] With more than a quarter million cattle on the trail in the spring of 1885, things began to look serious for the Texas cowman. There was but one thing to do; that was to drive west through Indian territory, south of the Kansas line, to Colorado, and comply with the quarantine law there. Another unexpected obstacle arose. The Cherokee Strip had been leased by a number of large operators and cattle syndicates. These men formed one of the most efficient associations known to the cattle industry.[45] This association announced that it would oppose with every means possible the passage of Texas cattle through its region, giving fear of "Texas Fever" as the cause of their action.[46] The Panhandle cattlemen did likewise.[47] New Mexico passed a quarantine law.[48] This completed the blockade on Texas trail cattle.

[42] *Albany News*, June 20, 1884.
[43] *Taylor County News*, July 17, 1885.
[44] *Ibid.*, April 3, 1885.
[45] See Dale, E. E., "The Cherokee Strip Live Stock Association," *Proceedings of Fifth Annual Convention of the Southwestern Political and Social Science Association.*
[46] *Taylor County News*, July 3, 1885.
[47] *Ibid.*, May 15, 1885.
[48] *Ibid.*, November 20, 1885.

With more than 200,000 animals marooned in Indian territory the drovers became desperate. They appealed to the Secretary of Interior. That official, Secretary Lamar, intervened in
their behalf. After no end of bickering, several arrests, bails, and
trials, a compromise was reached, whereby the herds were allowed
to proceed to Colorado.[49]

One naturally wonders what motive was behind so much
quarantining and so many anti-Texas laws. Joseph Nimmo,
chief of the National Bureau of Statistics, declared there was
very little danger "north of 36" from "Texas Fever." The drive
of two or three months was sufficient to cure that disease. The
motive prompting the action of Northern cattlemen he pointed
out, was selfishness. They were protectionists, pure and simple,
and desired to keep Texas cattle off the market, as well as off
their ranges.[50]

When the spring of 1886 opened, the old trouble began anew.
The Panhandlers and Cherokee Strippers established another
blockade of the trails.[51] The southern drovers became uneasy
and wondered if the experiences of the preceding year must occur
again. A compromise was finally achieved at a conference composed of representatives of those opposing the drives and those
sponsoring the trail interests. The meetings were held at Trinidad, Colorado, in May, 1886. The agreement, which was in the
nature of a treaty rather than of a private contract, provided that
Texas cattle from west of a line from Wilbarger County to Eagle
Pass could pass through the Cherokee Strip without delay, provided they stayed on the trail; cattle east of this line and west of
a line from Grayson County to Laredo by way of Cameron
County could be driven through the Strip without stops, provided
they had been driven all the way. If they were shipped part of
the way, forty-five days must elapse between the time they were
unloaded from the cars and started through the Strip; all cattle
east of the last named line had to be on the trail fifty days before

[49] *Ibid.*, August 21, 1885.
[50] *Ibid.*, July 3, 1885.
[51] *Ibid.*, May 7, 1886.

entering the Strip, or if shipped part of the way, seventy-five days must elapse.[52]

After 1886, fewer and fewer cattle were driven up the trail. The ever increasing paucity was due primarily to two things: first, to the stubborn opposition of the cattlemen to the north; and, second, to that new and rapidly spreading institution, the barbed wire fence.[53] The railroads eventually came to replace the trail as a means of cattle movement. The matter of quarantine lines within Texas, dipping and tick eradication, continued to vex cattlemen through the 90's and early 1900's.[54]

Trail difficulties were only a part of the cattleman's worries. There were the elements. Cattle had a way of drifting with the wind during the severe "northers" and blizzards. Many head from Tule Canyon and north of Pease River were known to have drifted as far south as Shackelford County.[55] Prior to 1883 most of the cattlemen employed a number of men known as "line riders" to patrol the southern boundary of their range during the winter months and keep the cattle turned back. When a blizzard would sweep across the country it was not unusual for herds of shivering animals to start moving southward *en masse*. As long as the blizzard lasted it was impossible for the "line rider" to turn them. He could only follow, and when the fury of the gale abated, turn the animals back to their range. At times in the coldest weather the rider would be in the saddle almost constantly for forty-eight hours at a time, or longer. It was a hard life.

A new system was adopted in 1883. Cattlemen combined and established long strings of line camps. One of these lines, composed of three camps, extended from Colorado City to Midland along the Texas and Pacific Railroad. Another, composed of five camps, extended from the vicinity of Baird to Eastland.[56]

[52] *Albany News*, May 20, 1886. *Haskell Free Press*, June 18, 1886.

[53] *Taylor County News*, April 23, 1886.

[54] *Ibid.*, March 29, 1895; July 9, 1897; October 28, 1898; November 18, 1898.

[55] *Fort Griffin Echo*, April 10, 1880.

[56] *Albany Echo*, October 27, 1883.

The patrol from each camp set out at daylight each morning and rode until it met the patrol from the next camp, and each patrol returned to its respective camp in the afternoon. All cattle encountered during the day were driven well back north of the line. The line camps were kept up from November until March.

Soon the drift fence came to replace line riding. Such fences were usually from thirty to more than a hundred miles long. Sometimes they were built by a single cattleman or cattle company, others were constructed by associations of cattlemen. The drift fence was still in use when the open range gave way to fenced pastures. Invariably, the first barbed wire introduced into the range country was for the construction of drift fences.

In spite of the vigilance of the cattlemen during the winter months, the cattle would stray and become badly mixed. The estrays were always caught in the spring round-ups. The boss of the round-up, however, did not know the owners of animals with strange brands. It behooved every cowman, then, to make his brand as widely known as possible. A system of brand advertising developed. Editor G. W. Robson of the *Frontier Echo* devised a method of printing a picture of a cow showing the brand and marks of the advertiser. The owner's name, post office, range, and location of his headquarters were given below.[57] This system of advertising was taken up by other newspapers and became almost universal in the cow country during the 80's and early 90's.

The cattle industry had reached its peak in 1885. The price had been gradually rising since 1874. By 1882 the increasing prosperity of the cattleman was taking the form of a boom. "Grass fed" steers were selling in Chicago at $6.80 per hundred pounds. Old conservative cattlemen began to make financial plunges. The books of cattle corporations were showing annual profits of forty per cent and more. The prospect caused English and Scotch syndicates, American companies, and rich individuals to pay fabulous prices for herds, grazing rights, and ranches. The whole proceeding was characterized by a recklessness which

[57] *Frontier Echo*, December 6, 1878.

knew no bounds. The market prices on the whole were slightly lower in 1883. The following year they held their own. The outlook was favorable in the spring of 1885, but there was a break in December. A few months later, a crash came.

The boom would have no doubt crumbled of its own weight, but the thing which made the disaster so complete was an unprecedented drouth. It began in the summer of 1885 and lasted for approximately twenty-three months. The few rains that fell during the time were local. Cattlemen moved their herds hither and thither in what was often a futile effort to find water and grass.[58] The market was flooded with animals too poor to sell. Before long there was no sale at all for range cattle. Cows which had been bought for $35 a year before would not bring $5.

Cold weather found the cattle in poor condition. The winter was very severe. Every blizzard left countless carcasses along the south pasture fences and the drift fences. The veteran cowman who still had memories of reverses of the early 70's and who had estimated his wealth in six or seven digits the year before, could view these scenes philosophically. The poor creatures might as well be dead; they were not worth anything anyway.

The years of 1887, 1888, and 1889 brought a series of disasters, though in modified form. The seasons were bad, the ranges overstocked, grass scarce, and prices low. In the spring of 1890 cattlemen were feeling more hopeful than they had felt in four years, but in the latter part of March a blizzard swept the country, dealing havoc to the cattle interests. The same thing happened again just one year later. The total loss in many sections went as high as twenty per cent.[59] Range conditions were favorable for the next two years, but the price was low. In the spring of 1894, the "die-ups" of the spring of '80 were repeated. The price continued downward until 1895.[60] Although range

[58] *Albany News*, May 20, 1886; September 23, 1886.
[59] *Taylor County News*, April 3, 1881.
[60] Pryor, Ike T., "The Past, Present, and Future," *The Cattleman*, December, 1924.

conditions remained practically stationary for the next ten years, they became better and losses due to blizzards less.

Prairie fires were a constant dread of the cattleman. The drier the weather became, the drier the grass, and the greater the danger from fire. During periods of drouths, there was always the possibility that the cowman's range would be swept clean of all nutritious vegetation within a few hours, provided, of course, there was anything there to burn.[61]

If a fire started there was but one thing to do—try to stop it. If the grass was tall and the wind high, all efforts were usually hopeless. The fire would race across the country until it came to a creek, canyon, or river sufficiently wide to stop it. If the grass was short and the wind not too high, the cowboys would kill a large beef, skin the animal, and tie two lariat ropes to the fresh hide. Then, two cowboys, with the hide between them, one riding behind the blaze and the other before it, parallel to it, would ride at full speed, dragging the hide, flesh side down, along the burning edge of the grass and snuff out the blaze. This method of fire fighting was hard on the horses and dangerous to the men. Later, cattlemen came more and more to rely on fire guards, that is, a series of furrows plowed across the range. If a fire started, it would burn to one of these guards and stop.

Predatory animals were a constant source of annoyance. Coyotes and prairie wolves always took their toll during calving seasons; and, at times, the toll was heavy. Ranchmen tried various plans to prevent these destructive raids.[62]

Eventually, they came to the opinion that the only effective solution would be an organized, widespread, and concerted effort to exterminate the predatory animals. Year after year, they lobbied in the legislature for laws granting bounties for the scalps of panthers, coyotes, wolves and so on. Such measures were repeatedly voted down by representatives from East Texas. It was left to the cowman to fuss and fume and do the best he could.

[61] *Frontier Echo*, November 1, 1878; *Fort Griffin Echo*, March 1, 1879; *Albany News*, November 2, 1883.

[62] *Taylor County News*, January 20, 1899.

Disease made periodical inroads into the cattleman's herds, as well as into his profit. "Texas Fever" played havoc until the state finally got it under control by means of tick eradication.[63] For a long time, the peculiar malady of "blackleg" was widespread.[64] Each severe cold spell in the winter brought on more or less pleuro-pneumonia.[65] Occasionally, more serious epidemics, such as "charbon" (anthrax) would break out.[66]

The antipathy of the cattleman for the sheepman is an old theme, the most exploited, perhaps, of any theme connected with the cattle industry. The controversy belongs to the free grass, open range period. The cattleman claimed the country by right of discovery, priority, seniority, preëmption, and conquest. It is well known that the cattleman claimed the credit of taking the land from the Indians and making it a safe place for women and children.[67] So did the buffalo hunters; so did the Texas Rangers; and so did the United States soldiers. He deeply resented the fact that while he was taking his chances against both red man and bad man, the sheep herder was snugly tending his flocks on hillsides in the old settled parts of the state, far removed from all danger. Then when the country "had been civilized" the herder arrived with his "woolies," disputing the right of the cattleman to monopolize the land the grass which "God had made." To hear the cowman talk, said the sheepman, one would think the cowman had created both the land and the grass; or, if the cowman did give God credit for the job, he assumed that God Himself was a Cowman. The cattleman asserted that the presence of sheep in a cow country was devastating, ruinous, and annihilating to the cattle interests. The sheep clipped the grass so closely that no other animal could eat it. Their white fuzzy bodies frightened the cattle. Furthermore, any decent, self-respecting cow would never again graze where a sheep had trod, or drink where a sheep

[63] *Fort Griffin Echo,* September 4, 1880.
[64] *Taylor County News,* January 24, 1890.
[65] *Ballinger Bulletin,* October 28, 1886.
[66] *Albany News,* August 8, 1884.
[67] *Fort Griffin Echo,* September 6, 1879.

had watered.[68]   The herder was a degenerate.   He slouched about, rode a nag, and wore one spur!

The antagonism of the cattleman and sheepman in all of its variations was set forth in a violent controversy between J. C. Loving, writing in the *Fort Griffin Echo,* and J. F. Lewis, in the *Graham Leader,* during the years of 1879 and 1880.   Lewis intimated that Loving and all other cattlemen of his kind were selfish, conceited, and foolish.[69]   After replying in several long broadsides in various issues of the *Echo,* Loving finally branded Lewis as "a tramp, an ingrate, a 'Nester,' and a liar."[70]   Editor Robson of the *Echo,* after stoutly seconding everything Loving had said and taking a few hard raps at Lewis himself, said he did not approve of indulging in personalities in newspapers; so the journalistic duel came to an end.

The feud was finally terminated by natural developments. With the passing of the free range and the establishment of inclosed ranches, the cattlemen saw the possibilities in sheep and goats and took them over.   He found that his old prejudices were largely without foundation, and that sheep and goats would thrive on weeds and bushes in his pastures which the cattle did not eat.[71]

Gunpowder revolutionized warfare in the medieval kingdom; barbed wire wrought a tremendous change in the cattle kingdom. Its introduction caused the open range, free grass era to give way to that of the inclosed pasture or ranch.   The economic aspect of the whole industry was changed thereby.   Under the old regime land ownership was a small factor.   Many of the largest operators did not own any land except the plot where their headquarters stood.[72]   With the fencing of the range land, ownership became the most basic element in the industry, frequently representing a much greater valuation than the cattle upon it.   The transition required nearly a decade.   Beginning in

[68] *Ibid.*

[69] *Graham Leader,* July 26, 1879.

[70] *Fort Griffin Echo,* January 3, 1880.

[71] Corder to Holden, December 26, 1926, Archives Texas Technological College.

[72] *Taylor County News,* April 24, 1885.

South Texas in the late 70's, the fencing movement extended toward the northwest. By 1883, practically all of the cattle country of South and Southwest Texas had been converted into ranches. A herd law, making it a penalty for any person to permit his cattle to graze on land not owned by him, introduced in the state legislature by Senator Terrell in 1884, was strongly supported by the southern ranch owners and opposed by the western open range interests. Had the bill passed, it would have been disastrous for the range cattlemen. Some of the newspapers of the region openly predicted revolution.[73] The transition was shortly to come, but not so suddenly. The methods used by the cattleman in acquiring ownership to the land is a thesis subject in itself, and an interesting one. Before the decade of the 80's ended, all the cattle country was inclosed with barbed wire, and the open range was a memory.

Contemporary with the fencing movement, and often an important factor in it, was the restless and constant pressure of the settler, or "nester." This fellow, pushing relentlessly on into the range country, homesteading the most fertile lands along the watered streams, fencing the waterholes, and provoking the fence-cutting war of the early 80's, was a creature distrusted and despised by the retiring cattle barons. He forced the cattle interests farther and farther into the arid parts of the state and away from the natural watering places. This fact led to the development of another feature of the cattle business—the construction of earthen tanks, or reservoirs and the use of windmills.

Tanks for the catching of surface water were used extensively in the rolling country east of the Staked Plains where creeks and draws abound. For a number of years people doubted that the Staked Plains would ever be a cattle country. The grass was fine, but the only water was that in the surface lakes. These did not last long in dry weather. In 1881 the Quakers in Blanco Canyon, digging a well, found an abundance of water at a reasonable depth. Three years later, a cattleman by the name of W. V.

[73] *Albany Echo,* January 26, 1884.

Johnson conducted an experiment of far-reaching consequences in Lubbock County. His idea was to discover if well and windmills could be made a practical means of watering cattle. He contracted for the drilling of six wells on his land. The water used in digging the wells had to be hauled in wagons for forty miles. The plan worked. Within five years all of the Staked Plains was a cattle country.[74]

The replacement of the open range by the ranches brought something else in its wake—a general improving of the herds. As long as the grass was free, the cattleman had a relatively small overhead expense, longhorns could be raised at a profit. When he had to invest huge sums of money in land, and still more money in fencing and watering it, old-fashioned longhorns did not pay. With a limited amount of grass, and it at a premium, it was necessary to raise fewer and better cattle. A few cattlemen in West Texas foresaw the future and began to bring in small nuclei of blooded cattle as early as 1876.[75] The necessity for improving the grade of cattle was not forced upon the average cowman until he became the owner of the land he used. Then, he immediately became an apostle, preaching the gospel of thoroughbred Durhams, Herefords, or Polled Angus.[76] Some tried Brahmas. For a few years, during the late 80's, it seemed as if the Durhams would come into general use.[77] The Herefords took the lead in the early 90's and eventually came practically to monopolize the whole stage.[78]

As trail troubles thickened in 1886 and 1887, the active and alert mind of the cattleman began to ponder over closer and more available markets. Fort Worth had become a local "stocker" market in a small way as early as 1876. The next year the stock yards there were increased to a 12,000 head capacity.[79] A small plant operated by the Houston Refrigerator and Canning Com-

[74] Taylor County News, April 24, 1885.
[75] Frontier Echo, June 9, 1876.
[76] Fort Griffin Echo, July 10, 1880; July 2, 1881.
[77] Mason News, November 25, 1890.
[78] Taylor County News, August 23, 1895; November 4, 1898.
[79] Frontier Echo, May 18, 1877.

pany was exporting some dressed beef.[80] These items seemed to give the cattleman his cue. Why not build refrigeration plants and let Texas export her beef? The question was eagerly agitated throughout 1887. Everywhere in the cow country mass meetings were held to discuss it; cattlemen's conventions, both local and regional, talked about it long and earnestly; and the local newspapers made it the chief topic of discussion.[81] The matter became so familiar to the public mind that the idea came to be called "the refrigerator" in everyday parlance. Several plans were proposed; but, for some reason, no definite action was taken. The matter died down in 1888, but came to life again with more vim than ever in 1890.

In the meantime, two small private refrigeration plants had been erected, one at Columbus and one at Victoria. The successful operation of these was, no doubt, the occasion of the renewed agitation for large-scale refrigeration in the state. A cattleman's convention assembled in Fort Worth in March, 1890, primarily for the purpose of taking action on the refrigeration business. A committee of seven was appointed to make investigations and recommendations, and to report to a future meeting of the convention.[82] The committee proceeded to Columbus and Victoria, examined the plants there, studied their methods, possibilities, and contracts with foreign exporters. In their report, they enthusiastically recommended that a refrigeration corporation be organized with a capital stock of $1,000,000, part of which should be used to purchase the plants at Columbus and Victoria, and the remainder to build a huge plant at Fort Worth. The stock was to be in $100 shares, to be sold to the cattlemen of the state.[83] No positive action was ever taken on the report, and the matter dropped from sight. Fort Worth was eventually to become a

---

[80] *Mason News*, September 17, 1887.

[81] *Albany News*, August 4, 1887; *Mason News*, January 29, 1887; March 19, 1887; April 2, 1887; April 9, 1887; September 3, 1887; September 17, 1887; *Ballinger Leader*, October 7, 1887.

[82] The committee consisted of Charles Goodnight, Ike T. Pryor, R. E. Madox, J. L. Brush, A. L. Matlock, and Tom O'Connor.

[83] *Taylor County News*, April 25, 1890.

packing center, with the establishment there of plants of Swift
and Company, Armour, and other concerns, but that phase of the
Texas cattle industry belongs to the 1900's rather than within the
scope of this treatment.

Among other afflictions which beset the cattleman was the
cattle thief. The frontier had been a rendezvous for question-
able characters during the Civil War. Draft dodgers and desert-
ers had gathered there by the thousands toward the close of the
war. These fellows were forced to live by their wits. Their
palates craved beef more than anything else, and they were not
particular about whose it was. With peace, many returned to
their homes, but others had come to like this new occupation of
shifting or "rustling" for themselves. These remained and
became the nuclei of bands of lawless characters. Their numbers
were swelled by "young bloods" from the East, lured by the
adventure of outlawry. The state left the six ranger companies
of the Frontier Battalion in the field for years after the Indians
were gone, for the primary purpose of curbing the activities of
the "bad men." The cattlemen were eventually forced to an
organized effort to counteract widespread stealing. The result was
the Stock Raisers Association of Northwest Texas, organized at
Graham on February 15, 1877.[84] The association expanded, and
later consolidated with the South Texas Association, and became
the Cattle Raisers Association of Texas. Later still, it formed a
union with the Panhandle and Southwestern Stock Raisers Association and the new organization became the Texas and Southwestern Cattle Raisers Association.[85]

The original purpose of the association was to stop cattle
stealing and to afford a more adequate means of apprehending
each cattleman's estrays. Salaried inspectors were employed in
1883 to "cut" trail herds for stolen or stray animals. As the
association expanded, the number of inspectors increased.

When trail driving went out of vogue the inspectors were
located at the advantageous shipping points and stockyards. As

[84] *Fort Griffin Echo,* April 6, 1877.
[85] *The Cattleman,* March, 1924, p. 16.

time went on the association assumed other functions. A legal department was established to prosecute, without charge to the members, persons indicted for cattle theft. The association became very adept in the art of lobbying in both state and national legislative circles. It kept a vigilant eye upon all matters pertaining to transportation, accommodations, rates, and traffic schedules. Anything considered burdensome to the cattleman's interest brought forth a lusty protest.

The cattle kingdom, like the cotton kingdom, was forced to give way by the changing order of things. It required many armies of soldiers, nearly two million of them, battling for four years, to shatter the cotton kingdom. It required an army of millions of settlers a much longer period of time to break the strength of a few hundred cattle barons with their retinue of seventy-five or a hundred thousand cowboy vassals. Along with the onslaught of settlers came developments of the industrial revolution which, in themselves, would have tended to change the use of the land of the Great Plains area. The invention of barbed wire and the use of the well-drill and windmill would, no doubt, have caused the free range system to give way to the ranch, or inclosed pasture, even though the settlers had not been pushing in and homesteading the most fertile lands and the water holes. The building of railroads and the improvement of gang plows, grain drills, and reapers would have caused in time great portions of the cattle country to be diverted to grain culture by large individual operators and corporations, even though the small farmers had not appeared. The years of the old time cattleman were numbered, settler or no settler. Had the settler not arrived, the cattleman would have retained possession of the fertile and arable regions much longer. As things came to pass, however, he was pushed into the byplaces which were too arid, too rocky, too infertile, too rough, or too mountainous for agriculture.

CHAPTER IV

IMMIGRATION AND SETTLEMENT

ALTHOUGH the passing of the frontier across western Texas was a part of the great westward movement extending from the Rio Grande to Canada, there were two things which tended to make the Texas movement distinct and separate from that of the remainder of the Great Plains region of the United States. In the first place, Texas, on entering the Union, retained her public lands. This fact wielded a silent influence upon every settler who became a land owner. When he purchased a piece of land, his negotiations were with the state instead of with the central government. When he made his annual payments on his land he paid the state. When he paid interest, he remitted to the state. When he "proved-up" on his wilderness homestead, he did so to the state. When a dispute arose, during that period of the settlement of West Texas which corresponds to the territorial stage of other states, he carried on his litigation in a state court. When he felt the need of a law, during the same period, he petitioned the state legislature. When federal frontier defense against Indians bcame inadequate, and it usually was inadequate, he petitioned the governor for military aid. In short, the eyes of the original settler were turned to Austin instead of Washington as was the case in the settlement of the public domain of the United States. The influence of this fact is still evident. Perhaps, there is not to be found in any state, with the exception of the original thirteen, so much expression of state pride and patriotism as in Texas.

In the second place, the advance of the Texas frontier was separated from the major westward movement by the Indian Territory. When the United States government moved the southern semi-civilized Indian tribes west of the Mississippi River in 1834, the reservation policy was inaugurated. The Indian territory was destined to reach from the western boundary of Arkansas into that region known as the "Great American Desert." Henceforth the western migration was forced to plow in two directions. The major part of the movement went north of the Indian country along the valleys of the Arkansas, the Platte and the Missouri, while a very considerable minor movement extended south of the designated Indian region into West Texas. The Texas prong of the advance constituted a problem somewhat different from that of the northern. It was more completely isolated, and its position was more precarious. The settlers there found Indians to the right of them, in Indian territory, to the left of them across the Rio Grande in Mexico, and in front of them in the wild tribes of the plains.

Since the days when Stephen F. Austin first advertised for settlers for his Texas grant, the cheapness of Texas lands had been a foremost thought in the minds of thousands of land hungry Americans in the older parts of the United States. Under the Mexican régime a man might become the owner of a league of excellent land for a mere song. Such an attraction caused enough people to migrate to Texas within a period of twelve or thirteen years to carry out a successful revolution. One of the first acts of Congress under the Republic was to enact a law providing that any immigrant who was the head of a family might acquire from the state 1,280 acres, or two sections, of land by paying the fees of office and surveying. Any unmarried man might obtain 640 acres upon the same terms. A steady procession of land-seekers came to Texas during the ten years of the Republic. Many more would have come had peace with Mexico been assured. Mexico was still in an ugly mood and occasionally let out a muffled threat to reconquer her lost province. Then came annexation and the Mexican War, which tended to check immigration from 1846 to 1848. With Texas securely a part of the United States, the lure of its cheap land in 1849 was second only to that of gold in California. More than 5000 "movers," Texas bound, crossed the Arkansas River at Little Rock during November of that year. Of 315 wagons crossing at one ferry alone 214 were going to Texas.[1]

The frontier settlements at the time extended roughly from Cooke County on the Red River to Fredericksburg and thence to Corpus Christi, running just west of San Antonio. Once started, the never ending column of immigration moved steadily westward for the next ten years. Throughout November and December of each year the covered wagons on the main roads were seldom out of sight of each other.[2]

In 1860 the extreme frontier line of settlement extended roughly from Henrietta in Clay County, to Fort Griffin in Shackelford County, to Kerrville in Kerr County and thence to Del Rio in Val Verde County. Immigration practically ceased during the Civil War. It began to some extent in 1866, but the new comers did not settle near the frontier. There was still plenty of reasonably cheap land to be had in the Grand Prairie and Black Prairie regions of Central Texas,[3] and the immigrants preferred to pay a higher price for it than to take their chances in the country exposed to Indian depredations. Although, many people who had fled from their homes west of the Western Cross Timbers in 1866 and 1867 had returned in 1868 and 1869, the

[1] *Northern Standard*, March 2, 1850.

[2] On November 2, 1850, the *Northern Standard* observed: "For the last two weeks scarcely a day has passed that a dozen or more mover's wagons have not passed through our town. Most of the immigrants here seem to be well prepared to meet the hardship, expense and inconvenience attending the establishment of new homes in the wilderness."

On December 6, 1851, the same newspaper said: "Day after day it comes increasingly. Whenever we step to the doors or south windows of our office, looking out over the square, we see trains of wagons halted, until supplies are purchased and inquiries made about the country and the roads. . . . Upon the southern line of travel through the state, as we hear, there is the same ceaseless stream, ever moving westward." . . .

On November 11, 1854, the *Standard* stated: "The town is almost daily filled with wagons of immigrants from Tennessee, Kentucky and Alabama." Again on December 11, 1858, the same newspaper commented: "Immigration exceeds everything we have ever seen. At least fifty wagons per day pass through Clarksville."

[3] See Simonds, *Geography of Texas*, p. 16.

census of 1870 shows that the extreme frontier was considerably farther east in 1870 than in 1860. The population of all the counties west of the Western Cross Timbers was decidedly less in 1870 than in 1860. The frontier settlements advanced slowly, but steadily in the face of Indian depredations, and by 1875, they had reached the line of federal military posts. After the decisive Indian campaigns in 1875, immigration increased tremendously.

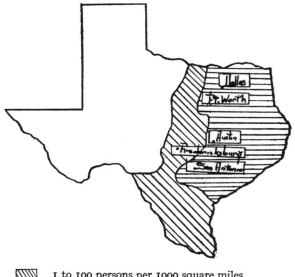

◫ 1 to 100 persons per 1000 square miles.

▤ More than 100 persons per 1000 square miles.

DISTRIBUTION OF POPULATION FOR 1860.

(Based on Federal Census, 1860.)

The movement for the next twenty-five years reached, and even exceeded, that of the 50's. People came in wagons, on horseback, and, after 1881, by train.[4] They came as individuals, as families, and as colonies.

It was estimated that over 400,000 people migrated to Texas during the year 1876. Of this number, 212,000 were brought in

[4] *Frontier Echo*, March 17, 1876.

by the Iron Mountain and the Texas and Pacific railroads. The *Frontier Echo* stated that at least half of the total number of immigrants for that year came from states north of Arkansas and Tennessee.[5] These newcomers settled in practically every part of the state east of the 100th meridian, but the region most intensely settled by them included Cooke, Montague, Clay, Wise, Jack, Young, Archer, Stephens, Erath, Comanche, Brown, and

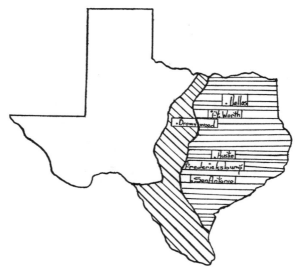

▨	1 to 100 persons per 1000 square miles.
▤	More than 100 persons per 1000 square miles.

DISTRIBUTION OF POPULATION FOR 1870.

(Based on Federal Census, 1870.)

Mills counties. A contemporary writing of the rapid settlement of Jack County, said:

"Passing to the Northwest we found farm homes thick where fifteen months ago one might travel half a day and see no human habitation. Ten Mile Prairie, situated in the north part of this county, has a new farm house on nearly every quarter section. The

[5] *Ibid.*, May 4, 1877.

inhabitants are mostly of the kind who come to stay; and realizing the fact that industry begets wealth, they have gone to work in earnest, and with good results."

This description is fairly representative of what was taking place from Montague County to Mason County. Between June, 1876, and June, 1877, almost five million acres of land was taken up under the land laws of the state. Towards the close of the year, 1877, the *Frontier Echo*, in a jubilant mood, commented:

"We will be compelled to annex Mexico and Indian territory in order to obtain elbow room. All these things are in the near future for Texas unless this immigration question is squelched."

So rapid had been the settlement that the governor issued proclamations during the first months of 1878 declaring several counties on a line with Jack County to be no longer frontier counties and forbidding the carrying of weapons therein. In the spring of 1878 the military post at Jacksboro was abandoned. Within a period of eighteen months the frontier settlements had advanced from thirty to fifty miles along the entire northwestern part of the state. From the middle of 1878 to the close of 1879 the immigrants found a halting place in the tier of counties extending from Wichita County to Coleman County.

In March, 1878, a party of farmers from Pennsylvania purchased 54,400 acres of land in Throckmorton County. The new town of Williamsburg was established, and before the close of the year the colony numbered more than four hundred.[6] About the same time a colony of four hundred German families arrived in Baylor County from the vicinity of Indianapolis. They bought 100,000 acres of land at $1.50 an acre and paid cash for it. The lot of these Germans during the first few years after their arrival was better than that of the average settler. They brought with them sufficient tools and capital to run them until a crop could be made.[7]

It is interesting to notice the effect of the coming of the actual

[6] *Ibid.*, March 8, 1878; December 14, 1877.
[7] *Ibid.*, March 15, 1878.

settlers upon the few buffalo trading posts and cow towns which
had grown up far in advance of the general frontier of settlements. They began to take on new life with the coming of the
small settlers. The town of Fort Griffin in Shackelford County
had developed from a trading post established there after the
military post was located in 1868. During the period of the
buffalo slaughter it became the chief supply station for the
hunters. Before the slaughter had ceased the new Dodge Cattle
Trail, passing through Fort Griffin, had been established, and
Fort Griffin became an important supply station for the cattle outfits going up the trail. With the influx of settlers into Shackelford County in 1878, it seemed that the future of the town was
assured. Not so, however; for the failure to secure a railroad
three years later caused the town to decline in favor of its rival,
Albany, fifteen miles south. The population of Albany, already
for several years the county seat of Shackelford County, had been
exceedingly small. After 1878 its future began to be more
promising. The same was true of Belle Plains, the county seat
of Callahan County. The town was established in the winter of
1877-78. By the summer, 1879, it had a number of stone business houses and a Methodist college.[8] Buffalo Gap in Taylor
County felt a quickening of life in 1878. The town had grown
from a buffalo camp established in 1876. When the county was
organized, in 1877, it became the county seat. From 1877 to
1881 the town was an important supply center for the cattle
range. Snyder had a like origin. A buffalo supply camp in 1876
and 1877, it took the name of Hide Town in 1878, which shortly
was changed to Snyder. Tascosa on the Canadian River in the heart
of the free range cattle country, and 300 miles beyond the line
of settlements, was established in 1876. For years it was a trading point on the cattle trail which led through the Panhandle into
Colorado, sometimes known as the Goodnight Trail. Afterwards, the town became the county seat of Oldham County.[9]

[8] *Frontier Echo,* August 23, 1879.
[9] The first decade of Tascosa's history, like that of Fort Griffin, was the
history of the typical frontier cow town or mining town. Tascosa achieved

Mobeetie, afterwards the county seat of Wheeler County, had its beginning in 1876 as a buffalo supply camp. It soon became a trading point for cattlemen, and its history as a cow town was not unlike that of Fort Griffin and Tascosa.

The several frontier towns mentioned above managed to survive, after a fashion, the coming of the settlers, the railroads, and the establishment of rival towns. With the exception of Albany, none of them were as large in 1925 as they were in 1879. Another buffalo town, Reynolds City in Stonewall County, was established in 1876 and enjoyed a remarkable boom for two years, and then disappeared almost as quickly as it started. At one time it had four general stores, a dozen saloons, a Chinese laundry, a hotel and a livery stable. The towsmen "pointed with pride" to its remarkably large graveyard and at the same time boasted of the healthy climate.

In the fall of 1877, Hank Smith, a typical and energetic frontiersman from the vicinity of Fort Griffin, trekked more than a hundred miles beyond the line of military posts, and settled in Blanco Canyon in Crosby County. The next year, Paris Cox, a Quaker from Indiana, visited the Blanco Canyon region in company with a party of buffalo hunters.[10] In the autumn of 1879 a colony of Quakers from Ohio and Indiana, under the leadership of Cox, purchased eighty-two sections of land in Lubbock and Crosby counties. Within this tract of land the town of Marietta was established. The colony continued to grow until at one time it numbered two hundred persons.[11]

With the rapid advance of the settlements after 1876, the

a national fame as the result of a cemetery known as Boot Hill. It contained the graves of twenty-seven men, all of whom died suddenly with their boots on. This cemetery came into existence at the same time as another famous Boot Hill at Dodge City.

[10] Cox Letters, McMurry College Library, Abilene, Texas. J. W. Hunt to C. V. Hall, January, 1922.

[11] In 1887 the Quakers established the Central Plains Academy with junior college rank. The colony continued to operate as such until 1891, when the organization was abandoned. Some of the Quakers went to other states, while some scattered out among other new and growing settlements in the Plains region.

cattle industry was forced to give way with equal celerity. The
movement went on in a leap-frog manner. In 1876 and 1877
cattlemen from Parker and Jack counties were busy moving their
herds from that vicinity to Stonewall, Haskell, and Knox counties.
In 1878 and 1879 cattlemen from Palo Pinto and Stephens coun-

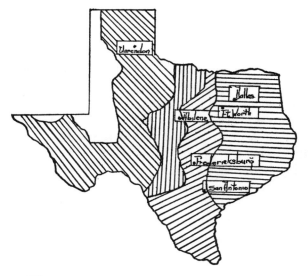

> ▨ 1 to 100 persons per 1000 square miles.
>
> ▥ 100 to 1000 persons per 1000 square miles.
>
> ▨ 1000 to 10,000 persons per 1000 square miles.
>
> ▤ More than 10,000 persons per 1000 square miles.

DISTRIBUTION OF POPULATION FOR 1880.

(Based on Federal Census, 1880.)

ties were looking for locations at the heads of the Double Mountain, Pease, and Wichita rivers.[12]

Immigration took a slightly unusual turn in Baylor County in
the spring and summer of 1879. Traces of copper had been previously found there. When the line of settlements reached the

[12] *Fort Griffin Echo,* August 2, 1879.

county, the mining prospects induced a considerable number of immigrants to go there who might have gone to other vicinities. The county seat, Seymour, was founded in June, 1879, and six months later, it had fifteen business houses with six more under construction.

Late summer, 1879, found the tide of immigrants beginning to trickle into Wilbarger, Knox, Haskell, Jones, Taylor, and Runnels counties. The country to the east was by no means thoroughly settled, and there were isolated, widely scattered settlers to the west. By actual count, forty-seven wagons passed through Fort Griffin during one week in August, 1879. Most of them were going to Haskell, Jones, and Taylor counties.

Until 1880, the settlements on the Northwest frontier advanced, on the whole, fairly evenly. In that year something happened to disturb the usual trend of things. The building of the Texas and Pacific railroad caused a long finger or prong of settlements to push out along the route of the road in Taylor, Nolan, Mitchell, and Howard counties. The railroad overtook the line of settlements in the eastern edge of Taylor County. Abilene was laid out in the fall of 1880, and within a few months was a "tent city" with more than two thousand people. Sweetwater, Colorado, and Big Spring came into existence within a year. After the arrival of the railroad, more than half the people who were to occupy the adjacent lands came by train.

In February, 1881, excitement over immigration began in a new place. Up to that time, El Paso had stood on the Mexican border, almost isolated so far as its relations with the settlements of Texas and New Mexico were concerned. The population had long consisted of "only Mexicans, old Texans, and a few hardy adventurers from other states."[13] About the middle of February, the Southern Pacific Railroad entered the town from California. For weeks the trains were crowded with passengers from the Pacific Coast, all eager to get to Texas and secure a location. Before the end of the month, the Atchison, Topeka, and Santa Fe reached the town from the north. The effect of the coming of

[13] *Ibid.*, February 26, 1881.

the two railroads was the introduction of a rough, mixed, and energetic population. Within a short time El Paso began to throw off the lethargy of an isolated Mexican village and take on the aspect of a growing American town.

The building of the Texas and Pacific caused the northwest line of settlements between 1880 and 1885 to take the form of a vast semi-circle extending from Hardeman to Midland counties by way of Haskell, Jones, and Fisher counties. The settlement of the counties along the route of the railroad was at the expense of those lying north and south of the road. The farming frontier did not advance more than forty miles west of Throckmorton and Seymour during the five years while it advanced 175 miles west of Baird.[14] The settlements in Crosby County remained isolated about the center of the semi-circle, almost due north of Big Spring and due west of Seymour. Editor Robson of the *Albany Echo* made a trip from Albany to Yellow House Canyon, Lubbock County, and back in the summer of 1883 and passed by one house on the way. The intervening country at the time was strictly a cattle region, and the house he passed was a ranch home.[15] Some eighty miles south of the route Robson traveled, and almost south of Crosby County, was a young city with almost 5,000 people, cosmopolitan airs, scores of saloons, rollicky dance halls, and a street railroad. Colorado City was the trading center for the cattle country for a hundred miles to the south and for more than 200 miles to north and northwest. Haskell, county seat of Haskell County, was not founded until the winter of 1884-85.

The influx of immigration from 1879 to 1885 had been fairly constant and normal, but in the late summer and fall of 1885 it took on unusual proportions. The good crops and general prosperity of the state set many of the people of the states north and east agog. The ferrymen along Red River worked overtime transporting covered wagons "whose tongues were pointing

[14] Throckmorton, Seymour, and Baird are approximately in a line north and south.

[15] *Albany Echo,* June 2, 1883.

west."[16] Sad times were ahead for their occupants. A West Texas drouth was setting in. Just one year later many of the same wagons with their forlorn occupants crossed the same river again. This time their tongues were pointing east.

The newcomers were optimistic enough in the fall of 1885. They continued to arrive until the spring of 1886. Not all of them were going on to the extreme frontier. Many were settling on the vacant lands in the counties considered already "settled." For instance, the line of settlement had definitely passed Callahan County during 1880. At that time the county had 3,000 population. In February, 1886, the county had 10,000 people. Regardless of where the people settled, they soon felt the pinch of dry weather. The drouth of 1886 gave the settlement of West Texas a setback from which it did not recover for several years.

Fortunate indeed was the town of Ballinger in its timely origin. The Gulf, Colorado, and Santa Fe, extending a branch line from Coleman Junction, reached the Colorado River in Runnels County in February, 1886. A town site was laid out by the railroad company on land previously purchased. A lot sale was held, and the town started off with a boom. By the middle of March, more than a thousand people were living on land which a month before had been a cattle pasture.[17] Had the railroad arrived two months later, the establishment of the town would have been delayed, no doubt, two years or longer. The building of the railroad into Runnels County stimulated, until late spring, 1886, immigration into that entire region.

By midsummer the drouth conditions had become acute. People were soon leaving the country by hundreds. The roads were full of covered wagons going east. Many of the wagons were conspicuous for the inscriptions crudely written upon the wagon sheets. One said, "In God we trusted; went west and got busted." Another, with more sentiment, had, "Last fall came from Rackin Sack, got sorry and now go rackin back"—a rather dry and cynical thrust at Fate. The drouth was broken in the

[16] *Taylor County News,* November 6, 1885.
[17] *Ballinger Bulletin,* July 9, 1886.

late spring of 1887. By midsummer, many of the drouth refugees were returning. During the summer, fall, and winter a constant line of wagons loaded with household plunder and children were daily passing through Abilene going west.[18]

A prong of settlements pushed out into the unsettled north-

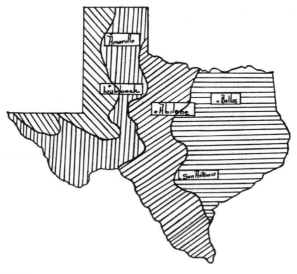

1 to 100 persons per 1000 square miles.

100 to 1000 persons per 1000 square miles.

1000 to 10,000 persons per 1000 square miles.

More than 10,000 persons per 1000 square miles.

DISTRIBUTION OF POPULATION FOR 1890.

(Based on Federal Census, 1890.)

west in 1887; for in January of that year, the Fort Worth and Denver Railroad had started building northwest beyond the line of settlements. By April, 1888, the road had been completed through Childress, Donley, Armstrong, Potter, Hartley, and Dallam counties to Texline. The towns of Childress, Clarendon,

[18] *Taylor County News*, January 7, 1888.

Amarillo, and Dalhart sprang into existence. Soon farms began to checkerboard the country adjacent to the railroad as far to the northwest as Amarillo. The building of the Fort Worth and Denver caused the North Plains to be settled approximately twenty years before the South Plains.

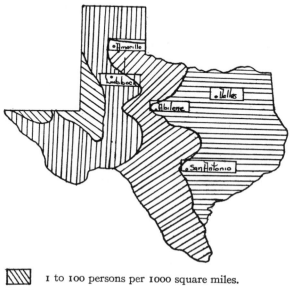

	1 to 100 persons per 1000 square miles.
	100 to 1000 persons per 1000 square miles.
	1000 to 10,000 per 1000 square miles.
	More than 10,000 persons per 1000 square miles.

DISTRIBUTION OF POPULATION FOR 1900.

(Based on Federal Census, 1900.)

A considerable change in the direction immigration was taking became manifest about 1889. Prior to that year, perhaps as many as nine-tenths of the immigrants had been diverted towards the northwest. Throughout the year, 1888, the most of them went to the North Plains, but the next year interest began to shift to the southwest. The *San Antonio Express* predicted as

early as 1883 that the southwest would have to wait for the major
part of the northwest to settle up before it could expect to make
much headway.   Some progress had been made, however.   The
Southern Pacific Railroad was extended west from San Antonio
to Del Rio in 1882 and 1883.   The building of the road stimulated some immigration along its route in Medina and Uvalde
counties.   The rise of Hondo, a new railroad town, replaced the
old German town of Castroville as county seat of Medina County.

The population of the region west of a line drawn from Lampasas, Lampasas County, by Castroville, Medina County, to
Corpus Christi, Nueces County, made a slow but consistent
growth from 1850 to 1870, and after 1870, a faster growth.
Gillespie County, for instance, had a population of 1,240 in 1850.
The German colony at Fredericksburg had been established in
1846.   In 1860 the county had 2,736 persons; in 1870, 3,566; in
1880, 5,228; in 1890, 7,056; and in 1900, 8,229.   Uvalde County
had 506 people in 1860; 851 in 1870; 2,541 in 1880; 3,804 in
1890; and 4,647 in 1900.[19]   By 1880, all Southwest Texas as far
west as the 100th meridian was fairly intensively settled, to the
extent the arid nature of the country would permit.   The building of the San Antonio and Aransas Pass Railroad from San
Antonio to Kerrville in 1886 had some influence on the number
of immigrants settling along its route.   The population of Kerr
County doubled between the time the road arrived there and 1890.

As the frontier of small settlers pushed on in the Southwest,
the aridity of the country in Kinney and Edwards counties, in the
tier of counties adjoining the Pecos River on the east, and in all
of the counties west of the Pecos caused that entire region to
remain sparsely populated.   With the exception of some small
irrigated districts along the Pecos River and at Fort Stockton,
agriculture has made but little progress in that section.   The line
of movement in the southwest took a northwesterly direction.
Beginning about 1860 with a line extending from Bandera to San
Saba counties, the settlements advanced by 1870 into Kimble,
Menard, and Concho counties, and a few venturesome spirits

[19] *Federal Census,* 1900.

were already pushing into the Concho region. A ranchman by the name of R. F. Tankersley had settled on the South Concho in 1864. The next year another, G. W. DeLong, made his headquarters at Lipan Springs in the same vicinity. When Fort Concho was established in 1868, less hardy souls had the courage to move their herds in the neighborhood of the lower Conchos where protection could be had within a day's ride. By 1874, the Concho country was deemed to have sufficient population to warrant the organization of a county. The Legislature, March 13, 1874, accordingly created Tom Green County from a region which had previously been a part of Bexar territory. The southern boundary of the new county extended from the northwest corner of Menard County to the Pecos River, and the northern boundary extended from the northwest corner of Runnels County to the Pecos. The county contained 12,500 square miles, an area larger than the State of Maryland, from which have since been carved thirteen counties.[20]

At the time of the organization of the county its legal voters numbered 160. There were but two towns in the entire area. Ben Ficklin at the stage stand of the El Paso Mail Company was located on the South Concho River five miles south of Fort Concho, and San Angelo—Santa Angela as it was originally called— on the Middle Concho, just across the river from the fort. Both places aspired to be the county seat. Ben Ficklin had the stage line, the drivers, the large force of men necessary to operate such an enterprise, and the postoffice. San Angelo had the fort, the soldiers, the payroll, and the larger array of saloons. The race waxed exceedingly warm. Tactics were used very similar to those in Kansas during the days of its territorial organization. Ben Ficklin imported the clerk of the Federal district court at El Paso, paid his expenses for a month while he quietly naturalized sixty-five Mexicans, voted them *en masse* on election day, and, much to San Angelo's chagrin, became the county seat. An

---

[20] The original Tom Green County has been divided into the counties of Coke, Sterling, Glasscock, Midland, Ector, Winkler, Loving, Irion, Reagan, Upton, Crane and Ward.

angry Fate seems to have decreed that Ben Ficklin should pay for her perfidy, however, for in August, 1882, the town was almost completely washed away. Sixty-five people lost their lives—the number of Mexicans naturalized seven years before. The county seat was moved to San Angelo, because there was nothing else to do.

The removal of the Indian menace in 1875 had some effect upon stimulating immigration into the Concho country, although not nearly so much as in the northwestern part of the state. The population of Tom Green County, which was less than a thousand in 1875, more than tripled during the next five years. In 1880 it was 3,615, of which 645 were negroes. It was not until the best available lands in the Northwest had been taken up, about 1890, that immigrants began to give serious attention to the Concho region. By 1900, the territory which had originally been included in Tom Green County had a population of 11,350, and twelve counties had been cut from it.[21]

By 1890, every part of West Texas had been settled, the greater part of it sparsely. The choicest lands had been taken, but there was still plenty of room. Immigrants continued to come and fill in the gaps. The movement was unusual in 1892 and 1893. Nearly every train from the north and east throughout the early part of 1892 was loaded with immigrants and homeseekers.[22] The same was true just a year later. The *Dallas News* reported that in one day during the first week of January, 1893, more than 500 immigrants passed through Fort Worth, some on the train, some in wagons, going northwest and southwest. And so it continued until, by 1890, the intensive settlement had gone as far in the Southwest as the arid nature of the country would permit, had reached the foot of the South Plains and had made enormous inroads into the North Central Plains. According to the Federal Census, which can never be accurate in a new and rapidly developing country, West Texas had increased from a population of 4,142 in 1850 to 755,260 in 1900.

[21] *San Angelo Standard*, May 3, 1924.
[22] *Taylor County News*, January 15, 1892.

One naturally wonders where all the people who migrated to West Texas, an area three times the size of all New England, were coming from. An analysis of their origin shows that the great majority of them came either directly or indirectly from the older states. It was a very common thing for a family to come to Texas, settle in East Texas or Central Texas for a while, and then move on to the frontier where cheap land on long time payments at a low rate of interest could be had. Judging from contemporary newspaper reports, it appears that more immigrants came from Arkansas than elsewhere; after Arkansas, in the order named, they came from Louisiana, Tennessee, Mississippi, Alabama, Georgia, Missouri, Kentucky, Kansas, Illinois, Indiana, Ohio, Pennsylvania, Iowa, Wisconsin, and the Carolinas. It is noticeable that immigrants from north of the Ohio River had a tendency to come in colonies. More than a dozen colonies, differing in size from twenty to four hundred families each, came from that region.

Prior to the building of the first railroads into the western part of the state in 1871, the greater part of the immigration from other states came by three main highways. Immigrants from the lower South, as a rule, came by way of Shreveport, Marshall, Dallas, Fort Worth, and thence to their destination. The Texas and Pacific Railroad later followed this route. Immigrants from Tennessee, Kentucky and north of the Ohio River, if they traveled overland, came by way of Memphis, Little Rock, Hot Springs, and Texarkana, at which place the route divided. One road led southwest to Dallas and Fort Worth; the other, west by Clarksville to Jacksboro.[23] With the building of improved roads in the first quarter of the century, the route from Memphis to Dallas, with some minor changes, became the Bankhead Highway. During the 70's the Iron Mountain Railroad was built, closely paralleling the wagon highway, and connecting with the Texas and Pacific at Texarkana. Immigrants from Kansas, Missouri, and Iowa, as a general thing, followed the old Butter-

[23] *Northern Standard,* December 6, 1851.

field Overland Mail[24] route. The road led by Fort Smith, Arkansas, through the southeast corner of what was then Indian Territory, crossed Red River near Denison, and thence to Jacksboro or Fort Worth.[25] During the 70's, the Missouri, Kansas and Texas Railroad paralleled this route at some distance to the west.

The hardships which the overland immigrants suffered while en route to their new homes were legion. They invariably traveled during the coldest season of the year. They could not leave the old states until they had disposed of their crops, if they were fortunate enough to have such crops, and had settled their affairs there. Then, it was necessary to make the trip to Texas, purchase land, build some kind of shelter to live under, and plow enough new sod land for a crop by planting time. To miss a crop or lose one would be disastrous. The great bulk of the moving came between November and February. Nearly all of the immigrants were on the road for weeks, many of them for months. Northers and blizzards often caught them poorly equipped to stand the rigors of cold weather. A family of four were caught in a blizzard a few miles from Clarendon in 1894. A few days later they were found frozen to death by a passerby.[26] The roads were not improved and there were few bridges. High water might delay one for days or weeks. A snow or a cold driving rain might force an encampment under the most miserable and disagreeable circumstances. Not infrequently sickness developed in the immigrant's family. After railroads were built, some of the people came on the train, but the hardships of those moving in wagons remained about the same.

One of the interesting characteristics of the whole immigration movement was the attitude which the early settlers had toward inducing other people to come and settle in their respective vicinities. As long as the country was strictly a cattle region, the cattleman looked with decided misgivings upon any attempt to

[24] The Butterfield Overland Mail was established in 1858 and ran from St. Louis to San Francisco. It was abandoned in 1860.

[25] *Frontier Echo*, January 26, 1877.

[26] *Taylor County News*, February 2, 1894.

induce farmers to come into the cattle domain. When he was forced to retire, sullenly and against his will, his successor's attitude towards immigration was the reverse. No sooner had sufficient people arrived to organize a county, than they began to take steps to encourage other people to come. They wanted neighbors, they craved the things which are made possible by community life such as social affairs, schools and churches, and they realized that land values would increase in direct proportion to the density of population. So with great zeal they turned their attention to the business of promoting immigration. Mass meetings were called. The response was spontaneous and enthusiastic. The methods used by these mass meetings were very similar to those used by chambers of commerce today, but the personnel was different. The town merchants attended the mass meetings to be sure, and furnished most of the leadership; but the great majority of those present were farmers who wore heavy shoes and long suspenders, who seldom shaved their sandy beards, and who chewed strong tobacco. The local mass meetings invariably formulated some kind of a permanent organization to carry on propaganda and entice immigrants. The permanent organizations took different names in different counties. Ballinger had the board of immigration, Abilene, the progressive committee, Brownwood, the bureau of immigration, Albany, the immigration society, and so it went. [27]

Soon the need of a state organization was felt. There was nothing new in the idea. While the state was under the Reconstruction Constitution, 1868 to 1876, a state bureau of immigration was maintained; but the whole affair was abolished by the Constitution of 1876.[28] This meant that in the future state-wide action would have to be sponsored by private enterprise. In the fall of 1887 the *Fort Worth Gazette* and *Dallas News* sponsored a state immigration convention composed of delegates elected by county mass meetings.[29] The response was enthusiastic, and the

[27] *Taylor County News,* January 25, 1887; *Ballinger Ledger,* May 20, 1887; *Albany News,* December 15, 1887.
[28] *Frontier Echo,* April 21, 1876. [29] *Albany News,* December 15, 1887.

meeting took place in December. The convention voted to organize a permanent committee on which would be one member from each senatorial district. Each senatorial district in turn was divided into county organizations. The local units were to work through the state committee, and were to be at liberty to launch any local plans they desired. To meet the expense of carrying on state wide propaganda to entice immigration, the convention asked each senatorial district to raise $600 for the use of the state committee. The district committeeman apportioned the amount among the various counties. The West Texas counties joyfully paid their pro rata share the first year. When called upon for a second year's subscription, their enthusiasm took a decided slump.

The state immigration committee did fairly good work with the means at its disposal. Much typical boosting propaganda was sent out. It served as an agency to receive and answer inquiries of prospective immigrants outside the state. It religiously and periodically sent to the various counties circulars containing the names and addresses of all persons making inquiries. It also published the same names in the *Galveston News* and *Fort Worth Gazette*. In all, the state committee did about all that could be expected of it. Yet West Texas soon cooled toward it. The real reason was not far to seek. The state immigration committee was working in the interest of all the state. West Texas wanted immigration for West Texas.

The *Anson Western* sounded the first discordant note. Why invest $50 in the state immigration bureau, when that amount of money spent in the county would pay for 10,000 circulars strictly advertising Jones County?[30] The note hit a popular response. In three weeks practically every newspaper in the surrounding region re-echoed the *Anson Western's* sentiments. That was the last year of the state immigration committee's existence.

Regional immigration associations fared better. The Southwestern Immigration Association was formed in May, 1883, at

[30] *Ballinger Leader,* September 20, 1889.

San Antonio.[31] It continued to function for more than ten years. The *Taylor County News* began to urge a West Texas Association in December, 1887. Three years passed by, and still there were no active steps towards a regional organization. The apparent lethargy was not due to lack of interest and enthusiasm on the part of the people. They had both, and an abundance to spare. They preferred to work as local units. A West Texas convention was finally called at Abilene in January, 1891.[32] The organization functioned vigorously for two months, and was heard of no more.

In September, 1889, the people of the eastern part of the state organized the East Texas Immigration Bureau. For once, West Texas was not jealous of something East Texas had done. The *Taylor County News* made the laconic comment:

"This will help West Texas, for fully half of the newcomers who may be induced to settle in East Texas will buy out and turn loose those who wish to come West."

The most successful of all the regional organizations was the Pecan, Colorado, Concho Immigration Association. It was comprised of the counties of San Saba, Brown, Coleman, Runnels, Coke, Tom Green, Glasscock, Irion, Menard, Concho, and McCulloch. The association was organized in the summer of 1890 and remained a going concern throughout the 90's. The central body, in the form of a board of directors, had the moral and financial support of active county organizations. Pamphlets were printed and broadcasted through the northern and eastern states. Agents were sent to the points where the Atchison, Topeka, and Santa Fe Railroad entered the state, for the purpose of intercepting visitors and immigrants and piloting them to the Pecan, Colorado, Concho country. Exhibition cars of native products were collected from time to time and sent to state and national fairs and exhibitions. It would be difficult to place an estimate upon the achievements of the association, but the Federal Census shows that the popula-

[31] *Albany Star*, June 1, 1883.
[32] *Taylor County News*, January 9, 1891.

tion of its constituency increased from 37,885 in 1890 to 52,890 in 1900.[33]

Aside from the activities of the Pecan, Colorado, Concho Association, the cause of promoting immigration in West Texas during the 90's was left almost entirely to the local and county organizations. They continued to function in an efficacious manner up to the close of the decade. Mass meetings retained their old popularity. County subscriptions, sometimes reaching into the four digits, were raised annually. How much good these local efforts did would be hard to say. They at least gave the earlier settlers something to do while they were waiting for the county to become thickly populated and land values to rise.

The railroads leading into West Texas became exceedingly active in promoting immigration during the decade beginning in 1889. The Texas and Pacific, the Fort Worth and Denver, the Santa Fe, the Fort Worth and Rio Grande, and the Cotton Belt vied with each other. All of them had immigration agents who spent all their time and a considerable part of the companies' earnings in making surveys, gathering statistics, publishing pamphlets with beautifully colored illustrations, elaborating on the wonderful possibilities of the country, getting up excursions from various points in the United States, arranging exhibitions, and doing scores of other things to entice hopeful immigrants into the transportation area of their respective railroads. Train loads of prospectors were hauled, at one-third to one-half fares, from Denver, Memphis and other points in the Mississippi Valley.[34] Exhibition trains, loaded with Texas exhibits, were sent through the northern and eastern states in 1891 and in 1898.[35] The effects of the railroad propaganda are not to be underestimated. The railroads, by virtue of their capital, organization, and extensive operations, held strategic places which enabled them to be a

[33] *Ballinger Leader*, August 8, 1890; *Ballinger Banner*, June 25, 1890; September 12, 1890; August 6, 1894.

[34] *Ballinger Leader*, November 1, 1889; May 23, 1890; *Taylor County News*, January 16, 1891; July 22, 1898.

[35] *Ballinger Banner-Leader*, September 3, 1891; *Taylor County News*, August 14, 1891; November 11, 1898.

powerful factor in arousing an interest on the part of prospective settlers in West Texas.

The peak in the matter of promoting immigration came in the opening of the Spring Palace at Fort Worth in 1890. A company was organized in 1889 to erect buildings and arrange annual exhibits of Texas mineral, agricultural, and horticultural products. West Texas counties responded energetically, and for the next several years tried to monopolize the whole show. Throughout the 90's the Spring Palace occupied a place in character and importance similar to that of the Dallas Fair today. Excursion trains were conducted over the various railroads leading to Fort Worth, and reduced rates were available from all points in the United States. The Spring Palace was later replaced as an annual attraction by the Fat Stock Show.[36]

The West Texas newspapers became crusaders *par excellence* in the cause of immigration. Local editors never tired of singing the praises of their respective vicinities. Several editors set aside one-eighth of the space in their newspapers for the express purpose of boosting the country and attracting immigrants.[37] Even then, they did not get to say all they wished. The result was that a surplus of unpublished propaganda was accumulated and the editors were forced to get out special boom editions periodically. These editions would sometimes contain as many as sixteen pages, fifteen of which would be devoted to booming the country.[38] They extolled the crops, the climate, the water, the people, the wind, the grass, the minerals, the potential resources, and everything else in sight. Often the editor's ingenuity exceeded his veracity. The *Taylor County News,* for instance, got out a special edition in the summer of 1898. Various local scenes were illustrated with pictures. One depicted the end of Lytle Dam at highwater. It was a reproduction of a scene showing seven children playing in the sand at the seaside, high waves, pavilion, sea

[36] *Ballinger Leader,* January 25, 1889; May 5, 1890; May 23, 1890; *Albany News,* February 28, 1889.

[37] *Taylor County News,* January 27, 1893.

[38] *Ballinger Leader,* March 8, 1889.

gulls. Another gave a glimpse in Lytle Park at Abilene, a boulevard, huge trees, a parkway, sidewalks, lamp posts, men in silk
hats, and victorias, the like of which had never been known within hundreds of miles of Abilene.

One newspaper carried in its columns, week after week, for
several months nineteen reasons why people should come and
settle in its particular locality. It began by saying "the climate is
perfect" and ended by saying "the growth of vegetation is so
rapid that in two years the home is surrounded by a growth of
trees and shrubs which would require five years to grow in a
colder climate." Another newspaper carried for months a similar
article listing "nine classes of persons who come to West Texas";
and it seemed that none were omitted. Still another editor, so
accustomed to the use of immigration terms, headed the weekly
list of births: *Our New Immigrants.* Oh, they had the fever!

Nor was that all. Every conceivable device possible was
resorted to disseminate the propaganda in other states. All
local readers were urged to send to the editor names and addresses
of prospective immigrants. Hundreds of extra copies of the
newspaper were printed each week for the purpose of being sent
gratis to such persons. Thousands of extra copies of the special
boom issue were printed. Several of the larger newspapers at
their own expense sent agents through the north and east to distribute literature and to arouse an interest in migrating to the
"land of opportunity." These efforts, put forth with such diligence by the newspapers of West Texas, could not fail to have
considerable effect in stimulating immigration to that region.[39]

The Federal government opened for settlement a district in
Oklahoma Territory containing 12,000 homesteads of 160 acres
each at high noon on April 22, 1889. More than 100,000
"sooners" were lined up on the boundary of the Territory when
the signal was given. In the grand rush that followed, there
were hair raising races, a mad scramble, violence, intimidation,
favoritism by the soldiers of the United States Army, and dis-

[39] *Ballinger Leader,* March 8, 1889; *Taylor County News,* July 22, 1898;
Mason News, March 8, 1890.

appointment for seven out of every eight who started. All of this seemed like a bit of irony to many immigration promoters in Texas, who had been begging and almost hiring immigrants to come to Texas, especially since hundreds of thousands of acres of land, practically as good as the Oklahoma land, could be had at as cheap a price and on better terms in the Panhandle of Texas.[40]

Towards the close of the decade, ending in 1900, the people of West Texas began to take a more sober view of the whole question of immigration. Many of them began to realize that in the most frenzied period of immigration and settlement many foolish and unnecessary things had been done to lure the all important settler. The *Taylor County News* sadly pointed out that "if Abilene had saved the money she spent on immigration fakes, she could have purchased sufficient land to settle 500 families on 160 acres each," and then added with a sigh that "the *News* can not afford to spend as much money during the coming year as we have in the past." The editor was unconsciously speaking a widespread sentiment. The immigration fever was passing.

[40] *Taylor County News*, May 3, 1889.

CHAPTER V

FRONTIER JOURNALISM

"THE *Coleman Courant* has pulled up stakes and moved to Colorado City, the new and growing city on the Colorado River at the crossing of the Texas and Pacific Railroad." This item appeared in the *Fort Griffin Echo* on January 15, 1881, and is typical of the shifting newspapers of the Texas frontier during the last thirty years of the nineteenth century. The editor's material equipment was scant and could be readily moved in a single wagon. It was not unusual, when an editor's business became dull, for him to box up his case of type and his hand press and follow the drift of westward migration as indicated by the advance of frontier forts or the new railroad terminals.[1]

On the Texas frontier this period is one of adventure, of action, and of change, and nowhere can a more authentic picture of it be found than in the columns of these isolated frontier newspapers where the price of buffalo steak appears casually in market advertisements, where complaints are written in no uncertain terms of the bold, bad cowboys who "shot up the town" in celebration of pay day, and where a detailed account of an accident befalling Mrs. Smith's cow finds room on the front page.

In the 70's the main interest centers about the Indian raids, General McKenzie's successfully waged Indian war of 1874-

[1] The following items are indicative of a widespread movement:

"Our neighbor and editorial brother, J. C. Son, formerly of the *Palo Pinto Star*, late of the *Mineral Wells Star*, put forth the first issue of the new venture *Albany Star* Christmas day. The *Star* is a neatly printed, well written five column folio, and is proof of Mr. Son's ability."—*Albany Echo*, January 6, 1883.

"The *Nutshell*, which lately moved from Blanco County to Bertram, has now moved to Burnett."—*Mason News*, August 27, 1887.

1875, the buffalo slaughter, 1873-1877, and the development of the cattle industry. In the 80's the cattle industry is even more important and extensive than in the previous ten years, but the all-engrossing topic is the westward movement of the railroads. With the 90's came many changes. The strife of sheepmen and cattlemen is stilled in many places by the necessity of both to push farther west as a result of the encroachments of the "actual settler" brought in by the railroads. The country gradually changes from a cattle range to an agricultural section; towns grow up, and journalism becomes a profession claiming the entire time of its followers. The editor settles down to tranquil existence in one locality and often loses much of his individualism. It is, however, with some of the characteristics of West Texas journalism in its earlier periods that we are to deal here.

The cattle industry exerted a strong influence upon the migrations of the local newspapers during the late 70's and early 80's. After the removal of the Indian menace in 1875 and the extermination of the buffalo in 1876 and 1877, the cattle industry spread over the western part of the state with great rapidity. The cow towns, as they were called, offered good opportunities for a newspaper. They were live, hustling, busy places. The cattleman used the local newspaper to advertise for his strays. The local merchants advertised their goods lavishly in order to bring their wares before the notice of the cattleman.

The *Frontier Echo* furnishes the best illustration of the tendency of a newspaper to move westward with the cattle industry. It was established in 1875 at Jacksboro in Jack County. At that time Jacksboro was a frontier cow town, and for two or three years the *Echo* thrived, but the cattle industry was hastily moving on. The story of the wanderings of the *Echo* can best be told by citing a few items from its files, which, fortunately, have been preserved. The following article appeared, December 1, 1878:

For nearly one year, we have had in mind that a newspaper published in the live stock interest of Northwest Texas would meet with public favor. This proposition being settled in the affirmative the next question is, where is the best point to issue such a paper; at one of the leading shipping places or near the center of the stock range. Good arguments could be adduced in favor of each place. We have determined upon the publication of such a paper. After careful thought and advising with many of the leading stockmen of the country, we are fully satisfied that the range is a better location for it than the railroad.

"But a few years ago, Jacksboro was headquarters for stockmen of Northwest Texas, but the settler, the small farmer, has driven the stockmen with their wealth clear to the outpost of civilization, close upon the track of the Indian. The cowboy is a picket-guard, in fact, a vidette, on the extreme outpost of Christendom and is, like the Indian, being crowded forward every year.

Fort Griffin is now headquarters for stockmen of the Northwest, and there we have determined to locate, believing we can better serve our patrons and add to our bank account there than here.

For three years and two months we have labored hard to make a living and a good newspaper for this place, how we have succeeded in our labors editorially, we leave our readers to judge.

During our residence in Jacksboro we have met with many persons whom we esteem highly and part from them with sincere regret. We shall ever cherish a warm feeling for Jack county and when occasion offers it will afford us much pleasure to say a good word. With this issue of the *Frontier Echo* we bid you all a kind adieu.

At Fort Griffin the newspaper took the name of the *Fort Griffin Echo* and flourished for almost three years. Then the natural course of development brought an end to the town's prosperity. The construction of the Texas and Pacific Railroad in 1880 and 1881 brought into existence the rival cow towns of Baird, Abilene, Sweetwater, Colorado City, and Big Spring. The fencing of the open range was causing the overland cattle trail to shift to the west. In 1881 the Texas Central Railroad arrived at Albany, fifteen miles south of Fort Griffin. When the military post was abandoned in 1882 there was nothing for the merchants, saloon keepers, and newspaper men to do but move to Albany or elsewhere. On January 6, 1883, the following item appeared in the *Albany Echo:*

Nearly one year ago the *Fort Griffin Echo* completed its third volume and closed its doors. We then said in due time would again make its appearance, but in a new place. Various causes, sickness being the principal one, have delayed the promised move and reopening until now.

The trials and tribulations of a frontier editor can be seen in a measure in the following article:

About five months ago we opened out the *Echo* in this place, issued one number, and, as most of our home people know, we then went to bed sick, and for several weeks were confined to our room. Only recently have we felt able to resume our task and even now we "tackle" it with fear and trembling for our physical ability to continue the work. So much by way of explanation. As of old, we shall endeavor to make the *Echo* a home newspaper. One fit to be read at any fireside. A long winded speech is unnecessary, but for two dollars cash we will give you the news of the town, county and a little state news, fifty-two times.[2]

Thus we see that in its migrations the *Echo* stayed three years at Jacksboro, five years at Fort Griffin and one year at Albany when it consolidated with the *Albany Star* and took the name of the *Albany News*, which it bears to the present.[3]

It was not unusual for newspapers to experience periods of boom and depression. During the 80's, while Lampasas was the terminus of the Santa Fe Railroad, the town became quite a health resort. A daily newspaper was established, but after a

---

[2] *Albany Echo*, June 2, 1883.

[3] The dates of the establishment of some of the West Texas newspapers will show the general westward trend of the journalistic advance: *Whiteman* at Weatherford about 1858; the *Weatherford Times* about 1872; *Comanche Chief* at Comanche, 1874; *Frontier Echo* at Jacksboro, 1875; *Henrietta Journal*, 1877; *Fort Griffin Echo*, 1878; *Albany Tomahawk*, 1879; *Texas Livestock Journal* at Weatherford, 1880; *Concho Times*, 1880; *Abilene Reporter*, 1881; *Mobeetie Panhandle*, 1881; *Seymour Crescent*, 1881; *Clarendon News*, 1881; *Texas Eagle*, Buffalo Gap, 1881; *Apache Rocket* at Fort Davis, 1883; *Big Spring Paragrapher*, 1883; *Albany Echo*, 1883; *Taylor County News*, Abilene, 1885; *Ballinger Ledger*, 1886; *Mason News*, 1886; *Throckmorton Times*, 1886; *Coke County Rustler*, 1890; *Coleman Enterprise*, 1890; *Devils River News*, 1890; *Fisher County Call* at Roby, 1890; *Appeal*, a religious journal at Abilene, 1894; *West Texas Stockman* at Abilene, 1896.

few months of fevered existence it was abandoned. The Fort Worth *Democrat* enjoyed a wide circulation for several years, but it was forced to suspend in 1880. The *Gazette* met the same fate fourteen years later. Buffalo Gap saw the alpha and omega of no less than three newspapers, one after another.

A noticeable characteristic of frontier journalism was that many editors had a hard time finding suitable names for their newspapers. In an old settled country names acquire dignity and prestige with age. The longer time goes on the more reluctant is the owner to change the name of his paper. Not so in a new country. There, a frequent change of names seems to help. A love of variety has precedence over reverence for the antique. The *Western Sun* in 1881, became the *Albany Sun*. An attempt to keep up with the fluctuations in the title of the Ballinger news-paper during the late 80's and 90's would make one fairly dizzy. It began as the *Bulletin;* then it became the *Banner;* next, it was combined with the *Leader* and became the *Banner-Leader;* for a while, it was the *Ledger;* and other variations followed. The Ballinger newspaper was rivaled in this rechristening tendency by the one at Albany. As a rule, a change in name resulted from a change of ownership, but not always. Sometimes, the owner merely became tired of the old name, or would conjure up some new name which he liked better than the old one. The change itself was an easy matter.

The life and success of the early newspaper depended upon the editor. He was invariably the owner, manager, editorial writer, circulation and advertising editor, and printer, in one. If business were good, he might have as an assistant a tramp printer, usually a sort of vagabond who got drunk on every possible occasion. The urge to write and something to say were the primary qualifications for an editor in the pioneer days. Teach-ers, doctors, lawyers, real estate dealers, preachers,⁴ government officials, railroad engineers, and what-nots mounted the editorial

---

⁴ All kinds of combinations took place. In 1886 the *Llano Rural* changed hands. One of the purchasers was the retiring county judge and the other was a Christian minister.

tripod with equal celerity.[5] Journalistic training was practically unknown and previous newspaper experience was not a requisite for editorial work. The editor's personality was clearly reflected in the pages of his newspaper. One can not read long in any of the old newspaper files without beginning to feel that he has an intimate acquaintance with the editor. Some of the editors were rather brilliant personalities, wide awake and aware of the historic significance of their period; others were dull, humdrum, and unimaginative.

Regardless of how droll or dull the editors were, they always had certain traits in common. Conspicuous among them was candor. The frontiersman was primarily an individualist. The frontier editor was no exception. He said whatever came into his mind. If he did not like the wart on a local citizen's nose, he said so. If someone criticized him or his paper privately, he retaliated by saying openly what he thought. Imagine the following item appearing in a present day newspaper:

"The old crank that presides over the hotel on the south side of the square, and who recently slandered another hotel, and was soundly thrashed therefor, objected to our looking over his register this morning."[6]

Caution and moderation in political affairs were unknown to the early editors. If they did not like a candidate or an office holder, they voiced their dislikes without regard to the number of subscribers they might offend. The *Throckmorton Times* in 1894 happened to mention that "Congressman C—— wrote a speech." The next week the *Wichita Herald* commented:

You are mistaken. That speech was taken out of stock, so to speak. It was a hand-me-down. Speeches of that calibre are always in stock by the regular speech peddlers in Washington, and cost only $2.40 a hundred. Of course when a Congressman wants one made

[5] *Taylor County News*, April 2, 1897; *Albany News*, July 11, 1884; *Frontier Echo*, December 3, 1875; *Mason News*, December 4, 1886; *Fort Griffin Echo*, May 1, 1880.

[6] *Albany News*, August 24, 1884.

to order, he has to pay more. Our Congressman chose the one, of course, that sold for a nominal rate.[7]

As a matter of fact, Congressman C—— was unusually popular, and such a thrust from the *Herald* was sure to alienate more patrons than it would amuse, but that made no difference.

Some of the frontier editors, seemingly realizing the power of the press, felt called upon to improve the manners and to uphold the social standards of their readers. Strange to say, they were especially adept in giving lectures in etiquette to the women. The writer has run across many such instances, and will give the following as a typical example:

A well bred girl thanks the man who gives her a seat in the street car, and does it in a quiet and not in an effusive way.

She doesn't turn around to look after gamblers or posing actors on the street, and she doesn't think that her good looks are causing the men to stare at her.

She doesn't go to supper after the theater is over alone with a man.

She does not declare that she never rides in the street cars.

She does not accept a valuable present from any man unless he expects to marry her.

She doesn't talk loud in public places.

She doesn't want to be a man, and she doesn't try to imitate him by wearing stiff hats, smoking cigarettes, and using an occasional big, big D.

She doesn't scorn the use of a needle, and expects some day to make clothes for very little people who will be very dear to her.[8]

Such bits of advice and admonition were given seriously, and were received in like manner by the readers. Much of the social advice was clipped from other newspapers and had little application in frontier communities. This fact made little difference, for the people received it eagerly.

For news frontier editors had to depend to a considerable degree upon correspondents in the various rural communities. This class of country reporters constituted a problem for the news-

[7] *Taylor County News*, March 23, 1894.
[8] *Mason County News*, November 2, 1889.

paper man. How different from the modern professional city reporter! The editors were constantly forced to give explicit directions to guide the rural correspondents. The *Mason News,* for instance, set forth specific instructions:

We want a correspondent in every neighborhood of the county to give us weekly reports showing the acts and doings of our people. We do not ask for long, prosy accounts on any subject; and these we can not publish. The items must be short and to the point. If a marriage occurs, give names of parties, date, place, and by whom married; if a death occurs, give name, date, cause and sex; if a house burns down, tell whose it was, when it burned, cause of fire, and if insured; if a murder is committed, state the simple facts; if your neighbor sells his farm, let us know to whom, price, etc.; if a house or barn is erected or other improvements going on, give us the names; give us the condition of the crops, whether there is a scarcity of rain, etc.; let us know about the schools, who are the teachers, number of scholars, etc. We do not want any gossip or slander. . . . We want facts, not fiction.[9]

It is hard to determine how well the rural reporters followed these admonitions. The editors themselves set a bad example. They could wax exceedingly long-winded over a marriage, a birth, or the real and imagined resources of the country. Their advice to their country correspondents was "do as I say, not as I do."

Early newspaper men engaged rather lavishly in "personals," —short items concerning local persons and happenings in the community. The tendency to deal in "personals" is not peculiar to the early period in journalism. It is still found in local newspapers with a small town and rural circulation. It was, however, much more prominent then than now. For instance, on one page of the *Mason News,* July 30, 1887, we find that Mr. W. sold his gin for $2,400, Mrs. C. had an attack of rheumatism, the cholera had killed Mr. B.'s chickens, the Grange was going to enlarge its store, and Mr. L. roped a steer and his horse fell with him. Similar items follow for several columns.

[9] *Mason News,* September 18, 1886.

One trait in which the pioneer editor excelled, and one which is seldom found today even among country journalists was the intimate and familiar tone with which he spoke of a local person's affairs. It was not uncommon to find items like the following:

While Frank Badger is a cripple by his horse falling on him, he thinks he would be supremely happy if he only had his best girl up in the Panhandle country to sit and read poetry to him.

Will Dodd says if he could persuade a certain young lady friend to go along, he would go to Nebraska, but he says to go alone he would feel lost and without her he would eventually be lost.

A dress that is soon to adorn the graceful form of a bride was purchased last Wednesday by a Mason young lady.[10]

Early editors were especially fond of publishing letters from citizens who traveled away from the home town. The entire front page was sometimes devoted to such a letter. Occasionally the editor would take a trip into a neighboring county; then, for several weeks after his return would give his readers an extended account in serial fashion of where he had gone and what he had seen.[11]

Early editors in West Texas were "natural-born boosters." Every editor sang the praises and consistently ignored the defects and drawbacks of his vicinity. The land was the best, the climate was superb, the rainfall abundant, the sunshine was wonderful, health was unequaled, and the people were of the highest and noblest type. Never ceasing propaganda was carried on to attract immigration. All that the immigrant had to do was to come west and settle in this or that particular locality; he would become rich, prosperous, and happy and would live to a ripe old age.

G. W. Robson, Captain Robson, as he was almost universally known, was typical of the frontier journalists. Except indirectly, we know too little about him. It seems that he had been a locomotive engineer for a while in Kansas. In 1875, he went to Jacksboro, Texas, and established the *Frontier Echo* as editor and

[10] *Ibid.,* August 13, 1887.
[11] *Ballinger Ledger,* October 23, 1887.

sole owner. In this capacity, he became one of the most influential men on the Northwest Texas frontier. He became the champion of the cattlemen. Although he never owned any cattle himself, he attended all the meetings of the cattlemen, and was one of the organizers of the Northwest Texas Cattleman's Association. He was a close friend of J. C. Loving, cattleman, journalist, and, for a generation, secretary of the cattleman's association. There was never a ball, barbecue, or meeting, professional or political, within a hundred miles to which Robson did not have a pressing invitation. People went far out of their way to extend him a favor. He was an anti-prohibitionist, and could take his "Tom and Jerry" straight. He had no fight to make on the various Temperance Unions as long as the "abstainers" clubbed together for mutual benefit and encouragement; but when they began to take an aggressive attitude, he opposed them with all the force of his straight-forward character. He was an individualist to the core. He was not a churchman, yet religious toleration never had a stronger advocate. In writing about the ladies, never was there a Kentucky colonel more gallant. He wrote up the weddings with a grand flourish, always devoting about 95% of the space to the bride. For his efforts there was always the reward of a big fine cake with white frosting. It became an unwritten law of the land, that every wedding "written-up" meant a cake for the editor. The only way to know Robson is to read the columns of the *Echo*. In that way one establishes an intimacy with him which can not be had in any other way.

Another pioneer editor of note was Edgar Rye, attorney, justice of the peace, poet, sign painter, builder, decorator, author, soap factory superintendent, and for a period quasi-vagabond, and editor. In 1890, he became joint owner and editor of the *Albany News*. Under his guidance for almost two years, the *News* became an extraordinary newspaper. Among his numerous duties, Rye found time to utilize his versatile talents in carving wood cuts with his pocket knife to illustrate his articles. Some one attempted to rob the First National Bank at Albany in

1890. Rye wrote a vivid story of the affair with all of the modern sensational frills, and illustrated it with a couple of drawings. Many local happenings were similarly illustrated. At one time, after a particular political campaign, all the defeated candidates were shown on board a steamboat going up Salt Creek to dissolve their chagrin in the briny waters. On another occasion, a den of skunks within the city limits became an intolerable nuisance. The city marshal was forced to exterminate the animals. Rye described the massacre with the most lurid terms and illustrations. In an editorial he advocated reciprocity between Albany and Cisco. Albany had an abundance of water and no whisky. Cisco was well stocked with liquor but had no water. The ingenious editor emphasized his idea by a cartoon showing the Ciscoites peering over the horizon for the Albany water tank while the express car at Albany was being emptied of kegs of assorted alcoholic beverages. For several months, he ran a series of illustrated articles which he called "Frontier Reminiscences." These were interviews which he had with old pioneer settlers who were then still living. The experiences of such men as Joe Mathews, J. C. Lynch, George Greer, the Reynolds brothers, cattle barons, Conrad and Rath, merchants, and other frontier characters were portrayed with appropriate illustrations from Rye's pocket knife.[12]

The casual reader who peruses the early files of the frontier newspapers will be struck by the controversies in which the editors engaged. Controversies seemed to be dear to their hearts,—not abstract controversies on religion, the tariff, science or philosophy, but intimate, personal, violent controversies. They were ready to cross journalistic swords over anything, and, if they could not find a *casus belli*, they crossed swords anyway. It was not long until the issue, if there was one, was lost from sight and the editors fell to abusing each other. If one should judge from the number and malignity of the epithets used, he would wonder if many of the pioneer editors did not lie awake nights

[12] Key, V. O., Jr., "A Journalist of the Texas Frontier," *Bunker's Monthly*, September, 1928.

thinking up bad names to call each other. The *Comanche Chief* and the *Eastland Review,* for instance, indulged in a journalistic duel in 1878. What the original point of dissension was the writer has been unable to determine, but the meaning of the following item from the *Review,* May 17, 1878, is unmistakable:

Boil down two or three curs and pour them in a mold the shape of a monkey. Take out as soon as cold, and you will have an animal similar in smell, form, and substance to the editor of the *Comanche Chief.*

Many of the controversies were carried on as a joke in order to keep up the interest of the local readers; but in some instances the editors were in dead earnest. For instance, the altercation between G. W. Robson of the *Fort Griffin Echo* and Edgar Rye of the *Albany Sun* was more than a mere controversy; it was a journalistic feud which lasted almost three years. Whatever inspired these two well-known and unique characters to develop such profound aversion for each other is not known. Time and again, Robson would relate something mean and despicable that Rye had said about him or his newspaper, stoutly contending that in spite of all his foe could say about him that he, Robson, would not be drawn into a controversy, and then proceed forthwith to lambaste Rye with all the fervor he could muster.

Whether the controversies were feigned or real, they amused the readers, and the editors intended that they should. The people, either consciously or unconsciously, demanded amusement. The editor had to do more than act as a mere reporter; he had to entertain. Pointed comments on local happenings were cleverly made, and large quantities of light reading were clipped from other newspapers.[13]

[13] Some of the most clever humorous writings which were reprinted by practically all of the early newspapers appeared under the title of the *Arizona Kicker.* The articles, much on the order of present day syndicated articles, were written by a staff member of the *Detroit Free Press.* They were exaggerated imitations of a small town western newspaper with all of their exceedingly personal journalism and glaring candor. They appealed to the western people, because they were as blunt in their sayings as the people in their thoughts.

Most of the early newspapers started their careers as "all home print" sheets. This period in the history of each newspaper invariably shows it at its best. It was a stupendous task for one man, sometimes alone and at other times with the assistance of a tramp printer, to rustle the news and compose editorials sufficient to fill a four-, six-, or eight-page paper, set the type by hand, and run the issue off on a hand-fed press. It was a time when editors worked at their jobs.

But, sooner or later, in almost every instance, the ardor of the editor would begin to cool. He would resort to "patent insides." This would leave the front and back pages, as a rule, for home print. Local happenings, local color, the reflected personality of the editor, and all the things which went to make the newspaper distinctive and individualistic would suffer a corresponding loss. Occasionally, but not often, a publisher realized the mistake and reverted again to all "home print."[14]

In the matter of advertising the early editors showed considerable ingenuity and originality. In 1877, just as the cattle industry was coming into its own in West Texas, G. W. Robson of the *Frontier Echo* devised a unique way of advertising for cattlemen wishing to recover their strayed cattle. Such an advertisement consisted of the cut of a cow on which was the cattleman's brand and mark: below the cow was the cattleman's name, the location of his ranch, and his post office address. The idea was popular with the cattlemen, and for several years the *Echo* had from one to two pages filled with "cow" advertisements every week. Robson applied for a patent on this system of advertising for strays. Whether he obtained it is not known.[15] In 1880, J. C. Loving, cattleman and publisher, issued from the office of the *Stockman's Journal* at Weatherford the *Stockman's Guide and Handbook* containing over 600 cuts of cattle and horses, similar to Robson's cuts, but smaller in size.[16]

[14] *Ballinger Leader*, October 25, 1889.

[15] *Fort Griffin Echo*, September 28, 1877.

[16] A short time later Loving moved the *Stockman's Journal* to Fort Worth. In 1882, he got out a revised edition of the *Stockman's Guide and*

It was quite a fad among West Texas newspaper men during the 80's to combine verses, rhymes, and jingles with advertising. The length of the verses depended upon the price the advertiser was willing to pay. It might be two lines, four lines or half a column. The following lines from the *Mason News*, January 5, 1889, are typical:

> The ladies of Mason, bless their sweet lives,
> The radiant maidens and the good queenly wives
> Dress finer than any who dwell in the West
> Because Smith and Geistweidt sell them the best.

The early editors carried on a continuous and militant crusade to increase their advertising business. Much time and space was devoted to advantages resulting from a liberal patronage of the local newspapers and the inevitable failure of those not devoted to advertising. When it suited their purposes the editors did not hesitate to call names. The *Mason News*, August 13, 1887, stated:

> Advertising is all that keeps the Park Hotel at Lampasas from being crowded with guests—the want of it, the want of advertising! Don't be so sparing of the cause and the effect will be there on time. All other industries of Lampasas are flourishing, but they use printer's ink.

The following week the *News* observed, no doubt with a silent chuckle, that "the Park Hotel at Lampasas had closed for the want of patronage."

Seldom a week ever passed that the average editor did not devote at least one paragraph, and occasionally, several columns, to educating the local citizenry to an appreciation of the value of advertising. The following item from the *Albany News*, July 18,

Handbook. A copy of this edition is in the Library of the University of Texas. It has a peculiar value to the student of the cattle industry in that it gives the name, owner, and location of every cattle ranch of any importance in West and Northwest Texas.

1889, is a mild example of the type of propaganda constantly being imposed upon the local townsmen:

Some men try advertising as Indians tried feathers. He took one feather, laid it on a board and slept on it all night. In the morning he remarked, "White Men say feathers heap soft. White man dam fool." Some men invest a quarter or fifty cents in advertising and then because they do not at once realize a great increase in business declare that advertising does not pay.

The problem of keeping on hand the necessary printing supplies was a source of much vexation for the editors. Some of the newspapers were located off the railroads, but on or off the railroad, shipments of paper, ink, and other supplies were constantly being delayed. In 1880, the *Fort Griffin Echo's* supply of black ink completely gave out. It was fortunate enough to have on hand a good stock of colored inks, red, blue, green, and violet. For several weeks the newspaper was issued first in one color and then in another. Variety was sometimes achieved by mixing colors.[17]

The collection of delinquent subscriptions was another source of constant worry and vexation to the printer. It seems as if newspaper men had not discovered the simple expedient of dropping a subscriber from the mailing list when his subscription expired. Perhaps they did know of it, but did not dare use it, lest they have no mailing list at all. Maybe they thought it best to keep on sending the paper year after year and then continually ding-dong at the delinquents with the hope that some of them would sometimes pay something on arrears. Regardless of what they thought, that is what they did. Week after week an urgent appeal was made for delinquents to come in and pay the printer.

In desperation the editors, sooner or later, advertised that they would take anything on delinquent subscriptions, wood, hay, fodder, corn, peas, potatoes, fence posts, feathers, scrap iron, honey, soft soap, shingles, syrup, cotton seed, tobacco, pigs, clothing, lumber, coal, eggs, live stock, ducks, pecans, axle grease, chickens,

[17] *Fort Griffin Echo,* June 26, 1880.

beer, hides, and what-not.[18] Editor Robson was feeling unusually optimistic and considerate when he wrote,

> If you expect to live all winter,
> Bring some wood and pay the printer.[19]

If editors had a hard time collecting what was due them, they had a few tricks of the trade to compensate for it in a small way. These tricks were universally used with a considerable degree of success, year after year. The editor would offer, early in the season, a year's subscription to the person who would present the editor with the biggest water-melon, the biggest potato, the best roasting ears, or the biggest and best anything else within reason. The contest lasted for months and the editor kept all of the "entries."[20]

The one thing which could make the frontier newspaper men more furious than anything else was a "dead beat," a person who was always trying to get something printed free of cost. Even the most staid editor could wax eloquent in his scathing denunciation of that particular variety of pest. A typical example of such an expression of editorial opinion is found in the *Frontier Echo,* September 29, 1876:

Time and again the *Echo* has received papers with a little slip of colored paper pasted on them begging us to insert a long notice of the Windy Bladder or some other tom fool thing and send marked copy of paper and the dead beat will be much obliged. Another says, "Do me the favor to canvass our town and country for subscribers to —— and I will give you a favorable notice."

Mold every mule the government ever owned into one mule and make him all cheek, but it would be as nothing compared to the amount of brass cheek this bummer exhibits.

We have favorably noticed this publication, but it has failed to mention this paper in any way.

Our merchants at home do not ask us to puff them gratuitously

[18] *Taylor County News,* July 23, 1897; *Seymour Weekly Crescent,* August 8, 1889; *Fort Griffin Echo,* November 17, 1876.

[19] *Frontier Echo,* November 17, 1876.

[20] *Frontier Echo,* June 23, 1876; *Mason News,* June 19, 1886; *Ballinger Leader,* November 24, 1890.

and we see no good reason why we should do so and "canvass our town and county" for them to boot.

From such Yahoos, good Lord deliver us.

We work for money. If you want the use of the columns of this paper, come down with the dust.

As early as 1876 (there were but few newspapers in West Texas then) there was agitation to establish a West Texas Press Association. Nothing was done at the time, and the matter was spasmodically raised from time to time for twelve or fifteen years. The ultimate outcome was two associations. The Northwest Texas Association, organized in 1888, was composed of newspapers located west of Fort Worth and north of the Brazos River.[21] The West Texas Press Association, organized at Abilene in 1891, was theoretically composed of the newspapers west and south of the Brazos River and east of the Pecos River.[22] The avowed purpose of these associations was to "make concerted effort in the way of doing all in their power to promote immigration and to raise the standards of the newspapers." It will be noted that the matter of boosting the country and promoting immigration was put foremost. In spite of all of the good intentions the associations had rough sailing. It is doubtful if much mutual benefit was ever realized. The thing which delayed the associations in effecting their organization for years, and severely impeded their usefulness after they were organized, was the extreme individualistic tendencies of the editors. Some of the editors refused to go into the organization at all, because they did not wish to take any chances of having policies dictated to them by some overhead organization. The innate love of controversy could not be quelled, and, ere long, a big row was going on between the independent editors and those in the association.[23] When this affair had somewhat subsided, the association editors got to squabbling among themselves. The associations had a feeble existence for a few years and finally ceased to function.

[21] *Seymour News*, February 19, 1891.
[22] *Taylor County News*, January 9, 1891.
[23] *Ibid.*, February 6, 1891.

Perhaps it would not be proper to close this chapter without a reference to the educational influence of the early newspapers. As an educational factor the newspaper was an institution taking its place beside the almost universal one-teacher school. There were at the time few books, magazines, or state-wide newspapers in the frontier country. The editors realized the need of the people for more than local news, and attempted to satisfy this need by introducing much syndicated matter on cattle and sheep raising, farming, diversification, bee tending, housekeeping, and even the more cultural matters, such as poetry, essays, and stories, especially those commemorating special holidays. He encouraged all kinds of local talent. Along with all his boosting tendencies, he never ceased to advocate better schools, churches, roads, courthouses, and other local municipal improvements. The influence of the local newspaper can not be as definitely measured as that of more formal educational agents. However, it may be remembered that the one teacher school reached a part of the children for only a few months each year, while the newspaper with its bits of information and inspiration reached the entire family every week of the year.

CHAPTER VI

DIVISION AND SECTIONALISM

A TALL, rangy, slightly bow-legged, sunburned man, with lines in his face which indicated one habitually accustomed to facing a wind carrying occasionally a bit of flying gravel, and with a squint in his eyes acquired by looking over great distances, was riding down town on the Illinois Central electric train in Chicago. The man next to him asked from what part of the country he had come. "West Texas," was the reply, with as much nonchalance as one might have said, "West Virginia" or "New Mexico." By no means did it occur to the tall man that the place he had named did not exist as a political area; moreover, that would be the answer of any person living in West Texas. He may answer "Texas" at first and then immediately qualify it by adding "West Texas." Perhaps unconsciously, he seldom lets an opportunity pass for impressing the stranger with the fact that he lives in West Texas.

West Texans have the feeling that their section constitutes all but a state in itself. This intense feeling of sectionalism belongs distinctly to the people of the western part of the state; the residents of the older part have had a self-satisfied, complaisant attitude. They have had all that they want; the institutions of the state were naturally placed in that part which was already settled when the institutions were built. They have always liked to think of Texas as it looks on the map, including West Texas. They have seen no reason why the property of the western part of the state should not be taxed to help pay for and maintain the established institutions of the state. They have left the West Texans to fuss and fume about "unequal distribution," "intolerable neglect," and the "need for unified sectional action."

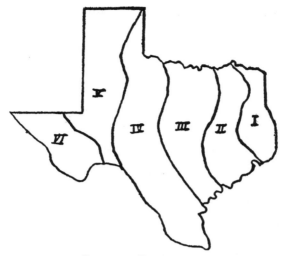

RAINFALL DISTRIBUTION

I. 50″ and above IV. 20″ to 30″
II. 40″ to 50″ V. 10″ to 20″
III. 30″ to 40″ VI. less than 10″

TOPOGRAPHICAL PROVINCES

I. Eastern IV. Central
II. Southern V. Great Central Plains
III. Eastern Central VI. Trans Pecos

It will be well to point out the difference between the various movements to divide the state and the rise of the present sectional feeling on the part of West Texas. The two movements parallel each other in part (one is as old as the other) but an analysis will show they are distinctly separate, have a different origin. Only in more recent years has the feeling of sectionalism in West Texas reached the point where division is considered a possible solution of the grievances of that section.

The division movement has had a more or less artificial basis. To trace it one must study the proceedings of the various constitutional conventions in Texas, the journals of the state Legislature, and the records of Congress. There have been numerous proposals by politicians to divide the state, but it is not clear as to how far these proposals represent the widespread and well-defined aspirations of the people of the various sections before 1876. In some cases, sectionalism did constitute a factor, but decidedly a minor one, in these division proposals. In other cases, it is very clear that the proposals originated with politicians whose ambitions and selfish interests constituted the dominating factor. In order to determine the degree in which the division movement, in its earlier stages, resulted from the aspirations of politicians rather than from the wish of the people, a brief summary of the proposals for division is desirable.[1]

The division movement began outside the state. Before annexation, the Texas question was the target which drew the main fire in the slavery controversy. Senator Benton on December 4, 1844, proposed that Texas be reduced in size, when admitted as a state, in order that her area should not exceed that

---

[1] The best study, as yet, of the division movement is by W. J. McConnell, *Social Cleavages in Texas*, in *Columbia University Studies in History, Economics, and Public Law*, Vol. CXIX. Mr. McConnell, by using the records of the state constitutional conventions, of the Legislature and Congress, has made an exhaustive study of the plans for division of the state. The writer has but one criticism to offer; i.e., the title is a little misleading. Only three or four plans of division out of almost two score treated by Mr. McConnell really represent "social cleavages." The remainder are predominately cleavages of politicians.

of the largest state then in the Union. The rest of Texas should become a part of the territory of the United States. The proposal was opposed by Texas and failed; it constituted a plan for division which did not result from a spirit of sectionalism in Texas.[2]

The desirability of dividing the state was fully and frankly recognized during the annexation controversy in 1845, and was provided for in the Joint Resolution, March 1, 1845. The first

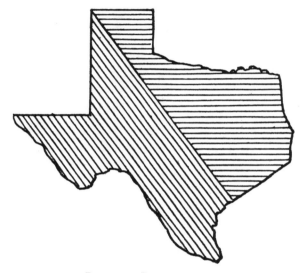

PROPOSED DIVISION, 1847.

West Texas to be a free state.   East Texas to be a slave state.

proposal for division after Texas was admitted as a state came from New England. Congressman J. P. Hale of New Hampshire offered a resolution proposing to divide Texas into two states of equal size by running the boundary line from the northwest corner of the Panhandle southeast to the Gulf of Mexico. West Texas would be a free state and East Texas a slave.[3] The resolution was not acceptable to the South.

[2] *Congressional Globe,* 31st Congress, 1st Sess., p. 165.
[3] *Ibid.,* 29th Congress, 1st Sess., p. 143.

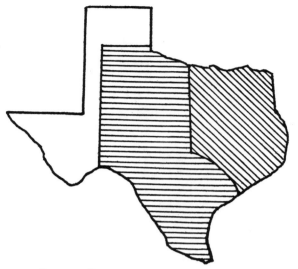

PROPOSED PLAN TO REDUCE AND DIVIDE THE STATE IN 1850.
Unshaded area shows proposed reduction.

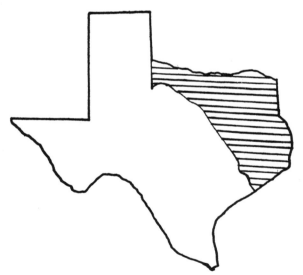

PROPOSED "STATE OF SAN JACINTO," 1850.
Shown by shaded area.

Isaac Van Zandt, the Texas minister at Washington during the annexation negotiations, favored an immediate division of the state. He became candidate for governor in 1847 with division as the chief plank in his platform, but died before the election was held.[4] This was the first time that division was proposed by someone within the state. It was three years before the division question was brought up again. Senator Benton, ever solicitous for the welfare of Texas, introduced a bill, January 16, 1850,

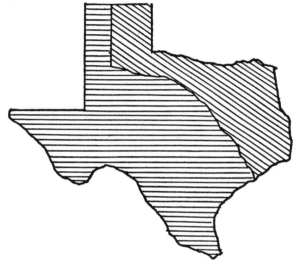

PLAN OF DIVISION PROPOSED BY FLANAGAN, 1852.

which would have reduced the size of the state by adding the Big Bend region and the north Panhandle to the territory of the United States; what was left of the state was to be divided into two states.[5] As a counter proposal to Senator Benton's measure, Senator Foote introduced a bill which proposed to erect the territory east of the Brazos River and the 100th meridian into the "State of San Jacinto." Neither proposal was seriously considered in the Senate, nor did they create any popular interest in

[4] Yoakum, *Texas*, p. 394.
[5] *Congressional Globe*, 31st Congress, 1st Sess., p. 166.

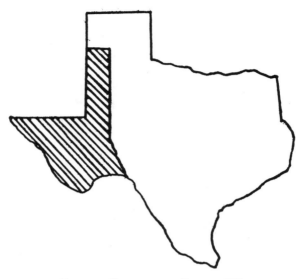

PLAN TO REDUCE THE STATE, 1866.

FLANAGAN'S PLAN OF DIVISION, 1866.

Texas. In 1852, the first division proposal in the state Legislature was introduced by Mr. Flanagan of Rusk. He would have divided Texas into two states by running a line up the Brazos River to meridian 101½, thence north along the meridian to the state line. The resolution was killed by a vote of 33 to 15, and there is no indication that the vote was sectional.

Division sentiment was strong in the Constitutional Convention of 1866. No less than three division and reduction proposals were introduced. Mr. Flanagan of Rusk would have created a new state east of the Trinity River, but this proposed ordinance failed on the first reading.[6] A few days later an ordinance failed which provided for the sale to the United States of the territory west of the Pecos River up to Fort Lancaster, then north along the 102d meridian to the Red River, and thence west to the New Mexico line. The third ordinance calling for a division of the state was before the Convention when it adjourned.[7] Agitation for division went on after the Convention adjourned. The question was used several times in the session of the Legislature which met in August, 1866.[8]

It was agitated more vigorously during the Reconstruction Convention, which met June 1, 1868, than at any other time. An aggressive minority, led by E. J. Davis and E. Degener, seemed determined to force the issue whether the Convention and the people were willing or not. An analysis of the motives of this group will show that sectionalism was not an important factor at this time. A few people favored division because they considered the state too large for effective and efficient administration. They pointed to the widespread lawlessness of the period as proof of the fact. Certain Germans in the southwest, in Comal, Kendall, Gillespie, Kerr, and Mason counties, considered that since the German element had been somewhat loyal to the Union during the Civil War, Southwest Texas, if erected into a separate

[6] McConnell, *Social Cleavages in Texas*, p. 42.
[7] *Convention Journal*, 1866, p. 202.
[8] *House Journal*, 11th Legislature, pp. 652, 687; *Senate Journal*, 11th Legislature, pp. 4, 6, 59.

state, could expect greater favors from Congress in the way of
Reconstruction. A more important motive than either of the
foregoing was a desire for spoils. A division of the state into
two or three units would double or treble the number of offices.
Such action would produce a veritable paradise for the mediocre
politicians comprising the Convention.[9]

The Convention had scarcely opened when Governor E. M.
Pease proposed to sell to the United States the territory west of

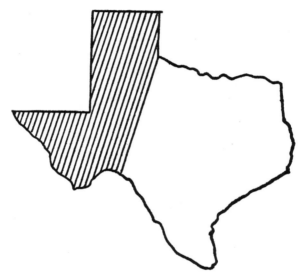

PLAN TO REDUCE THE STATE, 1868.
Shaded area shows proposed sale.

a line drawn north from the mouth of the Pecos River.[10] It happened that reduction was not what the Convention wanted.
Division would create more jobs. A committee of fifteen was
straightway appointed to make recommendations for division.
Before the committee was ready to report, something happened
at Washington to merit attention. A bill, providing for the

[9] McConnell, *Social Cleavages in Texas*, pp. 51–65.
[10] *Convention Journal*, 1868, First session, pp. 15–16.

division of Texas into three states, was introduced in Congress. The bill was called the Congressional Plan of Reconstruction. By its provisions the State of East Texas should have as a western boundary a line up the San Jacinto River to the western boundaries of Liberty and Polk counties, thence north to the Trinity River, thence up the Trinity River to the mouth of the East Fork of the Trinity, thence to the southeast corner of Fannin County, and thence north along the western boundary of Fannin County to Red River. The eastern boundary of the State of

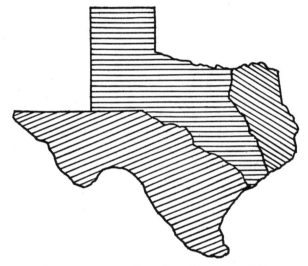

"CONGRESSIONAL PLAN" OF DIVISION, 1868.

South Texas was to ascend the Colorado River to its intersection with the 32d parallel, and thence west along the 32d parallel to the New Mexico line. The region between East Texas and South Texas would continue to be designated as Texas.[11] The bill failed on the second reading, but its significance lies in the fact that it became the basis of the plan under consideration by the committee of fifteen in the Texas Reconstruction Convention. The plan was making decided headway in the Convention when it was

[11] *Congressional Journal*, 1868, p. 143.

checked by a counter proposal. On June 25, W. W. Mills, from El Paso, suggested that Texas sell the extreme western region, the Big Bend country, to the United States on the condition that it be joined to Donna Anna County, New Mexico, and organized into a territory. The plan received little support. E. J. Hamilton then brought forward a new plan for a three-fold division. The region north of the 32d parallel was to be organized as North Texas; the region south of the 32d parallel and east of the Brazos River was to be East Texas; and that south of the 32d parallel and west of the Brazos, West Texas.[12] By July 14, the Convention had dilly-dallied so much with division and achieved nothing that a resolution was passed, by a vote of forty-seven to thirty-seven, which barred further consideration of the question until Congress should take the initiative in the matter. A futile attempt to re-open the matter was made by the introduction of a resolution proposing to erect the State of West Texas from the territory lying west of the Colorado River and south of the 32d parallel. The Convention then adjourned until December 7, 1868.

During the recess of the Convention the question of division became connected, in the popular mind, with that of railroad building. It was a time when the people were willing to pledge a pound of flesh and more to secure railroads. It became evident that railroad construction would be impeded as long as division was impending. No railroad cared to build through a region which might shortly become a new state with new railroad laws and regulations. A widespread sentiment developed during the fall of 1868 for settling the division question one way or the other once and for all. To this end, mass meetings were held in various parts of the state. A meeting of the citizens of Smith County at Tyler strongly urged division according to the Congressional Plan.[13]

When the Convention reassembled, December 7, the divisionists were more determined than ever to force the issue. They were

[12] *Convention Journal*, 1868, First Session, p. 148.

[13] McConnell, *Social Cleavages in Texas*, pp. 65-69; *Harrison Flag*, December 24, 1868; January 7, 1869.

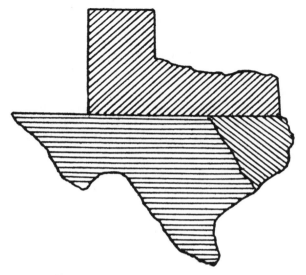

HAMILTON'S PLAN OF DIVISION, 1868.

NEWCOMB'S PLAN OF DIVISION, 1868.

now in the majority, but were divided as to whether the question should be settled by the Convention or submitted to the people. E. J. Davis and E. Degener, along with other radical leaders, had gone so far as to prepare a *Constitution for the State of West Texas*.[14] The first object of the divisionists was to get rescinded the resolution which barred the consideration of the division question. An active and determined minority prevented such action for almost a month by filibustering tactics. In the meanwhile, the matter was being warmly discussed by the people and press of the state.[15]

Throughout the controversy it is difficult to discover any clearly defined sectional feeling. The West was divided. Of the twenty delegates from the so-called western counties only seven were for division without reservation.[16] Some of the strongest leaders of the opposition came from the other thirteen delegates. Furthermore, mass meetings were held in San Antonio, the proposed capital of West Texas, to protest against division. The same thing happened at New Braunfels, the second largest town in the proposed new state. If the press of the state was indicative of public sentiment as a whole, it is evident that the people favoring division constituted a decided minority.[17]

The controversy in the Convention went on. Neither faction could effect its program. At last, the matter was compromised by an agreement to send a commission of six to Washington with the view of getting Congress to take the initiative; $6000 was appropriated for the purpose.[18] The commission lost no time in getting to the national capital. The members marshaled every conceivable argument to impress congressmen and senators.[19] To

[14] A printed copy of the *Constitution of the State of West Texas* is in the Library of the University of Texas.

[15] Ramsdell, *Reconstruction in Texas*, 250; McConnell, *Social Cleavages in Texas*, 71; *Texas Republican*, December 14, 1868; *Austin Republican*, December 2, 1868.

[16] McConnell, *Social Cleavages in Texas*, 78.

[17] *Ibid*.

[18] The commission was composed of Davis, Flanagan, Morgan Hamilton, Varnell, Whitmore, and Burnett.

[19] *Austin Republican*, April 7, 1869.

offset any influence which the Commission might have on Congress a number of citizens of Texas went to Washington at their
own expense to represent the non-divisionist sentiment. These
men presented to Congress a memorial, signed by twenty-three of
their number, in which they represented the great majority of the
people of Texas as being opposed to division.[20]

The outcome of the lobbying of the commission was the introduction of a bill in the House of Representatives providing for
the organization of the territory south and west of the Colorado

THE PROPOSED STATE OF LINCOLN (SHADED), 1869.

River into a state, to be known as the "State of Lincoln." The
bill was read a second time and referred to the committee on
Reconstruction, where it died when Congress adjourned, April 7,
1869.[21] The failure of the measure greatly discouraged the
divisionists, and their opponents drew a sigh of relief and considered the matter closed, at least for a while.

The question was not to be ignored long, however. E. J.
Davis had no sooner returned from Washington than he launched

[20] *Austin Republican*, March 31, 1869; *State Gazette*, January 22, 1869.
[21] *Congressional Globe*, 40th Congress, 1st Sess., pp. 100, 194.

into a political campaign as candidate for governor. Although
division was not an issue in the campaign, its partisans secretly
felt that the cause had won a victory when Davis was elected.
With the approval of the Governor, and perhaps at his instigation, a number of plans for division were brought before the
Legislature at its regular session in 1871.[22] A bill, introduced by
Representative Robinson of Bowie, provided for a four-fold

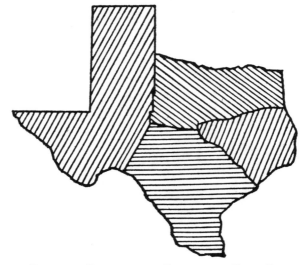

PROPOSED PLAN FOR DIVIDING THE STATES INTO FOUR PARTS, 1871.

division. The measure died in committee at the end of the
session.[23]

An analysis of the division plans prior to and during the
Reconstruction period seems to indicate most clearly the lack of
social cleavages within the state. Several of the plans were
formulated outside the state entirely. Moreover, a study of those
originating inside the state will show that they were the product
of interested politicians rather than the result of widespread pub-

[22] *Senate Journal,* 12th Legislature, Called Session, p. 34; *Ibid.,* 12th
Legislature, First Session, pp. 47, 112, 166, 187, 515.

[23] *House Journal,* 12th Legislature, First Session, p. 212; *Austin Republican,* March 9, 1871.

lic opinion within any section. Granting that sectional feeling was a factor in some instances, it was only temporary, as is evidenced by the fact that the proposed divisional boundaries were constantly criss-crossing each other and frequently new alignments were being made. A deep-grounded sectional feeling was at the time slowly rising in the western part of the state, but it had a long way to go before it reached the point of demanding division.

If one is to understand the rise of sectionalism he must go elsewhere than to the Congressional *Records* or the proceedings of the various conventions or legislatures. These sources are helpful, but they do not go far enough. It is argued that sectional aspirations are always reflected in representative political bodies. This is no doubt true, but the reverse is not. Discussions may arise in representative assemblies which are not prompted by sectional feeling. Conclusions concerning social attitudes drawn from a study of the doings of political bodies may be misleading and result in erroneous conceptions. To understand the basis of sectionalism one must ferret out the feelings, passions, prejudices, and personalities swaying the people. Sectionalism is almost invariably the outcome of the common interests of a particular section. When the interests of a section begin to conflict with those of another section with which it is politically associated, the rise of group consciousness is imminent.

Sectionalism in Texas had its beginning shortly after the organization of the Republic. The first Congress convened at Houston, but the quarters there were too crude and the climate too disagreeable for the comfort of the members. As those gentlemen splashed through ankle deep mud on their way to the improvised legislative hall, their thoughts turned towards a permanent seat of government farther back from the coast in the hill country. At a special session of the first Congress the two houses voted to appoint a committee of five citizens, not members of Congress, to consider and report to Congress all possible sites for a seat of government.[24] The sites to be considered were to be con-

[24] For a full account of the selection of a seat of government of Texas, see Winkler, E. W., "The Seat of Government of Texas," *The State Historical Quarterly*, X.

fined to the section of country between the Trinity and Guadalupe rivers, south of a line extending a hundred miles north of the old San Antonio road, and north of a line running from the Trinity to the Guadalupe river, crossing the Brazos at Fort Bend. Some ten places were reported by the Committee on November 20, 1837. By that time, the interest of people of the various sections was becoming sharply aroused. The sentiment of the western counties was expressed in an open letter by an inhabitant of that region:

"I have just reached this place from the far west where I reside and where it is difficult for myself and neighbors to acquire information in relation to the political operations of this government. It would be useless for me here to state that the citizens of the west have been the greatest sufferers in the war between Texas and Mexico. . . . Our only hope was in the protection of a munificent and just government, . . . I find instead of an eye to the interest of all, that local feelings and prejudices prevail, and at a time when the whole west is to be a considerable extent depopulated, we find members of Congress attempting to [entail] from the west a seat of government forever. Would it not be well for the gentlemen to reflect upon the probable result of such a measure? Would not the west in after days deny the right to thus bind them, and if the seat of government should be located and individuals invest in purchasing property, and a subsequent congress choose to remove the seat of government, would it not have a tendency to destroy faith? I trust that members of congress will consider maturely before they legislate to the prejudice of every part of this community. I do not object to moving the seat of government, but I do most sincerely object to any pledge on the part of this government that the seat of government shall remain at any place forever. First, because it is unjust in its operation—secondly, because I do not think that congress has the right to do so.

Very respectfully, your obedient servant,

A Western Citizen

Houston, November 23rd, 1837."[25]

[25] *Telegraph,* December 6, 1837.

Nothing came of the report of the first committee, nor of the second committee appointed in 1838. As long as the permanent seat of government remained undecided the sectional interest in the matter increased. It was a vital issue in the election of 1838. A correspondent of the *Matagorda Bulletin*, August 24, 1838, wrote George Sutherland, candidate from Matagorda for the Senate:

"He is truly Western in his feelings as well as interest, and therefore, when brought to the test in any great measure, in which the West is concerned, we know where to find him and what to depend upon—for instance, the location of the seat of government, and we know that this great question will come up, and be finally disposed of during the next three years. He has no interest in the East, to paralize his influence and cool his zeal; his entire interest is West of the Colorado—he was not barely 'desirous' to locate the seat of government on the Colorado; and did not manifest a simple anxiety for the location, as has been said of the others. But he was most zealous and active during the last session of Congress in obtaining the location of the seat of government at La Grange. To no one member, more than to George Sutherland could be attributed the success which the Western members had in that measure. . . . The Seat of Government will be permanently located during the next two years; and no measure can be so big with consequences to the West, and particularly to the citizens of this Senatorial District as its location on the Colorado. It will promote emigration to the West, thereby giving protection to the frontier settlements, and enhancing the value of our lands. It will also increase most rapidly the settlement of the lands of the Colorado, and of the country west of it, thereby increasing the capital and interest of that section of the country, which will result in important public improvements, increasing the facilities of commerce and trade. . . ."

The final selection of a seat of government was made by a joint commission of five. A. C. Horton of Matagorda and I. W. Burton of Nacogdoches were selected from the senate, and William Menifee of Colorado, Isaac Campbell of San Augustine, and Louis P. Cooke of Brazoria were selected by the House of Representatives, two from western, two from eastern and one from central Texas. The vote of these gentlemen in making their decision was strictly sectional as is indicated by their report:

City of Houston
April 13, 1839

"We, the commissioners appointed for locating permanently the seat of government of the republic of Texas, having met this day by appointment at the Capital, the question was put by the chairman, A. C. Horton, as to which river, the Brazos or Colorado, with the respective selections on each had the highest claims to our consideration in the discharge of the duty assigned us. The vote stood as follows: For the Colorado, Messrs. A. C. Horton, William Menifee, and L. P. Cooke; for the Brazos, Messrs. I. W. Burton and Isaac Campbell.

The question was then put by the chair, as to which of the selections on the Colorado river, viz.: Bastrop or Waterloo [present site of Austin] was entitled to their preference. It was unanimously determined that Waterloo, and the lands condemned and relinquished around it, was the proper site and was therefore their choice."

When it became known that Austin, then on the outskirts of the frontier, had been selected as the capital, a storm of protest arose in the eastern part of the state. The West gave a shout of joy. The sentiments of the malcontents were lustily voiced by the *Morning Star* at Houston; the delight of the westerners was proclaimed by the *Matagorda Bulletin*. For months the *Morning Star* tried to get the action rescinded. Every conceivable argument was advanced for the purpose. Austin had none of the advantages of a city, timber was scarce, water was not abundant, the place was remote from the Gulf, there was no navigable stream near it, communication relative to carrying on foreign affairs would be slow and the results disastrous, the members of Congress might be scalped, and the archives might be wrecked by Mexican or Indian raiders. The contention did not cease until the government buildings had been erected at Austin and the various departments of government established there.

For twenty years after the sectional controversy relative to the location of the seat of government, cotton and slavery were causing sectional interests to become more nearly permanent. It was a period of rapid extension of both. The soil of the river bottoms near the coast and the upper Louisiana line was extremely fertile. The task of clearing the heavy timber and opening cotton planta- tions required the work of negroes, which in turn meant a heavy outlay of capital. A man without capital had to seek less desir- able land farther west. Before railroads were built, a person wishing to raise cotton on an extensive scale was forced to stay near the rivers, and the streams were navigable for only a short distance from the coast. It was not until a few years before the Civil War that a few short lines of railroad extending out from Houston, Indianola, and Shreveport began to tap the river bottom districts. Nature segregated and restricted the Texas planter and his slaves.

The west was settled by men of little or no capital; it offered them the inducement of cheap land. Furthermore, it offered them open land which would be easy and inexpensive to put in cultivation or to use for pasturage. These men grew little cotton and seldom owned slaves. Although much of the upland prairie land was well adapted to cotton, the cost of transporta- tion caused it, at that time, to be unprofitable.

With conditions so different in the two sections, it was inevita- ble that there should be a division of interest. In 1859 two-thirds of the assessed wealth of the state was located in one-fourth of the counties; and these counties were in the eastern and south- eastern part of the state.[26] The slavery element, in control of the legislature until 1860, did not hesitate to pass laws favoring the slavery section. In 1858, for instance, the planters enacted a law which permitted any settler upon the public domain to pre- empt one hundred and sixty acres for every three slaves owned by him within the state. The measure was extremely unpopular in the west. It became an issue in the campaign of 1859, and was repealed in January, 1860, after the frontier had forced the election of Houston as governor. The re-opening of the African slave trade was strongly advocated in the planter section during

[26] *Texas Almanac*, 1860.

the 1850's and was opposed by the westerners. The ever-increasing number of Germans on the frontier was causing a growing anti-slavery sentiment in the west. Had the Civil War not abolished the institution of slavery entirely, the cleavage between the slavery element and the small farmer and cattle raiser in the west would have become, no doubt, more and more clearly defined. Economic conditions in the west would probably never have made slavery profitable there.[27]

Frontier defense also tended to perpetuate sectional differences during the 1840's and 1850's. The people on the frontier were often much more alarmed at rumors of Indian raids than the occasion warranted. On the other hand, people in the older settled part of the state failed to appreciate, in their comparative security, the dangers to which the frontier was exposed. The frontiersman resented the attitude of the East. The feeling of sectional neglect caused the frontier to throw its voting strength to Houston in the gubernatorial race of 1859 and effected thus the defeat of Governor Runnels for re-election.[28] The same feeling caused the frontier to support Throckmorton for governor in 1866. Reconstruction interfered with any further political demonstration of sectional feeling until the constitution of 1875 became a matter of state-wide discussion. Although a majority of the people in West Texas supported that document, criticism there was strong, and it was prompted by sectionalism.[29] The main attacks were centered on sections 50 and 52 of Article 3, which prevented the legislature or any county or town from giving or lending credit to any person, association, or corporation. West Texas was almost unanimous in its desire to encourage railroad building and immigration by means of state aid.[30] One does not have to go far afield to find why the Convention of 1875 placed such restrictions in the Constitution, but hostility to

[27] Ramsdell, C. W., *The Frontier and Secession* in the *Columbia Studies in Southern History and Politics.*

[28] *Frontier Echo*, Jacksboro, November 19, 1875.

[29] *Ibid.*, Jacksboro, November 19, 1875.

[30] *Ibid.*, December 17, 1875; December 26, 1875; *Fredericksburg Sentinel*, January 14, 1876.

Republicans and the North was not so strong in West Texas as in the older parts of the state. The men of the frontier had served, for the most part, in frontier organizations during the Civil War, and had developed an aversion for Indians instead of for Yankees. During the period of reconstruction federal troops were more than welcome on the frontier, but their presence in the interior of the state was resented. West Texas did not inherit the profound fear of the carpet-bagger or the distaste for everything connected with reconstruction in the same degree as did the people in the older part of the state.[31] Consequently, West Texas chafed under the new constitutional restrictions which she considered detrimental to her interests.

Since 1875, various legislative problems have arisen wherein the cleavage between West Texas and the rest of the state has been clearly marked.[32] In 1881, a bill was introduced making it a severe offense for a cattleman to graze unleased school lands. The West Texas members of the legislature presented a solid phalanx in opposition to this measure. A wave of consternation and resentment swept the western part of the state. The press of that section voiced the sentiments of the people in most positive terms. In spite of the turbulent opposition, the bill passed the lower house of the legislature and all but passed the senate.[33] West Texas was continually at variance with the rest of the state over the sale of public lands. West Texas felt that it restricted immigration and settlement and retarded the development of their part of the state.[34]

In February, 1889, the *San Antonio Express* started a controversy which has never ceased by publishing some statistics in regard to taxation and the distribution of the school funds. It pointed out that the fifty-four counties comprising what was known as West Texas at that time, paid to the state an excess of

[31] *Frontier Echo,* Jacksboro, December 3, 1875.

[32] For convenience the West Texans always referred to the rest of the state as East Texas. The term as they used it included everything not in West Texas. The limits of West Texas are defined in the Preface.

[33] *Fort Griffin Echo,* March 5, 1881.

[34] *Taylor County News,* May 31, 1889.

$250,000 in school taxes over what they received from the state as their *pro rata* part of the school funds.[35] This information was republished in every local newspaper in West Texas with long editorials on the injustice of the system of taxation. It was pointed out that not one institution of higher learning was located in West Texas. The entire matter became a much discussed topic, and tended to build up a feeling of unity in West Texas.[36] Politicians and demagogues lost no opportunity to remind the people that they were oppressed by "the selfish interests of East Texas."

Another fruitful source of dissension between the two sections of the state was the continued demand of West Texas for predatory game laws. The demand came primarily from the cattle and sheep industries, but was sanctioned by all the people of the western part of the state. The citizens of the rest of the state were not bothered by predatory animals and looked upon the whole thing as class legislation. Every time a state bounty law was introduced it was voted down; West Texas became furious.[37]

To augment the chagrin of the West, the older part of the state, by virtue of superior numbers, made and executed laws expressly passed for the benefit of the eastern section. The feeling of unity in West Texas was materially increased by opposition to such measures.

The grievances which West Texas nursed led eventually to a demand for a division of the state, from certain leaders, local newspapers, and associations in West Texas. As early as 1878, the *Dallas Herald* advocated a division.[38] When the free grass question was up in 1885, a number of West Texas editors stoutly

[35] *Ballinger Leader*, February 8, 1889.

[36] Various towns began to agitate for the establishment of state colleges. Dallas tried to capitalize the movement by attempting to get an agricultural and mechanical college established there for the benefit of "West Texas." San Angelo loudly voiced her demand for a state normal college.—*Ballinger Leader*, February 15, 1889; September 26, 1890.

[37] *Taylor County News*, March 17, 1891; January 15, 1897.

[38] *Frontier Echo*, August 9, 1878.

contended that the only solution for the problem was the division of the state.[39] In 1891, a West Texas representative stated on the floor of the House that the best way to obliterate the sectional question would be to annex East Texas to Arkansas. The Legislature would then, he thought, be able to get on with its business unvexed by the jealousies eternally bobbing up between East and West Texas.[40] A wave of division sentiment swept across the western part of the state in 1893.[41] A number of mass meetings were held.[42] A meeting, held at Vernon, in May, 1893, had an unusual influence.[43] Its resolutions were published and republished throughout that entire section. The division question subsided in time, but has since periodically been revived.

[39] *Albany News,* August 29, 1894.

[40] *Taylor County News,* April 10, 1891.

[41] Editors tried to outdo each other in thinking up biting things to say about East Texas. One of the favorite similes was to compare her to a vampire gently fanning her victim with her wings while she was slowly sapping the life blood of her victim. *Taylor County News,* May 12, 1893.

[42] *Taylor County News,* May 28, 1893.

[43] The *Taylor County News,* May 23, 1893, in speaking of the Vernon meeting made the following comment:

"The *News* has heretofore hinted that a division of Texas would become necessary as a relief from the unjust discriminations of state officers, legislatures and conventions. It now seems that this feeling is not confined alone to any one locality of northwest Texas, but it is pretty general and daily growing. The citizens of Vernon held a mass meeting last week and set forth their grievances and feelings in the following set of resolutions:

" 'Whereas, all the state schools, public buildings and higher courts are situated in the eastern and southern part of the state, and

" 'Whereas, the state legislation has always ignored northwest Texas, including the great panhandle country in the distribution of its public institutions and appropriations, and

" 'Whereas, all the school lands are located in the western and northwestern part of the state and the annual payment of the western part of the state into the state treasury is $300,000 more than it draws out, and

" 'Whereas, the present legislature continues in line with its predecessors, and

" 'Whereas, the interests of this section are altogether different from southern and eastern Texas, be it

" 'Resolved, that unless these matters are remedied our association favors the calling of a convention at some date in the future for the purpose of creating out of the northwestern portion of Texas a new state.' "

A small flurry in sectional feeling took place in 1909. The prohibition question was the foremost political issue just then. The northern and western parts of the state were predominately dry, while the eastern, central, and southern parts were wet. Some of the candidates talked of the feasibility of creating the "State of Northwest Texas" with its capital at Abilene and the "State of Northeast Texas" with its capital at Dallas. These two new states could at once adopt state-wide prohibition and could begin to experience all the joys and blessings in store for a bone-dry commonwealth.[44] It is well to note that this proposal came from a few politicians, and was not prompted by sectional feelings. These interested candidates evidently understood the futility of proposing a single prohibition state of all North Texas. The antipathy of the West for the East was too strong for that; hence, the two-state proposal.[45]

The clouds which had been slowly forming for more than half a century began to gather and present a most threatening appearance in 1915. The first formal move was made on January 28 of that year, when Senator Johnson of Hall County introduced into the legislature a resolution providing for the creation of the "State of Jefferson" from the territory included in 117 counties of West Texas, including the 25th, 21st, and 28th, and 29th senatorial districts. Introducing his resolution, Senator Johnson enumerated a long list of grievances, such as, unfavorable land laws; failure of the West to get its share of the public school fund, of the institutions of higher learning, and of the eleemosynary institutions; the failure of the West to secure predatory game laws; and the use of West Texas land by the state to build railroads in East Texas. All of these afflictions West

---

[44] *Dallas News,* August 27, 1909.

[45] A rather novel proposal, which had no connection with the rising sectionalism in Texas, was made in 1906 by Congressman Bede of Minnesota. The bill provided for the division of Texas into four districts. Each district was to have a separate legislature and two Senators in the United States Senate. The whole state was to have but one Governor. The plan received little encouragement in either Congress or in Texas, but it did provoke considerable newspaper discussion.

Texas had long been nursing. He pointed out that the State
Constitution provided that the state should be redistributed after
each Federal census for state senatorial and Congressional purposes. Two regular sessions and five special sessions had passed
since the last census and no move had been made towards re-
districting. At the time West Texas was entitled to twice as
many state senators as they had and two additional Congressmen.
The delay to act could only be interpreted as additional evidence

THE PROPOSED "STATE OF JEFFERSON," 1915.
Shown by horizontal shading.

of the determination of East Texas to dominate the Legislature.
West Texas was supplying all the public school lands, and was
paying many times more taxes to the state than it was receiving
from the state.

The resolution would have submitted to the people on the
first Tuesday in July, 1915, a constitutional amendment providing for the creation of the "State of Jefferson." The new state
would retain all unsold lands and receive that portion of the public school fund derived from the sale of lands located within

West Texas. It provided for a special election within the "State of Jefferson" for the purpose of selecting state officials for the new state. The temporary capital was to be Abilene in Taylor County.[46]

It is doubtful if Senator Johnson ever expected that resolution would make much headway in the Legislature. His real purpose was to jar the Legislature out of its lethargy and into a realization that West Texas was in dead earnest in the matter of getting an equitable distribution of the state institutions, and reapportionment of representation.

The same session of the Legislature witnessed two other proposals for division of the state. Senator Hall brought in a resolution which would divide the state into "North Texas," "South Texas," and the "State of Jefferson."[47] The measure died in committee. Representative Bates made a somewhat similar proposal in the lower House, and it, too, died in committee.[48]

An intense and widespread display of sectionalism occurred at Sweetwater during the first week of April, 1921. On April 2, Governor Pat M. Neff vetoed the West Texas Agricultural and Mechanical College Bill, a project upon which West Texas had set its heart. The same day an impromptu mass meeting was held at Sweetwater at which it was reported that "5000 citizens of Nolan and surrounding counties were assembled." The Resolutions of the day were drafted by R. M. Chitwood. Along with all the customary "whereases" were recited all the acts of "inequality and injustice" which had been perpetrated on West Texas. The people of West Texas had "appealed in vain for justice and for adequate educational facilities" in order "that prosperity might be blessed with enlightenment." "No free and vigorous people could be content to live under a government which denies them such rights and privileges." Under the final "be it resolved" the Resolution stated "that the citizens here assembled suggest that if our demands are not complied with by

[46] *Senate Journal*, 34th Legislature, pp. 119, 295, 1204.
[47] *Ibid.*, 34th Legislature, p. 749.
[48] *House Journal*, 34th Legislature, pp. 375, 755.

the next special session of the Legislature, we will call for the creation of a new state under which we hope to have equal rights and equal representation."[49]

The matter did not end there. On the evening of April 6, between three and four hundred people from various parts of West Texas gathered at Sweetwater to attend a protest banquet, given under the auspices of the Young Men's Business League. After lingering long over the lack of justice which West Texas had received at the hands of the rest of the state, the speakers proposed a division of the state. One of the most effective speeches was made by Judge R. C. Crane of Sweetwater. With the aid of a map he showed that the great network of railroads in East Texas had been built by means of West Texas land grants. Of all the lines receiving state lands, only three had been built in West Texas. He read a telegram from Austin which stated that 32,000,000 acres of land had been given to the railroads. Furthermore, he pointed out that 3,050,000 acres of West Texas land had been exchanged for the State Capitol building, and that the University of Texas had an additional 3,000,000 acres still unsold. West Texas, he said, had furnished the proceeds of land equivalent in size to sixty-five counties the size of Nolan to build up institutions, corporations, and buildings located almost entirely outside of West Texas. Argument like this has its fallacies, but in West Texas no one thinks of them or dares to point them out.[50]

For the next three years, West Texas assumed a militant air both inside and outside the Legislature. To stem the ever rising

[49] *Dallas News*, April 2, 1921; April 3, 1921; *Fort Worth Star-Telegram*, April 2, 1921; *Sweetwater Reporter*, April 2, 1921.

The particular grievance discussed at the Sweetwater meeting was the failure of West Texas to secure an Agricultural and Mechanical College; however, many past grievances were brought to life, such as unfavorable land laws; the failure of the West to secure predatory game laws; the giving, by the state, of West Texas lands to secure the building of railroads in East Texas; the unequitable distribution of the state's institutions; and the failure of the legislature to reapportion the representation of the state in both state and national legislative bodies.

[50] *Abilene Reporter*, April 7, 1921.

tide of western opinion, a new college bill, far more elaborate than the one vetoed by Governor Neff, was framed and passed. It was a sort of sop thrown out in exchange for temporary sectional peace. The Texas Technological College stands today as a living monument testifying to the existence of West Texas self-consciousness.

The feeling of local West Texas patriotism is likely to be exhibited upon almost any occasion. The West Texas Chamber of Commerce has become the guiding factor in directing this sectional patriotism. An almost unconscious manifestation of this feeling may be observed in all statewide meetings and associations. Delegations from West Texas are inclined to band together in such matters as the election of officers and the selection of the next meeting place. One may observe almost any day something in the newspapers indicating the ever-increasing distinctness which West Texas feels. For instance, the newspapers on November 7, 1926, carried an article telling of elaborate christening formalities by the Southern Steamship Company upon the launching of a new ship. The new ship was dubbed the "S.S. West Texas" with as much assurance as if it had been the "S.S. West Virginia."

Since West Texas has secured the Technological College, sectionalism has been quiescent. One must not conclude, however, that it is dying; rather it is in a dormant state, ready upon sufficient provocation to blaze up again with all of its old time ardor. West Texas is a distinct reality in the minds of West Texas people.

CHAPTER VII

DROUTHS

An immigrant's wagon, in October, 1885, moved slowly westward along the road which paralleled the Texas and Pacific Railroad. On the coupling pole were three joints of stove pipe, on one side of the wagon bed was attached a coop of chickens, on the other side a water keg, and on the rear a crate containing two pigs. The wagon bed itself was filled to a depth of three feet with household goods, from the top of which a half dozen children, tousled headed, sunburned, and dirty, peered from under the wagon sheet. On the seat rode an unshaved and uncouth man. Beside the man sat a woman, silent, patient, and persevering. Behind the wagon came a boy, barefooted, riding an old mare bareback, and driving three or four milk cows. A dog trailed along. The cattle and horses were not fat, but were moderately well fed and strong. The members of the family appeared road weary, but in their eyes there was a faint gleam of hope and eagerness. Occasionally the man would lean forward and view with satisfaction the brown, grass-covered prairies. He and his family were going west to become landowners.

Exactly one year later, the same wagon passed the same spot going east. There were no chickens, no pigs, no cows. The horses, rawboned and gaunt, pulled the wagon with difficulty. The family, bedraggled and undernourished, by their dull, expressionless faces, gave a hint of despondency. What had happened to bring about a change in the fortunes of these people? The answer was not far to seek. They had experienced a West Texas drouth.

From the earliest days of its settlement West Texas has had a reputation for frequent dry spells, and, at longer intervals, severe

drouths. In more recent years, the dry weather has not been
so noticeable. Many of the old-timers still staunchly contend
that it rains more now than formerly. An examination of the
records of rainfall as recorded prior to 1888 at the various
military posts and at the federal meteorological stations since
that time will show that the average yearly precipitation has
changed but little. The construction of artificial tanks and lakes
adequate to hold sufficient water to last through long periods,
the ever-increasing use of wells and windmills, and a greater
knowledge of dry-land farming have tended to make the dry
weather less noticeable. Prior to 1900, a drouth was a serious
matter. Most of the people depended upon creeks, rivers, or
natural lakes for stock water. A few months of dry weather
would cause these to dry up and the lack of water for the stock
to become serious.

The first severe drouth of which there is an account was in
1864. There were few people in the country at that time, and
no newspapers at all; consequently, information concerning the
conditions is limited. However, the old settlers who were in the
country at the time, and who lived through the drouth of 1886,
compared it to the "drouth of '86." According to their reports it
was the worst drouth prior to 1886.[1]

The year 1881 was reported a very dry year. By the last
of June, people were becoming alarmed; but the weather prophets
reassured the people that it would rain in the near future. By
the latter part of July there was still no rain. The water in the
Clear Fork of the Brazos had ceased to run. The Double Mountain Fork and the Salt Fork were practically in the same condition. All the small streams had dried up. Cattlemen reached
their wits' end trying to devise means for watering their stock.
In spite of all that could be done, many cattle died of thirst.[2] It
rained, however, in the fall, early enough to make late feedstuff
and a crop of fall grass.

The summer of 1883 was dry along the sources of the Colo-

---

[1] *Taylor County News*, June 6, 1886.
[2] *Fort Griffin Echo*, July 23, 1881.

rado River. The old settlers said they had never seen the river so low as at that time.[3] But no widespread shortage of water, grass, or feedstuffs was reported for that year.

The drouth of 1886 was a landmark in the history of West Texas. It has not been uncommon for old settlers to refer to events as taking place "before the drouth" or "after the drouth," just as the Civil War veteran dated everything as taking place "before the war" or "after the war." It was a colossal calamity, as disastrous for West Texas as was the Civil War with all of its privations. It caused as great a movement among the people as the recession of the frontier before the Indian onslaught of 1865-66. It gave West Texas a reputation over the entire nation as being a desert country of winds and drouths, a name which it has had a hard time in living down.

The drouth really began in June, 1885.[4] The rains had been fairly plentiful during that spring. The early crops of sorghum, corn, and spring grass had been made. The lakes, tanks, creeks, and rivers, being full at the beginning of the summer, lasted through the hot weather, and no real uneasiness was felt until January, 1886. By that time, the surface water began to give out in some places. The neighborhood of Brady, in McCulloch County, was first to suffer.[5]

By May, the dry weather began to show all its blighting effects. The grass for the stock was poor, even worthless. It had made but a feeble effort to put out in the spring. There was little water left anywhere in the country. Wheat, oats, millet, potatoes, and garden truck were all dead, or dying, and the prospects for corn, sorghum, and cotton were very gloomy, but there was still some hope.[6] By the latter part of May, all the water was exhausted at Cisco. The Houston and Texas Central Railroad ran an extra car daily with two large water tanks from Albany. The water was sold by the bucket and the barrel. Had

---

[3] *Albany Echo,* September 1, 1883.
[4] *Ibid.,* April 21, 1887.
[5] *Taylor County News,* January 22, 1886.
[6] *Ibid.,* May 21, 1886.

it not been for the railroad the town would have been completely
abandoned.[7] By June, the water had given out in other portions
of the country, and many people were compelled to move their
stock to the creeks, ten, twenty, or thirty miles distant, and
camp.[8]

The people's faces grew longer and longer. It became
habitual to look for clouds. The tiniest speck in the sky would
have hundreds of eyes turned upon it, studying its every movement. They were invariably dry-weather clouds which would
form, appear threatening for a while, and evaporate, giving off
nothing beneficial in the meanwhile but a shadow. Some of the
people tried to keep up courage by having picnics and fish-frys.
As the water holes in the creeks and rivers dried up the fish were
easy to catch; they could often be caught by hand in the shallow
places and mud holes.[9]

By June all industries and contemplated local improvements
were paralyzed. Immigration had stopped. Many people offered
their horses, cattle, tools, and land for sale to get money to
subsist on, but there was no one to buy. Labor of all kinds
could be had at a mere living wage. A good farm hand could
be employed for his board,[10] but there was no work to be done,
except move the horses and cattle from the region of a dried-up
water hole to the neighborhood of one which still had some water
in it, pull out of the mudholes the cattle which had bogged, and
"tail-up" the ones too weak to get up unassisted. By the middle
of July, the last mentioned job became a hopeless and endless
task, for the cattle were dying by the thousands.[11]

People began to leave the country. Those of small means
had no other choice. Their credit was gone; there was no work,
no sale for what they had; their families were hungry, and the
prospects were growing more dismal all the time. The exodus
from some of the drouth-stricken districts assumed the propor-

[7] *Albany News,* May 27, 1886.
[8] *Ibid.,* June 3, 1886.
[9] *Taylor County News,* June 11, 1886.
[10] *Ibid.,* July 16, 1886.
[11] *Haskell Free Press,* July 17, 1886.

tions of a panic; it arose more from demoralization than from the refugees' hope of benefiting their condition. Many left without any defined object or destination in view.[12] They carried with them what they could and left all else. Fortunate were those who did have a place to go. A deserted house in Blanco County had the following information chalked on a board which was nailed across the door:

"250 miles to nearest post office; 100 miles to wood; 20 miles to water; 6 inches to hell. God bless our home! Gone to live with the wife's folks."[13]

Throughout the summer and fall, the roads were filled with covered wagons, drawn by gaunt, rawboned horses, and filled with bedraggled families, going east. It is difficult to estimate how many people left the country. Some communities were completely deserted; others, because they were made up of people financially more able to stand the drouth, or because a few local showers had fallen, lost comparatively few of their inhabitants. If one should hazard a guess, based on such data as are available, one might say that one-half of the inhabitants left the country either temporarily or permanently.

As water for the cattle became scarcer and scarcer, the cattlemen dug wells in the beds of the rivers. The water trickled into these slowly; the supply was inadequate for large numbers of cattle. The cattlemen of Baylor, Throckmorton, Archer, and Young Counties began to let their cattle drift eastward, following the waterholes down the streams. By the last of July, something like 30,000 head were pressing on the settlements in Jack and Wise counties. The approach of these herds constituted a grave menace for the farmers. The starved, thirsty cattle would drink up their water, eat their grass, break into the fields and destroy any of the burned forage that might be left. The cattlemen could not control the cattle; in fact, they were desperate and did not care to control them. The farmers assembled and organ-

---

[12] *Taylor County News*, July 30, 1886.
[13] *Mason News*, June 18, 1887.

ized on Bear Creek in Wise County for the purpose of opposing
with force any further encroachments by the cattlemen.　For
a while, a collision seemed inevitable, and there was talk of calling out the militia; but, fortunately, nature intervened.　Some
local showers fell to the west, filling the water holes in a few districts, and it seemed likely that the grass would green up a little.
In a conference held between the contending parties, the cattlemen agreed to turn back their herds.[14]

The stock water famine was temporarily relieved towards
the last of August when a series of local rains fell.　It was
so late in the season, and the ground was so dry that
these did little good in the way of raising a fall crop.
Some of the sorghum which was planted, however, grew enough
to make a little forage.[15]

Winter found the people left in the country in desolate circumstances.　The horses and cattle were poor, and there was no
grain and little forage.　There were no Christmas trees that
Christmas.　The Sunday schools and other organizations used
available funds, usually spent on Christmas trees, to buy food
and clothing for the poor children.[16]

The dry weather continued through the winter.　The people
were bordering on despair.　By the latter part of March, 1887,
mass meetings were being held throughout the country to pray
for rain.[17]　It was beginning to look as if the history of 1886
was to be repeated again in 1887.　Hope began to revive when
showers started falling in April, and in May the long drouth
was broken by a general rain.　The drouth proper had lasted
twenty-three months.[18] Although the drouth was ended, its effects
were not over for a long time to come.

During the most dejecting periods of the drouth the local
editors and the people generally were not without a sense of

---

[14] *Mason News*, July 31, 1886.
[15] *Taylor County News*, September 3, 1886.
[16] *Albany News*, December 28, 1886.
[17] *Mason News*, March 26, 1886.
[18] *Albany News*, April 21, 1887; *Ibid.*, May 12, 1887.

humor; grim humor it was. A rural correspondent to the *Albany News* in June, 1886, wrote:

"Crops are failing fast for the want of rain. Wheat and oats are an entire failure, and corn is beginning to look very sick. I had thought of starting a hotel in Bugscuffle for the accommodation of candidates and other deadbeats at the remarkably low price of 25 cents per meal, but, alas! how soon our fond hopes are blasted by a Texas Drouth!"

About the same time, a correspondent from Hulltown, Shackelford County, remarked:

"The Farmers' Alliance organized here with fifteen or twenty members. But if it does not rain soon all the members may be expelled, as none can claim to be farmers.

"We remember hearing somewhere that an explosion in the atmosphere would produce rain, that rains on picnic days could be only accounted for in this way. If this be true, we want a meeting of candidates and have them explode.

"Many of our citizens will be compelled to seek greener fields and cheaper bread, for from recent appearances there will not be anything in the way of either wheat or corn raised in this part of the country.

"Stock are declining in flesh, and some are dying, and should the drouth continue much longer we will be compelled to move all stock."

The *Taylor County News* observed:

"The weather has been so dry here for the past three weeks that the wells are empty and the fish in the creeks are carrying toadstools for parasols to keep the sun from burning their backs. Water is getting so scarce that Baptists and Campbellites are beginning to favor baptism by sprinkling, and they have quit turning up their noses at Presbyterians. Potato bugs are crossing the creek like the Israelites crossed the Red Sea, and for the same purpose—in search of water. A prominent prohibitionist has ordered a case of beer from Decatur, not necessarily as a beverage, but as an evidence that he wants lather to shave himself."

On April 14, 1887, the *Albany News* described the following incident which had occurred at Anson:

"Monday morning an individual was seen in town with a long slicker under his arm, and it naturally created intense indignation. He was pursued until caught, and it was discovered to be J. P. Cole, who has displayed many eccentricities of late. S. C. Hines repaired to the sheriff's office and swore out a warrant against him, charging him with unlawfully carrying a slicker, against the peace and dignity, dampness and future prospects of rain, in the free state of Jones. Deputy Sheriff Scarborough at once gave hot pursuit, and after a short but exciting chase captured the offender in the City Drug Store. He offered various and sundry excuses but without avail for S. C.'s blood was up and he was determined that Cole should pay the penalty for his rashness. A good quantity of cigars restored the prisoner to liberty, and it is predicted that many moons will wane before he will again attempt such rashness."

In July, 1886, a wagon from a district where a local shower had fallen appeared on the main street of Haskell with its wheels clogged with mud. Everybody turned out to see the strange sight with as much enthusiasm as if it had been the elephant at a circus.[19]

One of the characteristics of the drouth was its spiritual effect. Never before had the people been more united. Everybody seemed burdened with the spirit of hard times, and bound together by a common sympathy. Everyone made some kind of an effort to cheer the gloomy spirit of his neighbor. A controversy developed, but it was the result of a difference of opinion as to procedure and not due to diversity of interests. Some optimistically religious persons went so far as to pronounce the drouth a blessing. Others claimed that the Almighty had sent it upon the people as a calamity because they had been too prosperous and too forgetful.[20]

As early as the first of August, 1886, it was evident that if those people who wanted to remain in the country did stay, they

[19] *Haskell Free Press,* July 31, 1886.
[20] *Taylor County News,* June 18, 1886.

would require aid from outside sources. A number of individuals and organizations petitioned the governor to issue a proclamation calling upon the people of the state to contribute as generously as possible and to send all funds and provisions to the county judges or relief committees of the counties asking for aid.[21]

The response was disappointing; in many places, the eastern counties called mass meetings for relief purposes. The people were indifferent, and the meetings were poorly attended. Committees were appointed to raise funds, but even they worked half-heartedly. Some money and provisions were raised.[22] A few counties did respond generously. Wilson County shipped a car load of provisions to Runnels County.[23] The people of Weatherford purchased 10,000 bushels of wheat and re-sold it to the farmers of Parker and adjoining counties on twelve months' time. The *Farm and Ranch* contributed one car load of mixed planting seed, and, in addition, established a bureau for "the drouth sufferers." A vigorous campaign for all kinds of aid was carried on through its columns.[24] By this means, numerous donations of money and seed reached the needy farmers of the West.[25] The *Fort Worth Gazette* and *Dallas News* sponsored a relief fund with fairly good success. When the money was distributed, it amounted to about $750 for each county in the drouth district.[26] The Grand State Alliance met at Waco on November 10, 1886, and made a distribution of the donations which had been contributed by the local alliances since the preceding August.[27] Various individuals and civic and religious organizations sent boxes of clothing.[28] Some of the most generous gifts came, unsolicited, from outside the state. Within three weeks after the Governor's

[21] *Taylor County News*, September 13, 1886.

[22] *Ibid.*, August 30, 1886.

[23] *Ibid.*

[24] *Taylor County News*, September 3, 1886.

[25] *Mason News*, September 4, 1886.

[26] *Ibid.*, March 12, 1887.

[27] *Ballinger Bulletin*, November 12, 1886.

[28] *Albany News*, December 23, 1886; *Ibid.*, March 3, 1887; *Mason News*, April 4, 1887.

Proclamation the merchants exchange of Saint Louis had taken steps to send ten car loads of provisions to the region of the drouth.[29] The Union Stock Yards of Chicago immediately sent Governor Ireland $1,850 to be distributed among the drouth sufferers.[30] Other organizations sent car loads of supplies and seed wheat.[31] At last, the Congressmen from Texas found somebody to appreciate their free distributions of garden seed. Large sacks full were packed off to the poor drouth sufferers![32]

The greatest sacrifices in the way of helping others came from within the drouth area itself. A notable example occurred in Runnels County. The Ballinger country, with the exception of the community of Content, was not quite so hard hit by the drouth as some of the neighboring sections; but Content was ruined. It was a choice between getting aid from somewhere and all the inhabitants leaving the country. A committee was sent to Ballinger to see what the prospects were for relief from there. The citizens of Ballinger, although they were having a hard enough time themselves, responded immediately by sending a wagon-load of flour, meal, and bacon. Within a month twelve more wagon-loads had been sent. The relief committee of the county, during the succeeding months, directed that the major part of funds and provisions from outside sources be given to the people of Content.[33] There is no reason to doubt the philanthropic motives of the citizens of Ballinger; incidentally, at the time there was a campaign on hand to move the county seat from Runnels City to that place, and the vote of Content was badly needed on the part of Ballinger.

By the latter part of August, 1886, donations of money and provisions were being received by the county judges of the drouth-stricken area, and methods of distribution had to be worked out. Each county devised its own. In Taylor, the county judge

[29] *Taylor County News,* September 2, 1886.
[30] *Mason News,* November 9, 1886.
[31] *Mason News,* February 5, 1887; *Albany News,* September 23, 1886.
[32] *Albany News,* January 13, 1887.
[33] *Ballinger Bulletin,* August 20, 1886; August 27, 1886; September 3, 1886; September 21, 1886; October 15, 1886.

appointed a relief committee, and called upon the people of each school district to meet and "select three good men to make out a list of needy families in that community who are asking for aid." These lists were used by the relief committees as a basis for apportioning the aid.[34] In Shackelford County the county judge called a mass meeting and turned over to it the matter of devising a plan. The result was a rather clumsy system consisting of three committees, a relief committee, a committee on investigation, and a committee to see that donations were properly distributed. There was an overlapping of functions, and in the end the relief committee, by acquiescence, came to manipulate the whole affair.[35]

The county judges of the drouth district held a meeting at Albany on December 27, 1886, to devise new means of relief and to effect a permanent organization by which a more equitable distribution of aid might be had among the various counties. Some counties did not need help as badly as others, and some of those needing it worst were receiving the least. To remedy this inequality a central aid committee was set up to apportion the blanket contributions. It was estimated at the meeting, at which twenty-one counties were represented, that 30,000 people were utterly destitute and that at least $500,000 would be needed for relief. A resolution was adopted, calling upon the Legislature to pass a relief appropriation, and steps were taken to get assistance from other sources.[36] This latter move was destined to lead to a widespread controversy which waxed hot and furious for several months.

Practically everybody was willing for the Legislature or Congress to set aside appropriations for part of the people in actual

[34] *Taylor County News,* September 3, 1886.

[35] Blank forms were furnished to any applicant for relief. This was filled out, stating the financial condition of the petitioner and the number in his family, and sworn to before a notary public. It was then passed upon by the committee, and the order for the provisions issued. The money donations received by the committee were invariably turned into the form of flour, meal, bacon, and molasses, before being issued.—*Albany News,* September 23, 1886.

[36] *Taylor County News,* December 28, 1886; *Albany News,* March 3, 1887.

distress, but a dissension arose over the question of starting campaigns for voluntary contributions, especially outside the state.
The difference of opinion was due to four things.   In the first
place, the uneven distribution of the drouth caused the people
in various places to form different opinions about the general
outlook of the country.   Some rains had fallen in Burnet, Llano,
Mason and Menard counties.[37]   Although little or no cotton was
made, there was some feed stuff, mainly forage, and grass; and
stock water was never as scarce there as in the region north and
south of this tier of counties.   A slow rain for three days during
April, 1886, caused Shackelford County to be in better condition than the surrounding region.[38]   There were a few small
isolated localities throughout the entire drouth region which had
received a few local showers just at the right time and made a
fair crop.   People did not travel far afield at that time, and, consequently, their ideas as to the general condition of the country
were formed from the conditions immediately around them.   The
Mason News was altogether opposed to any voluntary outside
aid.   It maintained that Mason County would be able to "pull
through" without such assistance and held that county up to all
the others as a model of thrift and frugality.   The *Taylor
County News,* in a region hard hit by the dry weather, worked
consistently and energetically for aid from all sources whatso-
ever.[39]   The *Albany News* adopted a middle course.   It admitted

[37] *Mason News,* February 26, 1887.

[38] *Albany News,* March 4, 1886; *Ibid.,* July 15, 1886.

[39] The *News* began its agitation on September 13, 1886, with the following
appeal:

"We regret exceedingly the necessity which compels us to report
to an appeal to the public for aid, but being satisfied that the time has
come when aid must be obtained from some source or many of our
people will suffer, we make and publish the following statement:

1. No rain has fallen in this country excepting local showers,
within the last fourteen months.

2. Not a grain of wheat, oats, barley, rye or millet has been gathered in the county.

3. The grass is burned up except in low places, and where local
showers have fallen.

4. Nearly all persons engaged in farming in this section are poor

that many people would require aid, but insisted that such help should, as far as possible, come from within the drouth area itself.[40]

In the second place pride caused differences of opinion. Very often, individuals and families in the direst need would refuse help because they could not endure the idea of being "objects of charity."[41] A few whole counties, apparently moved by a community pride, openly rejected all voluntary aid.[42] The amount of pride was usually determined by the degree of necessity in which the people found themselves. When they became hungry enough, their pride underwent a rapid decline. An example of this took place in Haskell County. The citizens of Shackelford County devised ways and means for aiding the farmers of Haskell County. On September 3, 1886, a mass meeting composed of the merchants and the more substantial farmers and ranchmen was held at Haskell courthouse, and the offer of

men who came here to secure cheap lands, and have expended everything they had in buying and improving their lands, who must leave the country or expose their families to great want and suffering.

5. The Commissioners' Court has used what available means were in the County Treasury, in giving aid to the people.

6. Under the laws of Texas no valid mortgage can be executed on a homestead of 200 acres, which, in many instances, will prevent farmers from securing loans.

[40] The following item represents the policy of the *Albany News*, September 16, 1886, represents a general condition:

"Most of the farmers say they are not in need of assistance but we understand there are a few who will need some assistance. We suggest that they let the people know their condition and we think they can get assistance at home."

[41] The following item from the *Taylor County News*, September 3, 1886, represents a general condition:

"The pride of the people seemed to be the biggest obstacle (to administering relief). Judge Porter says, 'Our distress has been brought on by no fault of the people, and no worthy man should feel humiliated by accepting aid.'"

[42] Midland county announced "that her people could 'rustle' a little more than usual to offset the shortage of crops."—*Ballinger Bulletin*, September 3, 1886.

"Tom Green County wants it distinctly understood that she is not an object of charity, and that the cry for aid comes from counties east of her."—*Ballinger Bulletin*, September 10, 1886.

Shackelford County was politely, but firmly, rejected.[43] The meeting was not representative; two weeks later, a second meeting composed of the small farmers in actual need, met at the same place. This meeting condemned the action of the previous one, and agreed to accept any donations offered.[44] It was quite common for those people who were able to maintain their pride to oppose all efforts to solicit aid from without.

The third element tending to cause a difference of opinion was the boosting spirit, of which West Texas had always had more than its share. Abilene was widely known during the 80's as the "Wind City," a term which had much more of a figurative meaning than otherwise. The spirit of the boosters was later taken over by the West Texas Chamber of Commerce. The booster instinctively looked askance upon anything which would reflect upon the reputation, the glory, or the land sales of the country.

The newspapers outside the state showed a decided tendency to exaggerate the accounts of the drouth.[45] In view of the fact

[43] *Albany News,* September 16, 1886.

[44] *Albany News,* September 23, 1886; *Taylor County News,* September 24, 1886.

[45] This tendency is illustrated by the following item from the *Ballinger Bulletin:*

"Texas cannot fail to appreciate the generosity of the North in its liberal contribution to the drouth sufferers within her borders; but the ignorance shown by the Northern press in regard to our state is fearful and surprising. Part of this, it is true, is the result of misinformation given by irresponsible and unauthorized agents, but not all of it. A Nebraska paper recently informed its readers that 500,000 in this state were suffering for food. Other statements almost as wild have circulated in the North and East. Some newspapers with noble motives, have asked aid for counties in Texas that are themselves contributing car-loads of provisions for the sufferers. There are 228 counties in Texas, and the few counties mentioned by Governor Ireland in his appeal for help are not all of Texas by a large majority. Erroneous and harmful reports have gained credence in true kindness, throughout the North, and for this reason we suggested that maps and statistical tables be reported to Northern editors in order that the people may be better enlightened as to the comparative size of Texas and the number and condition of her people."

that it was one of the most exciting things happening that summer, together with the Charleston earthquake, it was exploited for all it was worth, just as the Mississippi floods were heralded in the spring of 1927. But whether the outside newspapers magnified the disaster or not, the real estate agents resented it. Some of the West Texas editors became furious when they saw items from their own pens quoted in Chicago newspapers.[46] They could indulge in humor about their own adversities, but let a writer in Kentucky republish their home made humor and their wrath fairly blazed.[47] It is not strange that those who persistently insisted upon singing the praises of the country, regardless of whether they were motivated by local patriotism or personal interest, would oppose any movement to discredit their cause. Nothing could have done more to substantiate the rumors circulating out of the state than to put on a relief campaign.

The fourth cause of controversy was the antipathy of a certain class of cattlemen for the small farmer, "nester" as he was contemptibly called. This class represented the most unscrupulous cattlemen, and, in justice to the others, it may be said that they constituted a minority. These men opposed any kind of aid for the farmers, because they wanted to starve them out.[48] They looked upon the settler as a sort of pest which was steadily advancing westward and ruining the only industry which the Creator ever intended for West Texas, namely, cattle raising. They grimly viewed the drouth as a blessing just as the Texas farmer today rejoices over a blizzard sufficiently cold to freeze the boll weevil. Although the cattlemen suffered severely from the drouth, their plight was not nearly so bad as that of the

[46] *Albany News,* August 19, 1886.

[47] The following item, with the emphatic comment, was no worse than the local editors frequently published:

"The drouth in Texas is so intense that potatoes are cooked in the ground, and all the people have to do is dig and eat them. The workmen carry salt in their pockets and don't have to go home for dinner."—*Bourbon News,* Kentucky.

"If that don't take the cake! The writer of the above can beat the 'Father of Liars.' "—*Albany News,* August 12, 1886.

[48] *Taylor County News,* March 11, 1887.

farmers. The range to the west and northwest was open. They could drift their herds over great expanses in search of scanty grass, mesquite beans, and water holes filled by local showers. Even though they lost fifty per cent of the cattle, and many of them did, they still had something left. That was more than the average farmer had. A comparatively small number of cattlemen wielded an influence in defeating drouth relief far out of proportion to their numbers.[49]

When the county judges, at their meeting in Albany, December 27, 1886, proposed some "other methods" of relief, they started something they did not anticipate. One of the "other methods" was a suggestion that various relief organizations send representatives into the northern and eastern states to solicit voluntary aid. A number of such persons were sent out and the controversy started. The people divided into two factions. The affair, pro and con, may be best understood by the case of the Rev. John Brown.

The Rev. Mr. Brown was the minister of the Presbyterian church at Albany. As a man of enterprise and personality, he was selected by the relief committee of Shackelford County to go to Chicago and New York and solicit aid. At Chicago he found himself blocked by the counter-propaganda of some Texas cattlemen, who accused him of exaggeration and even misrepresentation. Some of the hostile Texas newspapers kept their readers informed on the wrangle in Chicago, and attacked Brown of their own accord. The friendly Texas newspapers retaliated. Brown then went to New York where he immediately enlisted the co-operation of the ministers of the city. Just as he had his relief campaign plans near completion and his forces organized, his secret adversaries appeared again and labeled him as an impostor. The attack greatly interfered with his purpose, but in spite of opposition he was able to procure sufficient funds to purchase several car-loads of seed wheat which were distributed to the destitute farmers of Shackelford County.[50]

[49] *Albany News,* October 7, 1888.
[50] *Albany News,* November 14, 1886.

Long before the Rev. Mr. Brown returned, to be repeatedly honored and thanked by mass meetings of appreciative farmers who had, through his efforts, got seed wheat to sow their land, the controversy had taken a new turn. It had become a question of whether the country needed any outside aid at all. The arguments of "anti-solicitors" would do credit to the chamber of commerce literature of the subsequent generation. The "pro-solicitors" insisted upon looking the facts squarely in the face, admitting a calamity, if there was one, and making an appeal for aid just as Charleston had done in order to relieve the suffering caused by the earthquake.[51] There is little doubt that the controversy materially hindered the matter of relief, not only the voluntary, but also the legislative, both federal and state.

In December, 1886, Congressman S. W. T. Lanham introduced a bill in Congress appropriating $50,000 to purchase seed for the drouth-stricken area. Before the bill got through the Senate, the domestic controversy, which had been raging for weeks, convinced the Senate that the drouth was not so serious as had been represented. An amendment reduced the appropriation to $10,000. President Grover Cleveland vetoed the whole measure on the grounds that it was unconstitutional.[52]

The first appeal for state relief came in connection with the land problem. To pay the interest on the unpatented school land was out of the question. Under the law the land board had no authority to postpone forfeitures because of non-payment of interest. Upon the instigation of Judge T. B. Wheeler and the recommendation of Governor Ireland, the Land Board passed a resolution that such land would be withheld from re-sale until the Legislature had met and had been given an opportunity to remedy the distress of the drouth-stricken farmers and settlers.[53]

The one form of relief on which the entire country could unanimously agree was the remittance of taxes by the Legisla-

[51] *Albany News,* October 7, 1886.

[52] *Albany News,* December 23, 1886; January 27, 1887; February 24, 1887; *Mason News,* January 29, 1887.

[53] *Albany News,* August 5, 1886; *Taylor County News,* August 6, 1886.

ture. The average American has always had an aversion for
taxes, and the West Texan was no exception. When the 20th
Legislature met it found itself flooded with petitions to that
end. One or two newspapers timidly raised their voices to
show the fallacy of such a procedure, and undertook to show
that the principal beneficiaries would be non-residents, such as
railroads and cattle corporations, who did not need relief.[54] The
Haskell Free Press pointed out that in Haskell county the property of the non-residents was rendered at $1,329,000 and that of
the residents at $249,000. A remittance policy in that county
would have meant the state would have lost about $5.25 for
each $1 saved for the actual drouth sufferers.[55] Be that as it
may, the idea of tax exemption was extremely popular with the
people,[56] but the Legislature was not to be stampeded by such
a demand.

Instead, it turned to another form of relief. A bill was passed
and approved in February, 1887, setting aside $100,000 to be
used to purchase corn, flour, and meal for the destitute people in
the drouth area.[57] Under the provisions of the Act a committee of three, appointed by the governor, visited the counties
of the drouth area and determined the amount which each county
should receive.[58] The county commissioners courts were authorized to prepare the designated provisions.[59] When the final distribution was made, approximately 29,000 people were aided;
the average amount was about $3.25 per person. As much
needed as the fund was, there were some people in the drouth
district who opposed it. The thing most desired was seed. One
infuriated editor wrote that "the people could live on prairie

[54] *Taylor County News,* February 11, 1887.

[55] *Haskell Free Press,* January 22, 1887.

[56] *Taylor County News,* January 7, 1887; *Ibid.,* January 14, 1887; *Albany News,* November 4, 1886; *Ibid.,* November 25, 1886.

[57] *Taylor County News,* February 4, 1887.

[58] *Albany News,* March 31, 1887.

[59] *Albany News,* January 29, 1887; February 10, 1887; *Mason News,* January 22, 1887; January 29, 1887; *Taylor County News,* February 4, 1887; February 11, 1887.

dogs and jackrabbits, but they could not raise a crop without seed to plant."[60]   So great was the demand for seeds that the commissioners recommended to the Legislature that an additional appropriation be made for that particular purpose,[61] but nothing resulted from the resolution.

The Red Cross sent its national president, Miss Clara Barton, to inspect the drouth area during the latter part of January with the view of utilizing its agencies of relief.   Miss Barton went first to Albany, a region not so hard hit by the drouth as other places.   From that point she made a study of conditions and visited a number of communities in Shackelford County.   She was much impressed by the adverse conditions of the people when she first arrived, but within two weeks three things happened to cause her to change her opinion.   The Legislature made the appropriation of $100,000 for food; Congress had appropriated $10,000 for seed; and some local rains fell in the immediate region she was visiting and caused the spirit of the people to rise. These things, in addition to the fact that spring was at hand when grass would be green and early gardens could be raised caused her to report to her organization that no help on its part was necessary.[62]

During the winter of 1886-87, the boosters, those persons who always went around with a "hip, hip, hurrah for this glorious country," a small and bedraggled group by this time, experienced a new uneasiness,—fear of the speculators.   They had visions of great hordes of these persons coming stealthily into the country, listening quietly while the settlers told their tales of woe; then, they would run down the country, praise another place where they used to live or some new El Dorado just discovered; in the next breath tell the impoverished farmer that if he wished to go there he, the speculator, would purchase the farmer's property for about one-third its value just to accommodate him and enable him to get away.   The people were warned over and

[60] *Albany News,* February 24, 1887.
[61] *Taylor County News,* February 25, 1887.
[62] *Albany News,* January 20, 1887; February 3, 1887; February 17, 1887.

over to hold their land and beware of the speculator. This calamity never materialized. The speculators were more afraid of the country than the residents were. A large amount of property changed hands at only a fraction of its value, but, as a rule, it was about as much a sacrifice for the one who bought it as for those who sold it.[63]

By May, 1887, the drouth was broken in West Texas, with the exception of a district in southwest Texas and another in the Panhandle where cattle died for lack of water and grass during the summer of 1887.[64] With rains in the spring of 1887, the price of cattle advanced. Cattle had been cheap during 1886, because they were so poor they were worth nothing for beef, and everybody was trying to sell. Cattle that could not be sold for $3 a head in 1886 were worth $10 in May, 1887.[65]

For several years after the drouth of '86, the newspapers were filled with various plans, schemes, and suggestions for preventing drouths. The professional rain-maker appeared. He could always get, not only an audience, but funds by popular donation to carry out his experiments.[66] Some people said that dry weather was due to lack of vegetation. This group strongly advocated a law to require every settler on school land to plant ten acres in trees. Other people urged plowing up the vegetation. Perhaps, the most sensible outcome of the agitation was an interest in the matter of dry-land farming.[67] Drouth-resisting crops were discussed; the *Abilene Reporter* urged the people to plant castor beans.[68] Many of the suggestions were impractical, but they all were helpful in that they tended to stimulate interest in dry-land farming. Irrigation was discussed enthusiastically as a drouth remedy; and the Texas and Pacific Railroad Company

---

[63] *Albany News,* January 20, 1887; March 3, 1887; March 10, 1887; March 17, 1887.

[64] *Ballinger Leader,* June 20, 1887.

[65] *Taylor County News,* May 17, 1887.

[66] *Taylor County News,* August 17, 1894; *Banner Leader,* September 10, 1891.

[67] *Taylor County News,* June 3, 1887.

[68] *Abilene Reporter,* April 29, 1887.

bored a number of artesian wells across the drouth area to see if underground water could be had in sufficient quantities. The company also sent a corps of engineers to California to study irrigation in that state and determine whether California methods could be used in Texas.[69]

Dry years continued to come, but none was so disastrous as 1886. In 1891, the country tributary to the Rio Grande suffered greatly from drouth. As the dry weather extended into the summer the cattle suffered more and more. The grass was completely stamped and eaten away for great distances from the water-holes. The animals were compelled to travel for miles from their grazing to water. In their weakened condition many would fall to the ground from mere exhaustion and die. The cattle-men offered whole herds for sale as low as $2 per head, but could not sell them at any price. A few of them, who started early enough in the season, managed to save their herds by driving them to the northwest; but the most of them, thinking it would rain, waited until the miserable condition of the cattle would not permit them to be moved.[70] The result was a heavy loss. The total amount of rainfall for all West Texas for 1891 was less than for 1886, but the most of what did fall came in the spring and early summer. Grass and some crops were made, and no great suffering occurred, except in the Rio Grande region.[71] In 1893, the part of West Texas lying north of the Texas and Pacific Railroad was in the extreme southern end of a drouth area which embraced Kansas, Missouri, and part of Arkansas and the Indian Territory. Although times were hard in that region, the conditions there were not comparable with those of Texas in '86.

[69] *Haskell Free Press,* April 2, 1887.
[70] *Banner Leader,* November 12, 1891.
[71] *Taylor County News,* July 21, 1893.

CHAPTER VIII

MIRAGES

A CONSIDERABLE mineral craze existed in West Texas during the 80's and 90's. This movement was not so widespread or intense as that of the railroads, but the difference was only a matter of degree. The people had the idea that minerals, precious and semi-precious, existed in abundance somewhere beneath the surface of the ground throughout the country. Strange to say, the greatest excitement was created by minerals that did not exist at all, as gold, silver, and tin. Those which were actually found, in more or less abundance, coal and oil, drew much attention, but were not to be compared to the ones which were long sought after but never found.

The movement existed for the most part in the people's minds. The country had a peculiar psychological effect. People came west looking for land, cheap land and good land. The land was cheap, and some of it was good, but there was one thing on which they had not counted,—the drouths. During extensive dry spells the people had little to do. Therefore, there was plenty of leisure to think about other sources of wealth than products of the soil. They listened with eagerness to all rumors of mineral discoveries.

The people especially loved rumors of gold. In the spring of 1879, a group of prospectors became convinced that both gold and silver were to be had in the hills west and northwest of Brownwood, and began to dig in that vicinity. The very fact that men were digging for gold caused excitement among the people. The correspondent of the *Fort Worth Democrat* gave the affair wide publicity. People began to go to the region of discovery from all sections of the country. The *Fort Griffin Echo* reported that "Leadville is laid in the shade and the days of '49 are to be re-enacted."[1] The excitement remained at white heat for several days, but as time passed and no gold was in evidence it gradually subsided.

Five years passed before the people experienced another thrill from a gold rumor. In the meanwhile, prospectors had been tramping about. In March, 1884, news spread that a gold mine had been discovered in Llano County.[2] General attention turned that way with great expectancy. It was too good to be true; but within a few weeks the people, hearing no more, forgot it.

Then came 1886, the year of all years in the gold excitement. The long, devastating drouth of that year caused the people to think of gold as never before. In desperation many settlers were all but ready to go out and dig up their own land to look for gold. They were especially susceptible to gold rumors, it mattered not if they came from far or near. A second report of a gold mine's being discovered in Llano County aroused interest as early as February, before the drouth had developed much.[3] In December, when many people were being fed by the state and district organizations, the interest became intense. Rumors flew hither and thither, with very little basis, to be sure, but the people loved to hear and tell them, whether they were true or not. It helped them to forget the drouth. The most prolific source of these reports was the vicinity of the old Spanish fort in San Saba County. To the West Texan the very name, "Spanish," has always been synonymous with gold and treasure. It still is. The whole country is alive with treasure legends today, and a majority of them are associated with the Spaniards. One legend represents Santa Anna in person as far west as Jones County. The fact that the Spaniards once had a fort in San Saba was conclusive evidence that there must be gold there. Reports of "traces" of gold, silver, and copper kept the public encouraged; people in that vicinity continued to look for the "traces" all winter.

[1] *Fort Griffin Echo,* June 7, 1879.
[2] *Albany News,* March 14, 1884.
[3] *Taylor County News,* February 12, 1886.

A rumor from Burnet County with a more authentic ring almost completely eclipsed San Saba for a short while. A Mr. John Bryan went into the town of Burnet one day with a pan of peculiar looking black sand which he had found on the farm of a Mr. Tate. The sand attracted eager attention. Some of the wisest men of the town were soon able to discover fine particles of gold in the sand. That was enough; the report spread with remarkable speed. Everybody had heard how gold had first been discovered in California in a somewhat similar manner. The next week the local press over the entire western part of the state spread the glad tidings.[4] The people waited with bated breath for their local papers the next week, expecting to read of a big rush, and, perchance, join it themselves, but no more was to be heard of the Burnet sand.

A new Eldorado appeared in May, 1887, when gold was reported "twenty miles above Austin, four miles from the crossing of the Missouri Pacific and the Austin narrow guage."[5] A "grand rush was expected out of Austin," but whether it ever took place or not we were never told.

San Saba's reputation as a gold country had been suffering, thanks to Burnet and Austin. In August, 1887, she revived her claims. A Mr. D. W. Kirkpatrick was digging a well and discovered about fifty feet underground what he thought to be a gold deposit.[6] San Saba was left to enjoy her find until it was completely forgotten. It was not until March, 1889, that a new rival appeared. A miner from New Mexico was prospecting in Mason County and found what he pronounced gold, at Hedwig's Hill on the ranch of Anna Martin and Sons. This announcement, coming from a veteran miner, had unusual weight. A land boom was experienced, and land values rose accordingly.

Very little more was heard of gold discoveries until November, 1891. Then, as a result of a rumor from Llano, excitement flamed up for the last time. The discovery was reported of a

[4] *Mason News,* December 4, 1886.
[5] *Taylor County News,* May 20, 1887.
[6] *Mason News,* August 27, 1887.

vein of gold, which was thought to be the "lost mine" worked
by the Spaniards two centuries before. The tradition of the
"lost mine" was an old one, and it had many versions in different parts of the country. There were few West Texans at
that time who had not heard it in one form or another.[7] Much
interest was manifested in its "re-discovery." After the excitement had died away, no more was heard of gold, except for a
continuous search for buried treasure, a movement which lasts
to the present.

Next to gold the people were interested in silver as a short
road to wealth. The editor of the *Taylor County News* seemed
determined, during the spring of 1885, to start a silver boom in
the Abilene country whether there was silver there or not. Some
peculiar looking rocks were brought into town by a Mr. Lee. He
had found them while digging a well one mile east of Abilene.
The editor pronounced them silver, and gave the discovery head-
lines. A silver company was organized with utmost speed. With
such tools as were at hand mining operations began at once. The
officers and directors of the company, in their enthusiasm and
excitement, handled the pick, shoveled the dirt, and made blisters
on their hands. In the meanwhile, the fame of Abilene's silver
mine spread far and wide. Work went on furiously for a week.
Experts were brought in; an intensive examination showed no
traces of silver. The editor sadly announced the fact, but added
"there is probably an extensive coal seam underlying the bed they
have been working on." At the same time he announced that
silver outcroppings had been reported in Jones County.

The silver interest was not allowed to lag for long. In
December, a silver mine was reported as having been discovered
in Stonewall County. The Abilene editor, a most resourceful
fellow, seized the report and made of it an unanswerable reason
why the Gulf, Colorado and Santa Fe should extend their railroad from Brownwood through Abilene on to the Stonewall silver
mines. This rumor was better founded than any of the other

[7] *Taylor County News,* November 6, 1891.

silver reports. It seems that there were actually some traces of silver there. For more than seven years, interest continued, with varying degrees of intensity. By 1892, two mining companies had started operations, and numerous other claims had been staked. One company, composed of Eastland City merchants, hauled ten wagon loads of the ore to Abilene, more than sixty miles, in June, 1892, from which place it was shipped to the smelter at El Paso, a distance of about five hundred miles. The hauling and freight charges amounted to about $20 per ton. The project evidently did not pay, for no more ore was shipped. There was much talk of erecting a smelter at the mines, but that was never done.

Just a year after the Stonewall discovery the general interest in silver turned in a new direction, and excitement took an acute turn. An unknown hunter walked into Mason about December 1, 1886, sought out a person who had a local reputation as a chemist, and had him analyze a specimen which the alleged chemist pronounced solid silver. The hunter refused to reveal his name or the location of the place where he had found the silver. He stated that he had found a rock which had been inscribed with several letters, many of which were erased. The remaining, disjointed ones spelled R. E. U. Q. He dug under the rock and found nothing. Subsequently, near an old oak tree, he picked up a piece of metal with a Spanish stamp on both sides. Later with farther search, he found an old mine, and, going in, found a ledge of ore from which he chipped his specimen. He alleged there was sufficient wealth to make him a millionaire and leave plenty for his friends. He left the town and promised to return within ten days, and was never heard of again. The fellow was no doubt a prince among liars, but he started something which has never completely died out. There was something in the whole episode which appealed to the popular imagination, mystery, the "lost mines" again, a three-foot ledge, and the specimen was genuine. What could have possibly prompted the conduct of the mysterious hunter, had he not been sincere? Excitement became rampant. It reached the greatest peak it ever reached, before or after, as far as silver was concerned.[8] People started out in droves to look for the old mine. Professional treasure hunters came from far and near. The writer met one of these characters in 1927 who had spent his whole life seaching for the fabled mine. An old man now, he has never become discouraged. He firmly believed he would find the mine before he died.

For the next several months, the people of Mason, Llano, and Burnet counties indulged in a triangular quarrel concerning the location of the mythical mine. The local editors said cutting things about each other.[9]

Strange as it may seem, the Mason, Llano, and Burnet affair, with no silver at all, almost completely eclipsed in the popular mind the Stonewall project which did have "traces" enough to encourage excitement. It held undisputed sway until 1891. In August of that year a Mr. J. B. Norris, while digging a well at Graham in Young County, struck a vein of what was reported to be silver ore "with a sprinkling of gold" at a depth of twenty feet. The mineral interest shifted to that region, and "great excitement prevailed."[10] Nothing was ever realized from this discovery. Later, that county found it had considerable wealth in the more lowly minerals, coal and oil.

The desire to find gold and silver became so intense that a large demand arose among the more enthusiastic and superstitious for mechanical mineral locaters, such as "mineral rods," and "indicators." Frequent letters were addressed to editors inquiring where such instruments could be purchased. On one occasion a Ballinger editor, who placed such things in the class with "rabbit's feet" and witches, returned an ironical reply through his columns. He suggested that the would-be prospector purchase a bologna sausage and use it as a "mineral rod," and added that when he became tired of prospecting, he could sit under the shade of a tree and eat his "indicator," thereby realizing some benefit from his investment. The general demand brought for-

[8] *Mason News*, December 4, 1886.
[9] *Ibid.*, June 16, 1888.
[10] *Ballinger Banner-Leader*, August 20, 1891.

ward a number of inventions. The local newspapers were filled, during the 80's and 90's, with advertisements of mineral indicators, which were "guaranteed to work."[11]

In order of time, the first mineral to be discovered and mined was salt. It was found on the Salt Prong of Hubbard Creek in Shackelford County in 1861.[12] Judge W. H. Ledbetter took up

[11] The following is a fair example of the advertisements of the "indicators":

THE GEOLOGICAL WONDER

Gold and Silver Indicator

The Geological wonder of the age, is an electrical gold and silver indicator for hunting gold and silver. The only apparatus of the kind that is entirely reliable, and fully warranted to do all that the proprietor claims for it.

All people who are interested in prospecting or hunting for gold and silver in its natural state, or buried treasure are requested to come and see the curiosity. It is especially adapted to prospecting the beds of creeks, rivers, muddy sloughs, and ponds, in which there has been money thrown, and rivers that have gold or silver lodged on the bed rocks, the instrument will immediately tell you by ringing a bell as on dry land. It tells just where the metal is by ringing a bell.

The bell will ring for the one hundredth part of a grain of gold or silver. It will tell you where gold dust is in the ground, and all placer mines on land or in water.

No trouble to work the invention. Come and see it.

The instrument will prospect in water and mud, eight feet deep. Patented October 15, 1889.

On exhibition at the fair grounds during the day, and at the St. James Hotel, during the evening, Dallas, Texas.

F. M. Kester, Ballinger, Texas.

[12] The following extract from *Shackelford County Sketches* (Albany, 1908), relates the unique incident by which the salt was discovered:

"It seems that the first knowledge white men had of the place was in 1861, at which time it was discovered by Cal Greer, William King, and Vol Simonds. These men were returning from a cattle drive to the Concho country, and when no considerable distance from Fort Phantom Hill, their horses got away and proceeded on their way back to their home ranges in the edge of Stephens and Shackelford counties, and this put it up to the three men to shoulder saddles and other effects and take a several mile jaunt across the country.

the matter of manufacturing salt on a commercial scale.[13] He hauled several kettles in ox wagons from Jefferson, and installed them in a single, large rock furnace. Between 1862 and 1866, the Ledbetter Salt Works turned out several tons of salt a month. It was the chief source of supply for the Trans-Mississippi Army on the northwestern frontier in Texas and Arkansas.[14] The greater portion of the output was sold to cattlemen and merchants throughout the western part of the state. It was estimated that practically all the ranches and towns within a radius of two hundred miles were furnished from the works. Big freighting outfits would come from long distances and haul the salt away by the ton.[15] After the war, Judge Ledbetter paid little attention to the works which fell into a state of disrepair. In 1879, he decided to operate the plant again, this time by solar heat.[16] For that purpose he built three vats, each sixty feet square. The new system enabled him to make several tons a week. The salt was coarse and was used mostly by cattlemen for stock salt as far northwest as the Panhandle. By 1881, competition and lack of railroad facilities made further operations impracticable, and the works were abandoned.[17]

Descending the mountain late one evening and finding nice pools of water, they decided to camp for the night. The snow whiteness of the earth made them skeptical as to the quality of the water for drinking purposes, and this skepticism was confirmed when they tasted the fluid, but the fact that the water was almost pure brine was a matter of great satisfaction rather than disappointment., for salt was a rare and essential article in the country just then. The story of the find was at once made as public as the population of the country would permit, and a few days later George W. Greer and George Hazelwood, two well known ranchmen, then living on Hubbard Creek, took some kettles and repaired to the place and laid in several months supply of salt."

[13] The title "judge" was acquired by serving as the first judge of Shackelford county, later.

[14] Martin to Pearce, February 3, 1862; Also, Barry to Dashiell, May 6, 1863.

[15] *Shackelford County Sketches.*

[16] *Fort Griffin Echo*, November 8, 1879.

[17] *Shackelford County Sketches.*

A short time later salt was discovered at Colorado City. A vein of solid salt rock eighty feet thick was struck while drillers were boring for artesian water. Beneath the rock was found an inexhaustible supply of salt water. A company was organized in 1885 to work the salt.[18] Solar evaporation was used until 1890, when a steam evaporating plant was added. A second deposit was found in 1889, and a company was organized to work it. The two companies continued to operate until competition drove them out of business about twenty-five years later. Since 1890, a number of extensive salt deposits have been found in various parts of West Texas but no attempt has been made to work them commercially.

The discovery of salt in Shackelford County during the first year of the Civil War was all but providential. The one other article needed as badly during the war was lead. The idea was generally prevalent that it existed in the hill country extending from Burnet County southwest towards Bandera County. During the spring of 1864, the state authorized a prospecting party to make a survey of the region and furnish supplies and ammunition for the expedition. The party was gone several weeks but no lead was found. When it broke up, a part of the men went to Mexico to escape military duty and the others returned home.[19]

After the war little interest was taken in lead. It was too low in the mineral scale. The people were looking for things of more value. One lone prospector appeared during the entire period when so much excitement was manifested for other minerals. He aroused little interest with his discoveries. People said bad things about him and he was obliged to defend himself in print. He found indications of lead on Little Bluff Creek in Mason County in November, 1890. He organized a company of farmers to develop the findings. The men worked vigorously until January, when they had to go home and start their crops. They were to meet again at the mine on July 6th, but their ardor

[18] *Taylor County News,* March 10, 1885.
[19] Erath to Culberson, June 30, 1864, Records Adjutant General's Office.

for digging waned as the hot summer approached. The company did not reassemble.[20]

Manganese was discovered in Mason County during the early 80's. A syndicate, the Wakefield Company, was formed and purchased, for less than $10,000, all the land on which deposits were located. The Spiller Mine was opened twelve miles northwest of Mason. It was more or less an experimental and testing project. In September, 1889, the company was reported to have sold its holdings for $925,000. For the next few years public interest in the manganese business was intense. Prior to the sale, the people had been more or less indifferent. Most of them knew nothing of manganese, but, hearing the amount of the consideration, they concluded that it must be something very valuable. The local newspapers printed long articles, in which scientific mineral terms were used in abundance, in an attempt to enlighten the people. The citizens read the articles and then knew very little more. But when the *Mason News,* in August, 1890, announced that the manganese holdings of Mason County were estimated to be worth $5,000,000, they began to wonder if all of that mineral was confined to Mason County alone. For some reason the deposits were never worked on a commercial scale.

Closely connected with the manganese movement was that of iron; that is, it was confined to the same locality and was going on at the same time. Some iron ore was found as early as 1886, in Llano and Mason counties.[21] The interest in iron did not spread beyond the immediate localities where it was reported to have been found, but was intense within these localities for a period of more than five years. The people there had visions of their region becoming a great industrial center like those in Wisconsin. There dreams were never realized, for the iron ore did not prove to be in workable quantities.

Copper was discovered in Baylor County sometime prior to 1870. Some attempts had been made to open up what was known as the Croton copper mines. Lack of transportation and the

[20] *Mason County News,* January 24, 1891.
[21] *Ibid.,* June 19, 1886.

Indian menace caused the project to be abandoned. After the
Indians had been subjugated by the campaign of the winter
1874-1875, a new company was organized to work the old Croton
mines. The party left Weatherford with implements and equipment in July, 1876.[22] How long the men worked is not known,
but no more was heard of them. Another company of Fort
Worth business men was organized in 1879, by a Mr. Clements,
county surveyor of Shackelford County. This company did
almost no mining but a great deal of advertising for the next
few years. The mines and the deposits attracted attention over
the United States and abroad. A Mr. P. H. Goldberg, of Chicago, acquired some copper land and began operations in Knox
County. In 1880, a French mining company became interested
and sent two engineers to inspect copper prospects. These men
found copper outcroppings in Baylor, Archer, Wichita, Clay,
Hardeman, and Wilbarger counties. They collected specimens
of the mineral and made an extensive and favorable report, but
nothing was ever done about it.[23] In 1884, another copper mining
company was organized with General George B. McClellan as
its president. Its claims extended sixty-five miles along the copper belt. The principal scene of its operations was in Wilbarger
County. By October, 1885, sixty openings had been made; the
most promising one was at Kiowa Peak, sixty miles west of
Margaret, Wilbarger County.[24] The copper movement, like the
iron movement, never created extensive interest in West Texas
outside the circles of copper operators and promoters.

The history of the coal movement is the most homely of all the
minerals. The coal deposits were widespread, abundant in quantity, but inferior in quality. The editors of the local newspapers
in the coal districts tried in vain to arouse public enthusiasm.
They continually commented upon the fine quality of the coal.
It resembled the semi-bituminous coal of Central Pennsylvania,
and in some cases was superior to Pittsburg coal. It was excel-

[22] *Frontier Echo,* July 28, 1876.
[23] *Ibid.,* October 16, 1880.
[24] *Taylor County News,* October 2, 1885.

lent for producing gas, and for blacksmith purposes was unsurpassed.[25] They pointed out its possibilities in manufacturing and its influence on the building of railroads. But the people did not respond. They were interested only passively. The entire coal movement did not produce as much fevered excitement as a single rumor of the discovery of gold or silver.

Coal was discovered in Lost Valley in Jack County, in April, 1876. The matter attracted the attention of some geologists and coal operators. A survey was made of the adjoining regions, and the beds were found to be extensive. In 1878, more deposits were found along the West Fork of the Trinity in Jack County. The discovery of coal in this region became a strong point of argument during the next fifteen years for the extension of a railroad to that section.

Two months after coal had first been found in Jack County, a bed of sufficient thickness to be worked remuneratively was discovered in Hamilton County. The next year, 1877, a stratum was found twenty feet below the surface by a well digger in Kendal County. Interest then shifted to Shackelford County. Three wagons appeared on the streets of Fort Griffin on June 13, 1879, loaded with coal which had been picked up in the bed of the Clear Fork River about a mile above the mouth of King's Creek.[26] The local editor gave the usual publicity. One of the Albert Sidney Johnston heirs, H. M. Johnston, came from California to inspect the Albert Sidney Johnston lands in Shackelford County with the view of opening a mine. The Houston and Texas Central Railroad became an ardent prospector. The company sank a shaft on Sandy Creek, and found some coal, but it was of such poor quality that it could not be used. Other tests were made with like results.[27] In the end, Shackelford County's coal resources remained undeveloped.

The first successful coal mining operations on an extensive

[25] *Frontier Echo*, April 21, 1876.
[26] *Fort Griffin Echo*, June 14, 1879.
[27] *Albany Echo*, May 5, 1887.

scale took place at Gordon in Palo Pinto County. The Texas and Pacific Railroad reached there early in 1880, and by January 1, 1881, the mines were producing thirty car loads a day.[28] Later, mines were opened at Strawn about ten miles west of Gordon. The coal at these two places was of better quality than the average grade found in West Texas. The Palo Pinto County mines became the chief source of fuel for the railroads, gins, and domestic users in that part of the state.

The next important coal discovery was in the vicinity of Crystal Falls in Stephens County. A vein five feet thick was found at a depth of a hundred and fifty feet. The coal was of fairly good quality, but the lack of railroad facilities prevented its development.[29] There was much talk of building a tramway from Crystal Falls to Albany. The cost of such a road was estimated at $23,000. The capital would have had to come from local sources, and that much money was not available. In spite of the fact that the road could not be built, Albany claimed the Crystal Falls coal field as her own and tried to start a boom on the strength of it.[30]

Coleman County came in for its share of coal. Sometime prior to the arrival of the Gulf, Colorado, and Santa Fe Railroad, a bed was found a few miles south of Santa Anna. As soon as the railroad arrived in 1886, the Colorado Coal Mine was opened. It was worked to some extent for a few years and then abandoned.[31] In 1889, a second deposit was found. As the *Taylor County News* expressed it, "a twenty-five inch vein of coal was discovered in Coleman County and the papers gave a fresh 'whoop' for the 'cattle trail' railroad." A mining company was organized to develop it.[32] Some tests were made, but no commercial quantities were produced.

The year 1886 was rather prolific in the way of coal dis-

28 *Fort Griffin Echo,* January 8, 1881.
29 *Albany Star,* January 13, 1883.
30 *Albany News,* April 8, 1886.
31 *Ballinger Bulletin,* July 23, 1886.
32 *Albany News,* March 21, 1889.

coveries. Beds were found in Hardeman County, at Eagle Pass, Lampasas, and White Oaks, near El Paso. The quality of the coal at White Oaks was pronounced unusually good.[33]

During 1887, there was considerable prospecting on the part of a few people for coal in Mason County. The purpose was to find coal and iron together and insure an industrial center. The people at large were so excited about gold, silver and manganese that they took little interest in the coal business. The local editor was forced to council his people "not to be backward even in the development of coal mines."[34]

The last coal development of the period took place in Young County. The beds there had been discovered during the late 70's. In fact, they were a continuation of the Jack County beds. Development was delayed on account of lack of railroad facilities until 1888.[35] With the coming of a railroad, mines were opened. The quality of the coal was fairly good, and, in time, Young County came to rival Palo Pinto as a coal producing county.

Little interest was taken in oil during the period. Some oil and gas were found in 1891 in Brown County.[36] The same year oil was discovered in Shackelford County. This discovery led eventually to the development of the Moran field. Oil had not come into extensive use, and the people did not appreciate its importance or foresee its possibilities.

They received the news of oil serenely enough, but, in 1881, they had become wildly excited about the discovery of a well of mineral water in Palo Pinto County. A stockman by the name of Lynch had previously settled there in the hills. Surface water becoming scarce, he dug a well to secure water for his cattle. To his immediate disgust, the water contained so much mineral substance that the cattle would hardly drink it. The well soon acquired a reputation for its curative properties. People rushed there from all sections. In the summer of 1881 a town site

[33] *Taylor County News*, February 12, 1886.
[34] *Mason News*, February 12, 1887.
[35] *Albany News*, February 16, 1888.
[36] *Taylor County News*, October 18, 1891.

was laid out, a lot sale held, and Mineral Wells came into exist-ence.[37]

Interest in the precious metals gradually died out. The people found other things to think about, as the country became more thickly settled and its agricultural resources developed. When the mineral movement was revived two decades later it had completely changed in its character.

[37] *Fort Griffin Echo,* August 6, 1881.

CHAPTER IX

AMUSEMENTS

LIFE in West Texas during the frontier period was not entirely made up of work, hardships, privations, and Indian scares. The people were gloomy enough during the drouths, but the productive years caused their spirits to rise. Friendliness, hospitality, and sociability were traits which seemed indigenous to the country. If the newcomer did not have them when he arrived he was sure to acquire them before long.

The people derived a certain amount of downright pleasure from the railroad agitation. It gave them something to think about, talk about, and an opportunity to hold mass meetings. They took it seriously but they liked it. The same is, in part, true of the mineral movement. These affable people craved other pastimes. There were few commercialized amusements, but the people were resourceful enough to devise their own.

One of the most interesting amusements was horse-racing. It stirred the sporting blood of the people. They loved horses and they loved sports with plenty of action; so a combination of the two could easily become their favorite recreation. There were two kinds of horse races, the big, much advertised, semi-professional race and the local race. During the 70's and before barbecues and fairs came into vogue the big race was the great event of the year. Crowds were drawn from a radius of a hundred miles. People would leave home one or two days beforehand, depending on the distance. It was not uncommon for entire towns, within a thirty- or forty-mile radius, to be practically deserted during the races.[1] At an early hour on the gala day, the people, in vehicles, on horseback, and afoot, would gather at the race ground, located in some nearby pasture where there

[1] *Frontier Echo,* March 2, 1877.

was enough level ground to admit of racing. There were no seats, grandstand, nor any of the equipment one usually considers essential to a race track. All the preparation required was to step óff the various distances and mark them with a stone or post. Sometimes, wires were stretched on either side of the track to prevent the crowd from surging out in the way of the horses.

The races usually did not begin until late morning or early afternoon. The spectators, who gathered hours beforehand, spent the time in "getting a line" on the various contestants, talking excitedly, and placing their bets. Betting was almost universal; few people at the time found anything morally wrong with it. As the country filled with settlers from "back east" and as religion became more and more a dominant factor in the life of the times, betting fell into disrepute and finally came to be looked upon by the majority as a sin. There was more or less drinking throughout the day; everybody did not drink and most of those who did managed to stay sober until after the races when they could collect or pay their bets. Then, if they cared to get drunk, they had a good excuse; those who lost could find solace, and those who won could afford to celebrate. There were several large horse ranches scattered through the country.[2] Although the ranchmen devoted their primary attention to the raising of saddle and work horses, many bred race horses. It was their principal diversion to train them carefully and enter them in the regional races.

The local race was almost always an impromptu affair. It usually resulted from an argument between two owners as to the running merits of their horses. They might not be race horses at all, but their owners were proud of them and were willing to back them against all odds. The race might take place immediately, and they would repair to the local race track accompanied by practically everybody in town. The bets would be hastily placed and the race run. If the affair was postponed for a few days, the news would circulate and a bigger crowd would be on hand. Not infrequently disputes arose over these local races.

---

[2] Albany acquired a national reputation during the 80's and 90's as a breeding center of Norman horses.

The owners were not as good sportsmen as the professionals. Fights sometimes occurred, and it would become necessary to return the stakes.[3]

Contemporary with horse races were the dances. As in races, people experienced much anticipation, made elaborate preparations, and traveled long distances. The big dances, or balls as they were called, took place on the most popular holidays, preferably Christmas, New Year's, and the Fourth of July. They were held at the courthouse, or, occasionally, at a schoolhouse or ranch house. The district court room was the most spacious in the country, and therefore, most desirable.

Regardless of where the event took place, plans were made long in advance. A general invitation was extended to the people in the adjoining counties through the medium of the local newspaper. For everyone, far and near, to hear of a ball, was to consider himself invited. Then came the preparation and anticipation. As the time drew near the anticipation became feverish. As in the case of the horse races, it was necessary to start from home in plenty of time, as a rule, early in the morning, if the drive could be made in a day. People came on horseback, in buggies, buckboards, and wagons. It was necessary for the guests to arrive in the afternoon in order to get the horses watered and fed, attend to their toilets, and eat supper. If the dance was at the courthouse or schoolhouse, each family brought food and placed it on temporary tables and the entire crowd was invited to partake, after the manner of "dinner on the ground" at various kinds of public gatherings. If the dance was given by a ranchman, he provided the supper.[4] He would previously barbecue a beef which was served with bread, pickles, black coffee with cakes, pies and other delicacies. After supper the house was cleared of furniture with the exception of seats around the walls. There were never chairs enough, and the deficiency was made up by laying boards across chairs and boxes. The fiddlers spent some time in "tuning up." When all was ready the manager,

[3] *Fort Griffin Echo*, September 6, 1879.
[4] *Taylor County News*, May 17, 1894.

or caller as he was termed, took his place and summoned the guests to prepare for the first dance. The primary prerequisites for a caller were a pair of "leather lungs," a sense of rhythm, and enough leadership and personality to get the crowd to enter into the spirit of the dance. Most of the guests were inclined to be shy at first, but when noise and action started, all shyness was forgotten. The whining of the fiddles, the scraping and stamping of the high-heeled boots on the rough floor, and the rhythmic shouts of the caller were all well adapted to dispelling any traces of self-consciousness on the part of even the most timid. A young lady from the east gave a description of her first western dance as follows:

"It was with many misgivings in spite of my partner's assurance that he would pull me through, that I took my place in the dance.

> " 'Hark ye partners.
> Rights the same.'

So far, I bowed as did the rest.

> " 'Balance you all.'

"With the plunge of a maddened steer, my partner came toward me. I smothered a scream as I was seized and swung around like a bag of meal. Before I could get my breath I was pushed out to answer to

> " 'First lady to the right;
> Swing the man that stole the sheep,
> Now the one that hauled it home,
> Now the one that ate the meat,
> Now the one that gnawed the bones.'

"Not being well acquainted with the private histories of the men in the set, I was at a little disadvantage, but I was seized, swung, and passed on to the next, until I finally arrived breathless at the starting point.

> " 'First gent, swing yer opposite pardner,
> Then yer turtle dove.
> Again yer opposite pardner,
> And now yer own true love.'

"I blushed in spite of myself at so publicly passing as my partner's 'turtle dove' and 'own true love,' while his sweetheart over in the corner, transfixing me with a jealous glare, saw no humor whatever in the situation.

"Again came the command:

> " 'First couple to the right,
> Cage the bird, three hands round.'

"I found myself in the center of a circle formed by my partner and the second couple and then exchanged places with my partner at the call:

> " 'Birdie hop out and crane hop in,
> Three hands around and go it again.
> All men left; back to the partner,
> And grand right and left.
> Come to yer partner once and a half
> Yaller hammer right and jaybird left,
> Meet yer partner and all chaw hay,
> You know where and I don't care,
> Seat your partner in the old arm chair.'

"By this time, feeling quite bruised and battered, I was ready for most any kind of a chair."[5]

The dance went on furiously until daybreak. Waltzes, quadrilles, and schottisches followed each other in rapid order.[6]

[5] *Lubbock Avalanche,* March 6, 1903.

[6] The *Taylor County News,* March 19, 1886, gave a typical program of a western ball:

Program for Cowboys' Ball

1. Grand circle round-up march.
2. Horse hunters' quadrille.
3. Catch-horse waltz.
4. Saddle-up lancers.
5. Broncho racquet.
6. Captain's quadrille.
7. Circular's gallop.
8. Round-up lancers.
9. Cut-out schottische.
10. Branding quadrille.
11. Cow and calf racquet.
12. Night-horse lancers.

There was more or less drinking. At the ranchman's ball egg-nog was often served.[7] Sometimes a reckless individual would become rollicky and would have to be ejected by his more sober companions. That was to be expected, and produced no undue commotion. About sunrise breakfast was served, the horses harnessed or saddled, and the guests, after taking an extra cup of black coffee, started sleepily on their long drives home.

Weddings were grand events. Although not attended by as many people as the big balls of the year, they had all the attractions of a ball and more,—the feasts, the dances, and the charivari. It was a protracted season of festivities, lasting two or three days.

Notwithstanding the fact that people, as a rule, married young, the courtships were usually long, often having their origin in childhood attachments. The engagements was announced several weeks in advance of the wedding. Then the necessary preparations followed. Among the well-to-do these took on elaborate proportions. The exact date of the wedding was determined by the arrival of the preacher, usually a Methodist circuit rider or a Baptist missionary on his regular circuit. A general invitation was sent out, by word of mouth, to all the neighbors. This included everybody within twenty, thirty or forty miles, depending upon how well the country was settled. On the appointed day the guests began assembling hours before the time of the ceremony, which usually occurred about the middle of the afternoon. The wedding often took place on the front porch of the home of the bride's parents, for the simple reason

13. First guard waltz.
14. Second guard quadrille.
15. Third guard Newport.
16. Fourth guard quadrille.
17. Day herders' waltz.
18. Maverick's polka.
19. Bull calves' medley.
20. Stampede all.

[7] *Mason News*, February 19, 1887.

that the crowd could not be conveniently assembled in one room of the house. After the ceremony came the congratulations, the wedding feast, and the dance. All the guests did not remain for supper. Some of the older people with their smaller children would leave after the congratulations, but all were urged to stay.

The matter of feeding from fifty to a hundred people in one small kitchen (the dining room and kitchen were generally one and the same) was no small task. But the food was already prepared. The bride's family and relatives had been cooking cakes, pies, hams, and other appetizing dishes for days. Perchance, a beef had been slaughtered for the occasion. The guests were served in relays. Some eight, ten, or twelve could eat at one time. When they had finished, the dishes were quickly washed and the tables "re-set," and so on until all had eaten. The bride and groom were given the places of honor at the first table and made highly uncomfortable by the jests of the others. For them it was more like an inquisition than a wedding feast.

After the supper, came the dance which lasted until daybreak. The guests were fortunate if they got a little time to rest before starting to the "infair." The infair was a reception held that afternoon and night at the home of the groom's parents. The merry gathering began in the afternoon, and the supper and dance of the previous night were repeated. Occasionally the festivities were continued into the third day, especially if it were the Christmas season.[8] These arrangements applied to the well-to-do, but even with the poorer people the differences were only a matter of degree.

A few nights after the wedding festivities the charivari took place. This affair was always planned with the utmost secrecy. On the appointed night the friends of the newly married couple would assemble at some designated place. Each person carried a tin pan, a plow-share, a cow-bell or anything to make noise. The party would leave their horses and buggies at a considerable distance from the house where the bride and groom were spending the night, and proceed the rest of the distance with

[8] *Fort Griffin Echo*, January 4, 1879.

great stealth. The most appropriate time for this was shortly after midnight. After surrounding the house, a signal would be given, and bedlam would turn loose. Beating, banging, whooping, yelling, the troupe would march around the house until the inmates arose and invited the noisy visitors to enter. The custom required that refreshments be served, but, refreshments or no refreshments, the crowd would have a party for an hour or two and then depart.

Life in the little frontier towns was by no means dull. The town itself was most unpretentious. Before the coming of the railroads most of them were county seats, consisting of a courthouse, blacksmith shop, wagon yard, a few picket or boxed stores, a half dozen saloons, a very plain hotel, and a few equally plain dwelling houses. There was no civic pride; the garbage and rubbish was pitched into the "main" street with as much nonchalance as into the alley.[9] But there was always plenty of excitement.

Every town had a group of loafers, who did nothing day by day but think up "practical jokes"—the most of them were highly impractical—and execute them on the first likely victim. In the morning these fellows sat on goods boxes and chewed strong tobacco in the shade on the west side of the "commercial row"; at noon when the sun was coming straight down, they disappeared and left the streets empty and silent; when the shadows began to lengthen in the afternoon, they appeared from somewhere and took their places on the east side of the buildings. They swapped jokes, spun yarns, talked about the weather, the cattle business, politics, anything and everything, and spent a goodly part of their energy studying out some new devilment.[10] There was always an objective to their jokes, namely, to get "the treats" as often as possible. After perpetrating a prank, if the victim were a good sport, he invited the crowd to the nearest saloon and ordered the drinks; but, if he took the affair in an ugly manner, and appeared to be indignant about it, he

9 *Albany News*, August 22, 1884.
10 *Frontier Echo*, October 1, 1875.

became a social outcast. Life for him would become very unpleasant so long as he remained in that town, and he was liable to open insult at any time.

There was more or less going on at all times of the year, but during the winter months excitement became very intense. This was "off season" for the cowboy; it was after the summer drives and the fall round-ups, and before the spring round-ups. All cowboys not needed for winter range duty spent the time at home "back east" or loafing in the frontier towns. Nobody can excel the idle cowboy in devising devilment. He, with the professional loafer, made the winter months unusually lively, and caused them to be referred to as "badger season." [11]

The most standardized and successful joke, one that was worked time after time for years, was "pulling the badger." Three classes of persons were selected as the "puller," any green, gawky tenderfoot who needed edifying, any "high collared" gentleman from the East, and any unsuspecting, respectable looking person who appeared to have enough money to buy the treats. When the loafers had selected their victims they would casually collect around the stranger and begin to talk excitedly about a big dog and badger fight which was about to take place. Their enthusiasm could not fail to engage the interest of any normal person within hearing distance. Everybody was placing enormous bets on either the dog or the badger. Then a heated dispute would arise over the selection of a referee. The chief duty of this official was to start the fight by pulling the badger out from under a barrel by means of a long rope which was supposed to be attached to the badger's neck. Several men would volunteer, but they would be challenged on the grounds of having a bet on one side of the other. Then they would begin to look for a disinterested person. Somebody would, for the first time, discover the proposed victim. Here was a stranger, he would surely be non-partisan, would he serve? He would consider it a great honor. Then the crowd would

[11] *Albany News*, April 18, 1884.

start *en masse* to the rear of a saloon, or the butcher shop, wherever the badger happened to be kept. On the way, several persons would whisper advice to the referee as to how he could help to throw the fight. If he pulled hard, he would help the dog; if he pulled easy he would help the badger. By this time the whole town had suspended business and collected to witness the fight. A dog was obtained and all made ready. The referee, feeling his responsibility seriously, took his position. His sympathy was invariably with the dog. When ordered to pull, he did so with much vigor. To his disconcerted amazement no badger appeared on the other end of the rope at all, but instead a certain domestic utensil which is not often spoken of in polite conversation. Then, the crowd exploded with laughter, and prepared their thirsty throats for the drinks.[12]

When one had "pulled the badger" he was considered as having taken the degree of the "Noble Texan." The greater the importance of the neophyte, the greater the delight of the perpetrators. No less a personage than a United States Senator took the degree. The "badger fight" came near becoming an institution of itself. It was one of the factors which tended to produce a leveling effect upon all social classes on the frontier. When a New England banker, who had just been made a "Texan," called for a napkin at the supper table of the hotel and was politely told by the waiter that he was just two hundred miles too far west to enjoy that luxury, he quietly accepted the explanation and reached for his handkerchief.[13]

The "badger fight" was reserved expressly for newcomers. When no such person was available and the townsmen felt that things were getting dull, they played pranks on each other. The writer has found accounts of no less than a dozen stock and trade jokes which were used from time to time. Aside from these, some of the loafers, endowed with more originality than the others, were always contriving something new. Items of

[12] *Taylor County News,* May 6, 1892; July 3, 1885; July 31, 1885; January 22, 1886; July 9, 1897; July 16, 1897; *Ballinger Ledger,* January 3, 1890.
[13] *Frontier Echo,* November 29, 1878.

the following type are not infrequent in the local newspaper of the time:

"A couple of little 'nigs' created considerable amusements on the streets last Tuesday evening by running foot races for the drinks; that is, they done the running and the 'Po' whites done the drinking."

It was considered an especially good joke to cut off the tail of the parson's cow. The idle cowboys would occasionally indulge for several days at a time in roping dogs, hogs, and goats and "canning" them. The local editor at Fort Griffin, who never hesitated to lift his voice against things of which he did not approve, looked on smilingly. "This is commendable," he added, "as it is an innocent pastime, affords the boys lots of amusement and keeps them out of other mischief." [15] The small boys seemed to have a mania for smashing the window lights of the church house, the school house, a vacant dwelling, or anything they could smash without getting caught. When all other forms of amusement failed, an idler could escape boredom by getting drunk. Saloons were plentiful. Every town during the 70's had more of them than all other kinds of business enterprises combined.[16] Hand in hand with getting drunk went fist fighting. Certain men, when they become drunk, want to fight.[17] They never had to wait very long in those days until they found somebody willing to accommodate them. Everybody would stop whatever he was doing any day to watch a good fight, and as long as no guns or knives were brought into action, no one interfered. Within a day or two the constable would carry the challenger and the challenged before the justice of the peace, where they would plead guilty and pay their dollar fines. The price of beer sometimes had a direct effect on the amount of fighting. In 1884, two new five-cent-beer saloons were opened in Albany. The old saloons stuck to the pre-war (the beer war)

[14] *Ibid.*, September 7, 1877.
[15] *Fort Griffin Echo*, February 26, 1881.
[16] *Ballinger Bulletin*, November 20, 1886.
[17] *Frontier Echo*, April 21, 1876.

price of fifteen cents a glass, but within a few days they were forced to come down. There followed a considerable increase in the consumption of beer. A man who never had money enough to get drunk at the old price, immediately went on a sixty-five-cent fighting drunk. As soon as he had paid his fine and got another sixty-five cents ahead, the occurrence was repeated. It was not uncommon for several fights a week to occur in a town.[18]

Moderate drinking was generally considered proper during the 70's.[19] But when a party of cowboys came into town in the afternoon, frequented the saloons until a late hour at night, and, after the people of the town were sound asleep, mounted their horses and rode through the streets, shooting their guns, yelling and making all kinds of noises, the citizens became exceedingly indignant. The next week the local editor would write a biting editorial, in the form of a lecture to the cowboys regarding their moral conduct and the rights of their fellowmen, all of which the cowboys cared for little and heeded less.

Frequent raffles tended to help keep up the excitement in the frontier towns.[20] Any kind of a game of chance was popular.

[18] The editor of the *Taylor County News* was a quiet, peaceful, law-abiding sort of person. His attitude towards fighting may be inferred from the following item of May 14, 1886:

> "The summer fights appear to have set in in earnest; only three in two days! It is rather warm to indulge in such pastime just now and we make a motion that they be deferred until badger time next fall."

[19] The editor of the *Fort Griffin Echo* did not hesitate to extend his thanks publicly to anyone who had generously treated him. The following item was a fair illustration of how such things were generally held:

> "Billy Burton, he of Casino Hall, knowing the *Echo* crew would work until a late hour last Saturday night, made our hearts glad and our stomachs warm by sending us a large pitcher of 'Tom and Jerry.' It is useless to say 'we 'uns' did not know what to do with it."— *Fort Griffin Echo,* January 11, 1879.

[20] Items like the following were common in early newspapers:

> "And now to keep up the excitement, some of the boys resort to raffles. The latest being for a fine black walnut bed-stead, good suit of clothes, a hat, a pair of boots, wash bowl and pitcher, boots and hat, and glass table set."—*Frontier Echo,* November 17, 1876.

It appealed to the gambling instinct. Seldom a month passed without having a horse disposed of by raffle. It was the best way to get rid of one. People would take a chance on a raffle who would not think of buying the horse outright, even at a nominal sum.

This old order of amusements, horse-racing, widespread gambling, balls, and respectable drinking, was destined to pass away. The influence of a new factor began to make itself felt in the life of the people as early as 1879. That was religion.

Religion played a curious part in the history of the west. It was more than a spiritual quickening; it was the cause of a social reformation. It had had very little place in the early frontier. About the end of the Civil War, the remaining settlers in Shackelford and Stephens counties "forted up" at old Fort Davis on Clear Fork. On December 24, 1865, a Baptist missionary arrived and preached to the people in the schoolhouse. It was the first sermon many of them had ever heard.[21] Religion made little headway until 1875. After the Indian menace had been removed in that year, a steady stream of settlers began to arrive in the frontier region. These people were from older settled parts of the state where religion had long been a vital part of their lives. They brought their convictions with them, along with very well defined ideas as to what kind of social amusements were morally right. The building of the Texas and Pacific Railroad in 1880-81 greatly accelerated immigration. By 1885, the new element was gaining the ascendancy, and many of the old forms of amusement became taboo. The old-timers who became an ever-decreasing minority, held on to the old amusements until they were, in part, abolished by law.

The religious element substituted new relationships to satisfy the social craving of the people. As churches were established, they tended more and more to become the center of the social life of the community. Protracted meetings, periodical revivals, and camp meetings were substituted for the western balls. The transition took place during the 80's, culminating in 1885 and

[21] Diary of Sam Newcomb in *Shackelford County Sketches*.

1886. The religious element had become strong enough to enforce a degree of Sunday observance by 1886.[22] From this time the major pastimes of the people began to take different forms.

More interest began to be taken in clubs and organizations, especially by the people in and near the towns. During 1877, a number of "Lazy Man's" clubs had been organized by the professional loafers of several of the towns. The rules of these organizations prevented any member from doing any kind of manual labor or putting forth undue mental exertion. The chief functions of the order were to initiate new members, see that the rules were strictly enforced, and summarily expel members for violating the regulations.[23] The activities and proceedings of all the clubs were published in full in local newspapers and furnished amusement for non-members as well as members.

Fraternal orders had been organized at an early day, but after 1886, their popularity increased immensely. The Masonic order, the Odd Fellows, and the Knights of Pythias, were to be found in every town. The lodges furnished a diversion; attendance at meetings was large; interest was genuine; and, the membership was far greater, in proportion to the population, than it has ever been since. So popular were fraternal orders and secret organizations that the few colored people organized their own in imitation of the whites. If they could not secure authentic data from the old established orders, they were wonderfully

[22] *Ballinger Bulletin,* September 10, 1886.

[23] One man was expelled at Jacksboro for "assisting, by looking on, while another man laid the floor of a house." His defense was that "he was little interested," but the club did not consider this sufficient excuse.

Another man engendered "bad blood" in the club by cutting an armload of wood, but he explained that the wood was rotten and easily cut, and that he had done it under protest. The club gave him a severe reprimand, but did not expel him.

One other member committed a double offense by borrowing a newspaper and reading it himself. If he had gotten someone outside the club to read it to him, the matter might have been winked at but the club withdrew all manner of fellowship.—*Frontier Echo,* April 20, 1877.

adapted at inventing complicated ritual and high sounding names, such as the Seven Stars of the Consolidation.[24]

Every town had its volunteer fire company, composed of practically all the single young men in the community and a few of the married ones. Theoretically, the purpose of the company was to fight fire; but, in reality, it was just another organization to give direction to the social welfare of the young people. As for fighting fire, no organization was really needed. Every time a fire broke out, everybody in town rushed to it anyway and did all that they could to extinguish it. First aid consisted merely in saving as many of the movable effects as possible. To put the fire out was usually impossible. The fire equipment consisted of one wagon with a few barrels of water on it or, perhaps, one big tank, and a score of buckets, and another wagon with a hook and ladder on it. The ladder was seldom needed. Its chief function was to aid in rescuing people from upper windows, and there were no houses in the frontier towns high enough to admit of such spectacular performances. So the fire companies carried on their social functions with great zeal. They gave dinners, dances, and balls, and then, benefits to get money to pay for them. Since it would appear unpatriotic for any citizen to refuse to support such a public-spirited organization, the companies prospered immensely.[25]

Along in the same category as the fire companies were the military organizations of the larger towns, units of the state militia. Each of these had as picturesque and romantic a name as could be found, such as the Abilene Light Infantry, the Ballinger Rifles, and the Fredericksburg Guards. They held about as many social functions as they did drill practices. They, too, were strongly inclined to giving plays and benefits, to raise money to pay for elaborate balls, at which they wore their blue uniforms and gleaming brass buttons.[26]

[24] *Albany News*, May 11, 1886.
[25] *Taylor County News*, March 9, 1894.
[26] *Ibid.*, March 23, 1894; March 30, 1894; *Banner Ledger*, November 1, 1891.

Gun Clubs came into vogue during the late 80's. Nearly every town had one. Shooting matches for beeves, turkeys, and almost anything else, had been common from the earliest days of the frontier; but, the gun clubs seemed to have resulted from a general "organization complex" which became prevalent after 1886. These clubs differed from the fire companies and military organizations in that the members had no desire to "sponge" on their fellow citizens, but paid for the fun themselves. Furthermore, the clubs existed for sporting, not social, purposes. Each organization conducted annual shooting tournaments for its own membership, and occasionally held a contest between a picked team of its own and one of a neighboring club.[27]

Other minor sports were indulged in, both in an organized and unorganized fashion. Bicycle clubs were common, and various kinds of races were fostered, such as handicap races, speed races, and distance races. When enough snow fell in the winters, sleigh riding would become the fad. Sleighs were quickly improvised by taking the wheels off buggies and attaching runners or skids, to the axles.[28] Hunting ducks, coons, fox, wildcats, bear, and buffalo, before they were exterminated in 1877, was exceedingly fine sport.[29] Trailing wild game with dogs on moonlight nights was always popular. Jack-rabbit coursing threatened to become as popular at one time as fox coursing in Kentucky.[30] Baseball clubs began to appear about 1880.[31] Their scope of matched games was restricted. If they played another town, the trip had to be made in hacks. The gate receipts were small, so they could not afford to travel long distances. In 1886, croquet became the rage. Everybody played it. It became one of the modes of entertainment at parties and dances. The croquet court would be lighted with oil torches, and all who did not care to dance could play croquet.

[27] *Mason News,* February 16, 1889; *Taylor County News,* May 1, 1886; *Ballinger Leader,* December 2, 1887.

[28] *Banner-Leader,* February 23, 1893.

[29] *Fort Griffin Echo,* January 24, 1880.

[30] *Taylor County News,* November 8, 1888.

[31] *Fort Griffin Echo,* July 31, 1880.

Bands had a strange fascination for the people during this period. Every town either had a band or wanted one. The people loved music, and especially they loved loud, noisy music. But it was not so easy to maintain a band as a fire company or gun club. It required a certain degree of musical talent, instruments, and an instructor. The citizens were willing to sacrifice more for a band than anything else. Jacksboro had one in 1875, Fort Griffin in 1880, Albany in 1883, and after that time practically every town intermittently maintained bands for several months at a time.[32]

School entertainments furnished a place to go. These affairs were crude enough, but the audiences were appreciative, never critical. The frequency of the programs depended upon the ingenuity of the teacher. If he or she were enterprising, there was a program every other Friday afternoon or night. If not, once a month, or once a session would have to suffice. But for a school to close without a final "concert" was not to be thought of. The programs consisted of speeches, or "elocutions," dialogues, songs, music, sometimes a play, and, occasionally, a spelling match.

Christmas trees were the brightest spot in the year for the children. They came into vogue rather late in the period, however. There were private trees and a few community trees during the 60's and 70's. The Christmas tree was long prevented from becoming a widespread annual custom by the lack of a suitable organization to foster it. It was not until Sunday schools had been organized in practically every community, during the late 80's and 90's, that the Christmas tree became a common custom.[33]

As dances became more and more taboo, parties came to take their place. These were strictly community affairs, held at someone's home. The party was announced and everybody invited.

[32] *Frontier Echo*, October 1, 1875; *Fort Griffin Echo*, September 25, 1880, December 18, 1880; *Albany Star*, January 19, 1883; *Albany News*, May 20, 1886; May 27, 1886; *Ballinger Banner*, June 18, 1890.

[33] *Taylor County News*, January 1, 1886.

At the designated time, the people gathered. No previous preparation had been made, except that the bedstead had been taken out of the "front room" and chairs, boxes, benches, and trunks had been placed around the sides of the room for the guests to sit on. No program was arranged. Everyone was supposed to entertain himself. Somebody would start a game of "snap," which would often be the only form of entertainment.[34] About eleven o'clock the guests would assure the host and hostess they had had a delightful time and go home. Occasionally, the activities would be slightly varied by introducing a candy "breaking" or an ice cream supper.[35]

As the country became more settled quilting parties became common. An enterprising housewife would piece several quilts from scraps of goods left over from her year's sewing; then, she would card the cotton, procure the linings, get out the quilting frames, prepare a big dinner, and invite the neighbor women in to help with the quilting. The response would always be generous. The prospects of a good dinner and the opportunity to visit and gossip all day had a powerful appeal. Two, three, or four quilts might be completed in a day.

Singings came to be an important diversion during the 80's and 90's and still are in many of the rural sections. They had a humble beginning and gradually grew into an institution. A few of the frontier homes came, in time, to enjoy the luxury of an organ. The neighbors would gather there occasionally for group singing. After churches and Sunday schools were organ-

[34] The game of snap has been used more at the country parties than all other modes of entertainment put together, including the square dance, and yet, it is the most senseless game ever devised. It is played by a boy and a girl standing facing each other in the center of the room, or in the yard, and holding hands. A third boy or girl "snapped" a member of the opposite sex to catch him or her. They run around the couple "holding up" until the "catcher" touches the "snapper." Then one of those "holding up" drops out, "the snapper" holds up with the other, and the "catcher" becomes the "snapper," and so the thing goes on until everybody is dizzy. It is all running, sliding, slipping, stumbling, and shoving. There is no dignity, rhythm, or grace to it.

[35] *Mason County News,* December 13, 1890.

ized, one of the first community undertakings was to purchase an organ to place in the church or schoolhouse where the religious meetings were held. A community singing class was soon organized to hold regular meetings every other Sunday afternoon.[36] As the country became more settled and singing classes appeared in a majority of the communities, county singing conventions were instituted. The convention, composed of delegates from the local classes, held one or two annual meetings. The honor of entertaining the convention was passed around among the local classes. The sessions lasted two days, beginning on Saturday and ending on Sunday afternoon. The community acting as host entertained the delegates and visitors in their homes and furnished the feed for their horses. Sunday was the big day. Singing was started early in the morning; at noon there was a dinner on the ground; in the afternoon came more singing for two or three hours; then a short business session was held, at which officers for the next year were elected, the next meeting place chosen, and the convention adjourned. The Sunday sessions were extremely popular; the building was never half large enough to accommodate the crowd.

When singing became popularized, it made possible another institution,—the singing school. One of the greatest ambitions of a majority of the young swains was to lead the singing at the local class meetings, and if they could get placed on the program to lead one song at the County Convention or at the Fifth Sunday singing, it was perhaps the greatest triumph they ever expected. It was necessary "to learn the notes," how "to get the pitch," and to "carry a tune." For this purpose a singing school was conducted for two or three weeks periodically, usually once a year. The teacher was invariably an unlettered man with some elementary knowledge of music, and an abundant

[36] The regular class meetings occurred on the first and third Sundays of the month or the second and fourth. Sometimes a month would have five Sundays, and the fifth Sunday was always reserved for special occasions, known as Fifth Sunday singings. These were regional singing conventions; they would last all day with dinner on the ground, and would be attended by people from all the neighboring communities.

supply of nerve. He was highly respected by his pupils, and conducted his school as if he were a czar. His salary was paid by tuition fees which varied from one to two dollars for each pupil.[37]

Singings had a strong appeal for the country people and a part of those living in the towns, but there was a certain element in each town which desired a more intellectual mode of diversion; hence, literary societies were organized. They flourished and prospered for an entire decade, from 1877 to 1887. Every town had one. Its membership represented the most lettered citizens of the community, the doctors, the ministers, the lawyers, the school teachers, some of the business men, and a few of the more educated cattlemen. The program included a wide range of subjects, but controversial matters had the greatest appeal. Debates were frequent.[38] The meetings occurred once a month or oftener, and took place at the Masonic hall, the hotel, or at the house of one of the members.[39]

Contemporary with the literary societies were dramatic clubs. A "little theater" movement swept over the country from 1875 to 1890; or, to be more accurate and judging from the amount of interest manifested, it was a "big theater" movement. Jacksboro had a local dramatic club in 1875. By 1885, nearly every town in West Texas had one.[40] Interest in dramatics, both amateur and professional, became so intense that every town had an opera house, which was decidedly the largest and most imposing public auditorium in the community, including the churches.

---

[37] Fort Griffin Echo, September 4, 1880; Mason News, September 11, 1886; July 4, 1888; Ballinger Leader, December 26, 1890; Taylor County News, December 9, 1892.

[38] They debated such questions as "Resolved, That capital punishment should be abolished," "That education should be compulsory," "That conscience is an infallible moral guide," and "Can a house contain both an attic and a garret, a basement and a cellar."

[39] Frontier Echo, November 9, 1877; November 23, 1877; November 30, 1877; December 7, 1877; November 8, 1879; March 6, 1880; July 17, 1880; Taylor County News, April 10, 1885; Albany News, February 25, 1886; Mason News, October 2, 1886; December 11, 1886.

[40] Taylor County News, May 8, 1885.

The club members took their work seriously. They would study, memorize, and rehearse their parts for weeks, and often for months. When time came to make a public appearance they were always repaid for their pains. The opera house would be filled and often standing room taken. Regardless of how poorly the players acted the audience thought they were good, cheered, applauded, and for weeks afterwards showered the amateurs with compliments.[41]

Aside from the dramatic clubs, other kinds of local-talent entertainments flourished. Before the military posts were abandoned, the soldiers would occasionally get up some kind of a program and present it in the nearby town. Ladies aid societies, lodges, fire companies, militia companies, and other organizations would get up plays and miscellaneous programs as benefits, which received a generous patronage. A minister took a trip to the Holy Land. When he returned he was prevailed upon to give lectures under the auspices of various church organizations upon what he had seen. So great was the craving of the people for diversion that the lectures were well attended, notwithstanding the fact that admission was charged.[42]

One man built a music hall at Fort Griffin in 1876, while the place was a supply depot for the buffalo range and cattle trail, and was still a military post. He employed ten or twelve so-called musicians, charged an admission fee, and gave nightly performances to crowded houses for months. Although the "artists" played badly, the same crowd would return time after time to hear them. The same year a sort of sleight-of-hand magician rented the district court room at Jacksboro and entertained every evening for several weeks before more or less the same crowd. He changed his performances a little, but his tricks, with variations and additional flourishes, remained the same.

[41] *Frontier Echo,* August 11, 1875; August 11, 1876; *Albany News,* February 29, 1884; March 7, 1884; September 26, 1884; May 6, 1886; March 12, 1886; *Taylor County News,* May 8, 1885; October 25, 1889; *Ballinger Bulletin,* November 12, 1886.

[42] *Mason News,* April 27, 1889.

Professional road shows were plentiful. Some carried their own tents; others played at the opera houses. Their programs were a kind of vaudeville, consisting of humorous sketches, songs, dances, and instrumental specialties. Any kind of a mind reader was always a good drawing card. Elocutionists were especially popular. At rare intervals a theatrical troupe came through. In 1898, a grand opera company toured the country, attempting a part of the opera "Martha." [43]

A phrenologist could always get an audience. In July, 1884, a lady lectured two nights in the Presbyterian church at Albany on the "Science of Phrenology." The people paid their money to hear her. As she went on her way the local editor commended her to the people of Baird as a woman of great ability and one who merited their patronage.

The type of show that thrilled the children, and everybody else, was the circus. The circuses which traveled in West Texas prior to 1900 were small. They moved from town to town on wagons. They had a small tent, one or two elephants and a few other animals, and a small group of performers, but it was a circus, nevertheless.[44] The Legislature, in 1898, placed a heavy tax on circuses. A general wave of protest swept across West Texas. Some editors went so far as to declare that it was an outrage against the boys and girls, that to deprive them of seeing the animals was to deprive them of certain educational advantages. No doubt, the editors were fond of seeing the pretty girls ride the horses themselves.

Above all, the people loved a picnic. They enjoyed nothing better than to come together with well-filled baskets, and, before religion had made it taboo, well-filled bottles.[45] They could meet

[43] *Taylor County News,* April 6, 1894; *Mason News,* September 17, 1887; *Ballinger Ledger,* October 7, 1887; *Taylor County News,* December 2, 1898.

[44] The most famous circus known to the country during the 90's was that of Molly Bailey.—*Ballinger Banner,* June 4, 1890.

[45] Such items as the following were not uncommon in the local newspapers prior to 1879:

"Each gentleman in the picnic party carried a quart bottle of liquor, but said bottles were empty before the home stretch was made; but as their old friends and make new ones. The Fourth of July was invariably celebrated in that way. As time went on picnics became more elaborate. By 1883, barbecues were taking the place, in part, of the basket picnics. Brass bands were employed, and horse races, shooting contests, and pink lemonade were added diversions. By 1890, several regular annual fairs had been established. The most outstanding of these were the Concho Valley Fair at San Angelo and the West Texas Fair at Abilene. The attractions, exhibits and prizes drew people from an extensive area. The local wagon yards and hotels were crowded during the week of the fair.[46]

Such were the amusements of West Texas prior to 1900. The introduction of the automobile, improved roads, and moving pictures were shortly to revolutionize the amusements and social conventionalities of the people. Whether the change has been for weal or for woe, we are not called upon to say. However, that may be, the generation which grew up under the old order of things still bemoans the passing of the "good old days," as is the custom for people to do when approaching the age of senility.

the ladies all belonged to 'the Temperance' they did not drink, but were very lively before reaching home; wood ticks and chiggers did it."—*Frontier Echo*, July 19, 1878.

[46] *Ballinger Ledger*, September 27, 1889; *Mason News*, September 20, 1890; November 15, 1890; *Ballinger Banner*, February 26, 1890; *Taylor County News*, October 15, 1897; November 15, 1897; November 14, 1898.

CHAPTER X

RAILROADS

PRIOR to the time the Texas and Pacific reached Fort Worth in 1876 there was no railroad within the limits of West Texas, and this fact worked a great hardship on the people of that region. Merchants were obliged to purchase their goods from jobbers at San Antonio, Austin, or Denison, and have them freighted overland in wagons drawn by oxen, mules, or horses.[1] Up to the close of the Civil War, goods were often freighted directly from Shreveport or Port Lavaca. The long distances and difficulties of transportation also limited the market for the produce of the western settler to a few staples and the quantity of these was necessarily restricted.

The cost of freight was almost prohibitive.[2] The average settler made one trip a year to market. He could count on being gone from home two weeks to three months, depending on the distance and the weather. There were no bridges and few ferries. He might have to camp for weeks on the bank of a stream waiting for it to run down. Until after 1875, most of his journey lay through a country frequented by Indian raiding

[1] Oxen were used for the most part before the Indians ceased to be a menace about 1874. This was due to the fact that the Indians were not so apt to molest a freighter with oxen as one with mules or horses because the oxen were much harder to drive off. The Indians were usually in a great hurry on their raids, and the only thing they could do with oxen was to kill them for food, and they seldom had time for that.

[2] The cost of freight per hundred pounds from Port Lavaca to San Antonio was about $1.25; from San Antonio to Fort Chadbourne in Coke County, $2.75 or $4.00 from Indianola; from San Antonio to Fort Belknap, $4.50 or $5.75 from Indianola; for each hundred miles beyond Fort Belknap $1.40 per hundred was added.—36 Cong., 1 Sess., House Ex. Doc., No. 22, p. 7.

parties. To him it seemed that his future prosperity, cultural advantages, in fact, all his progress depended upon a system of transportation. The coming of the railroad constitutes a West Texas movement within itself. The word "movement" does not convey the full meaning. It was a fever, almost a craze. It began in the late 70's, extended through the 80's, reached its climax about 1886, and moved westward across the Plains and Panhandle in the 90's and early 1900's.

During this period the building of railroads was foremost in the minds of the people. They took it seriously. They held frequent mass meetings to which delegates would sometimes travel hundreds of miles. They discussed railroads at the round-ups, at the post office, at the court house and at church on Sundays. Two neighbors meeting on the public road could not converse long without bringing up the all-important question.

The people had reason to take the matter seriously, both individually and collectively. The land owner could foresee the possibility of his land's increasing in value many fold as the result of a railroad nearby. To the towns, the securing of a railroad, or the failure to secure one, was often a matter of life or death. If they secured the road it meant a boom, a rapid increase in population, and prosperity for the merchants and property owners. If they failed to secure a road, there was a danger of the town's disappearing entirely. This calamity actually happened in a score of instances. When the Texas and Pacific missed Belle Plains by eight miles the town died completely. Previously it had had a splendid prospect, even having a flourishing college.[3] The same thing happened to Buffalo Gap, county seat of Taylor County, which had been a lively trading point from the days of the buffalo slaughter. In 1880, the Texas and Pacific passed twelve miles north, and Abilene was founded. Buffalo Gap practically disappeared until 1912, when

---

[3] The *Fort Griffin Echo*, May 29, 1880, has the following news item, "This noon the telegraph brings the news that the road will run half way between Belle Plains and Callahan City, thus killing both towns."

the building of the Santa Fe partially revived it.   Perhaps the most striking example, however, was that of Fort Griffin.   During the 70's it was the greatest trading point in the state west of Fort Worth and San Antonio.   It was the depot and supply station for the buffalo range during the extermination of that unfortunate animal, the supply station for the cattle industry for more than a hundred miles to the west, north and southwest, and it was the last important supply station on the cattle trail to Kansas.[4]   With the building of the Texas Central to Albany in 1881, the town's population began to dwindle.   Store buildings and residences were torn down or transported bodily to the successful town, and today Fort Griffin is identified only by the stone ruins of the old fort.

The extension of these railroad lines was the occasion of a constant shifting of population.   Although the bulk of the population of each new town was permanent, there were many transients who moved their saloons, eating houses and stocks of goods with the railroad, always managing to be in the town which at the moment was the western terminus and therefore experiencing a boom.[5]   The inevitable slump which marked the moving on of the road was due in large part to this drifting class.[6]

The newspapers as natural spokesmen of the people did not hesitate to proclaim their hearty approval of the railroad move-

---

[4] Doan's Store on Red River was the only supply station between Fort Griffin and Kansas, but drovers used it only in emergencies, having stocked their chuck wagons at Fort Griffin.

[5] Items such as the following are very common in the newspapers of the period: "John Shanssey has moved his Saloon from Palo Pinto to the booming railroad town of Gordon."—*Fort Griffin Echo*, November 9, 1880.

[6] "When you go to the terminus of the T. & P. railroad be certain to visit Mr. M. T. Tallant at his Occidental Saloon where he keeps just as good lickers as he formerly set before his patrons in Weatherford. . . . At present he is located at Eastland, but as regular trains run on West he will follow and set up the Occidental at the terminus."—*Fort Griffin Echo*, December 18, 1880.

"Yesterday Jim Massey bid his friends an affectionate adieu and lit out for the end of the T. & P. Railroad."—*Fort Griffin Echo*, November 20, 1880.

ments.[7] The rumor of a surveying party in any part of the West furnished sufficient impetus for a new wave of railroad discussion among local editors over the entire section. In 1887, Jay Gould made a tour of the state, and his every move was carefully catalogued by the West Texas scribes. They served their patrons well, giving them what they wanted most to hear.

Rivalry between neighboring towns attempting to secure the same road sometimes became very bitter. These controversies, sponsored chiefly by the newspapers, often gave rise to local feelings which continue to the present. The rivaly between Fort Worth and Dallas dates back to a dispute over which of the two should be the terminus of the Texas and Pacific Railroad.[8]

The actual arrival of a railroad was always the occasion of general rejoicing and celebration on the part of the successful town. The event was invariably commemorated by a barbecue and ball to which people for a hundred miles around would come and to which citizens from the unsuccessful towns would receive especially pressing invitations.[9]

Another characteristic of the railroad movement was the non-committal attitude maintained by the railroad companies themselves. The road officials had a tantalizing way of maintaining a Sphinx-like silence as to their intentions. No one ever knew where an extension was going until the contract for the grading was let or actual construction begun. The air of mystery and uncertainty only added to the interest. For instance, had the Gulf, Colorado, and Santa Fe made public its exact route when it started west from Lampasas in 1855, everbody would have accepted its decision as final, and that would have settled it. As it was, no one knew where the extension was going. Every town in West Texas from Cisco to El Paso was kept in suspense for two years, and their interest was manifested by mass meetings, permanent committees, subscriptions, raising of bonuses, correspondence, and interviews.

[7] *Mason News,* February 5, 1887.
[8] *Fort Griffin Echo,* August 11, 1876.
[9] *Mason News,* October 1, 1887.

The Texas and Pacific Railroad

The Texas and Pacific was the first railroad to build into the western part of the state. It monopolized the attention and interest of the people of that section from 1875 until 1881, when competition was begun by other roads. The company was incorporated March 3, 1871, under the Act of Congress of July 27, 1866, and under the general railroad laws of Texas.[10] The line was to extend from the eastern boundary of Texas to San Diego, California, and follow as nearly as practicable the 32nd parallel.[11] For road constructed outside of Texas the company was to receive from the United States the twenty alternate odd-numbered sections of land on either side of the road for every mile constructed in the territories, and ten sections for every mile in the states. For each mile of road constructed in Texas, it was to receive sixteen sections of land. There was in both cases a time limit for the completion of specified sections of the road. Should the company fail on any of these, the remaining lands due the company would be forfeited.[12] Two branches were provided in the charter; one from the eastern terminus, near Marshall, to New Orleans, a distance of three hundred miles, and one from a point one hundred miles from San Diego, connecting with the Southern Pacific of California.[13]

Construction began in 1871, and by December, 1874, the line was completed to Eagle Ford, seven miles west of Dallas. By this time the people to the west were thoroughly aroused, and began to take a great interest in every activity of the railroad. On October 23, 1875, *The Frontier Echo* gave public expression to what was in the minds of the people:

"The proposed railroad will have at least seven eastern terminal points on the Mississippi, and radiating branches in West Texas,

[10] *Frontier Echo,* February 18, 1876.

[11] Haney, J. H., *A Congressional History of Railroads in the U. S.,* Democrat Printing Co., Madison, 1910.

[12] *Ibid.*

[13] Poor, H. V., *Manual of the Railroads of the U. S.,* Poor, N. Y., 1871, p. 548.

and also constituting the Grand Trunk line to the Pacific Ocean. Some of the immediate results of such an enterprise would be, it would bring millions of foreign capital into Texas, it would add to the rapid development of West Texas. It would bring into this section a multitude of industrious immigrants. It will secure us the highway from the Mississippi to the Pacific."

But at this juncture something happened to delay the early realization of the western hopes. A resolution, passed in Congress in December, 1875, suspended all government subsidies in money, bonds, land and endorsements to all public and private enterprises. This included the operations of the Texas and Pacific which had just arrived at a point seven miles west of Dallas.[14] The road was still entitled to land from the State of Texas, but there was no immediate sale for these lands, and, furthermore, title could not be acquired to them until after the road was built. The funds on which the company had been operating had been realized from the sale of bonds indorsed by the United States Government. The railroad now found itself in a serious predicament. The date by which a hundred miles of road should be completed west of Eagle Ford was rapidly approaching. An appeal was made to the State Legislature for an extension of time. The question created statewide interest, and a clear indication of sectionalism appeared. The newspapers of the eastern part of the state appealed to the Legislature to use this opportunity "to recover the magnificent domain conveyed to the Texas and Pacific."[15] *The Frontier Echo,* which, unfortunately, is the only western newspaper of this period whose files have been preserved, at first was also opposed to an extension of time. It took this attitude because it believed such a policy would force the company to hurry to fulfill its contract. A fervent editorial on June 2, 1876, closed with this statement: "Extension of railroads is what we want, not extension of time." But as matters proceeded, the *Echo* changed its tone and came out flatly against the demands of the eastern newspapers. Tom

[14] *Frontier Echo,* December 12, 1875.
[15] *The Statesman,* June 25, 1876.

Ball, State Senator from Jacksboro, became the champion of the railroad in its plea for an extension of time. In a speech on July 20, he opposed an amendment which excluded the Texas and Pacific from participating in a general bill giving all the railroads thirty days' extension of time.[16]

During the summer of 1876, the company concentrated its efforts on completing the road to Fort Worth. On September 29, 1876, the *Echo* announced with much pleasure,

"Trains are now running on the Texas and Pacific Railroad through to Fort Worth. This, in connection with the change in the arrival and departure of the stages east of this place cuts the time down between here and the east by twenty-four hours. Bully for the T. & P. and for Bain!"

Dallas was much opposed to Fort Worth's becoming the terminus, and brought all pressure to bear to have the road pushed on to Weatherford. The citizens of Weatherford, aided by those of Dallas, prevailed upon the officials of the road to attempt this extension, notwithstanding the fact that means for financing the project were, as yet, uncertain. Weatherford, aided by all the citizens of Parker County, offered to donate the depot grounds and right-of-way across that county. In the drive for funds for this purpose the city council loaned the citizens $465 of the city's money to make up a deficit. The company decided to try to raise the money for the construction of the grade by issuing three-year eight per cent bonds. In asking the people to buy these bonds the *Weatherford Times* urged that

"this is a good investment, and if our people who have lands to sell, produce to carry to market, spare cash to invest, will look to their own interest, they will assist in the building of the road to Weatherford. . . . Our stock men say the country is already too thickly settled for them and that they will be compelled to move in a year or two. Build the railroad to Weatherford and it will accelerate their removal, they say."[17]

[16] *Frontier Echo,* August 11, 1876.
[17] Exchange in the *Frontier Echo,* November 2, 1877.

Meanwhile, the company was appealing to Congress for aid. Congress was asked to authorize the Treasury to indorse the bonds which the company under its charter had the right to issue up to $30,000 for each mile of road built. Congress hesitated for several months and during this time the discussion on the matter became nationwide. The retirement of Chairman Potter from the Texas and Pacific Committee left Congressman Throckmorton of Texas at its head. "Old Throck," as his admirers affectionately called him, was always the champion of West Texas. His efforts caused the bill to pass the committee, and it received a favorable vote in the House, but was "tabled" in the Senate until December, 1878, when it was called up and made a law.[18]

From that time work on the road was pushed forward with vigor. Excitement arose by leaps and bounds among the people and towns to the West. Every local newspaper began to speculate as to what route the road would take west of Weatherford. Each editor conclusively settled the matter in the interests of his own constituency. The *Texan* at Breckenridge was satisfied that the route would go through Breckenridge and ignored Albany's chances; on the other hand, the *Tomahawk* at Albany was equally confident that the road would pass several miles south of Breckenridge, and would of necessity pass through Albany.[19] It seemed a freak of irony that the road, when actually constructed, passed more than thirty miles south of both places.

On February 21, 1880, the contract was let for the first sixty-mile section west of Weatherford. By July 10, the construction train had reached the Brazos River in Palo Pinto County, southeast of Mineral Wells. On August 21, 1880, the *Echo* carried the following item:

"The terminus of the Texas and Pacific was changed Tuesday

[18] "The Senate put the kibosh on the Texas and Pacific Railroad Bill until next fall; therefore Fort Worth is happy and Weatherford is as mad as can be."—*Frontier Echo*, June 14, 1878.

[19] *Frontier Echo*, January 17, 1880 (exchanges).

from Weatherford to Gordon, thirty-five miles this side west of Weatherford. Grading is being pushed forward with all possible speed, contractors being at work all along the line over one hundred miles west of the track layers. Soon the railroad point for this county, Shackelford, will be Eastland."

On August 28, the same newspaper announced:

"A new town on the Texas and Pacific Railroad near Simpson's Ranch (Abilene). It is thought it will be the railroad town west of Dallas and that it is to receive the especial patronage of the railroad company by making it a division and locating machine, and repair shops at that point."

By January 22, the road had reached the Colorado River in Mitchell County. The work was pushed with all dispatch, but in spite of haste it ran far behind its scheduled time. The Southern Pacific had been authorized by Congress to build east from California until it effected a junction with the Texas and Pacific. It was believed the junction would take place in New Mexico or Arizona, but it reached El Paso before the Texas and Pacific. The junction actually took place at Sierra Blanca, about ninety miles southeast of El Paso. By the close of 1883, the southern transcontinental route was open to traffic. An avenue of commerce and communication had been opened up across West Texas; land values had risen and the people had been given a taste of what railroads could do for the country.

The Texas Central Railroad

The first rival of the Texas and Pacific in westward extension through Texas was the Texas Central, a branch of the Houston and Texas Central. On May 28, 1879, the Texas Central was incorporated. It was owned and controlled by the Houston and Texas Central, but the organizations were separate. The charter of the new road authorized the construction of a main line to the northern boundary of Texas with a branch road from the eastern terminus to the northeast border of the state.[20]

[20] *Railroad Charters,* A, 131, office of Secretary of State (Texas).

During 1879, forty-three miles of road were completed from Ross to Morgan.[21]

By that time the road had attracted the attention of the West. Mass meetings were held and committees appointed to negotiate with officials of the road in an effort to get the line extended through their respective towns.[22] In the fall of 1881, construction was completed to Cisco, about a year after the Texas and Pacific had reached that place. This was the first town west of Fort Worth and San Antonio to get two railroads, and that within a year; the citizens could hardly contain themselves.

Albany had been beside herself with excitement for more than a year after the Texas Central had begun building. Mass meetings had become a habit. The permanent committee had been doing its utmost. Extraordinary inducements had been offered. Great was the joy of her citizens when the road started construction out of Cisco towards Albany. December 20 was designated as the date for arrival in Albany. The occasion was to be commemorated by a general celebration and lot sale. Plans were made to run an excursion train from Cisco. Owing to the heavy rains on December 18 and 19, and the severe norther on the 20, attendance at the celebration was small and but sixty lots were sold at the public auction.[23] The proposed boom which the citizens hoped to inaugurate was not realized.

Albany remained the terminus of the road from 1881 to 1890. During this time the Texas Central dropped from the attention of the people, who became occupied with other roads. Little mention is made of the Central except for an occasional complaint at the service, until 1887, when a rumor was spread that the road was considering an extension of the line. There seems to have been no basis for the rumor, other than that the company had been accumulating large quantities of bridge and

[21] Poor, *Manual of Railroads*, 1886, p. 805.
[22] *Fort Griffin Echo*, April 23, 1881.
[23] The average price of a lot was $75. The highest price was $150 and the lowest $35.—*Fort Griffin Echo*, December 24, 1881.

other materials at Cisco; but the people did not require that rumors be authenticated before they began to act. Interest ran high for a few weeks. Would the road go west, northwest or north? Nobody knew, but it was the consensus of opinion that it would be northwest or north. Mass meetings were held in the towns in that direction.[24] Seymour and Haskell were especially active in their efforts. The company took no steps to carry out the reported extension and the excitement died out. When the extension was made in 1900, it was laid to the west where the new town of Stamford, in Jones County, was built. The terminus remained at this place until 1907, when the road was extended into Fisher County and another new town, Rotan, became the terminus.

The Fort Worth and Denver Railroad

The Fort Worth and Denver Railroad was chartered May 26, 1873.[25] The line was to extend from Fort Worth to the Canadian River, where it was to connect with the Denver and New Orleans, and form a through line from Fort Worth to Denver.

For nine years after obtaining its charter the company retained the status of a "paper railroad." This long delay caused the railroad-hungry people in the northwestern part of the state to fret and worry.[26]

It was not until 1882 that actual construction began. In that year about one hundred miles of track were completed from Fort Worth to Henrietta. Thus far, the work had been pushed vigorously, but, much to the discomfiture of Wichita Falls, a lull came. It was not until September 24, 1883, that the twenty-mile stretch from Henrietta to Wichita Falls was completed and opened to traffic. There was no construction of road in 1884. In the spring of 1885, the line was extended about 35 miles

24 *Albany News*, April 14, 1887.
25 *Railroad Charters*, A, 422, office of Secretary of State.
26 "The wind work for the Fort Worth and Denver Railroad is now being prosecuted with vigor, and let us hope the work with pick and shovel will soon follow with the same energy."—*Frontier Echo*, December 14, 1877.

to Harold, and here the road rested again for about fifteen months. In September, 1886, construction was resumed with vigor. The road reached Vernon, October 15, 1886; Quanah, February 1, 1887; Clarendon, October 1, 1887, and Texline, January 26, 1888.[27] Two months later a junction was made with the Denver and New Orleans, and the third trans-state railroad was opened to traffic. The building of the Fort Worth and Denver across the North Plains caused that region to be opened up for settlement twenty years before the South Plains.

The Santa Fe Railroad

The Atchison, Topeka, and Santa Fe Railroad Company was incorporated under the laws of Kansas, March 3, 1863.[28] The Gulf, Colorado, and Santa Fe was chartered under the laws of Texas, May 28, 1873, and construction begun in May, 1875. Although the two railroads had no official connection until 1886, they were associated in the minds of the people of West Texas. This was probably due to the fact that the word, Santa Fe, was common to both names, and was the term used when referring to either. In March, 1886, the Atchison, Topeka, and Santa Fe acquired control of the Gulf, Colorado, and Santa Fe by an exchange of bonds.[29]

By 1877, the Gulf, Colorado, and Santa Fe had completed forty-three miles of road from Galveston to Arcola. Notwithstanding the fact that the end of the line was, as yet, one hundred and fifty miles southeast of Austin, several communities in West Texas had observed its movement, and began to take action to attract the line to their towns. The citizens of Comanche were especially active at the time.[30]

By an Act of Congress, in July, 1884, the Southern Kansas Railway Company, an auxiliary line of the Atchison, Topeka and Santa Fe, was given the right to extend a line from Arkansas

[27] Poor, *Manual of Railroads*, 1886, p. 345.
[28] Poor, *Manual of Railroads*, 1886, p. 722.
[29] *Taylor County News*, March 5, 1886.
[30] *Frontier Echo*, March 2, 1877.

City, Kansas, south through Indian Territory in the direction of Denison and Fort Worth, and also another line in the direction of Wolf Creek, Indian Territory, and the Panhandle of Texas.[31] No sooner had news of this reached Texas than all the towns in the northwestern part of the state from Fort Worth to Wichita Falls became excited, and each began to talk of the possibility of securing the road, and perhaps, becoming its terminus. Henrietta claimed a boom on the strength of its prospects.[32]

The Gulf, Colorado, and Santa Fe reached Belton in February, 1881, and Lampasas on May 15, 1882. The Fort Worth branch was completed from Temple on December 8, 1881.[33] Lampasas remained the terminus of the main line from May, 1882, until April, 1885. During this time the towns to the west and northwest spent a great deal of time in speculating as to the probable route the road would take from Lampasas. When the company began to make arrangements to renew construction in 1885, these towns became active in pushing their claims. Brownwood, Coleman, San Angelo, Abilene, and Colorado City vied with each other, or co-operated, according to their interests.[34] Brownwood offered a bonus of $25,000, and free depot grounds, as well as a right-of-way across Brown County to the Coleman County line. This offer was too generous for the company to turn down, especially since it had seemingly been their intention to go through Brownwood all along.

San Angelo had been advocating a route due west from Lampasas by San Saba and Brady. This would have left Brownwood thirty miles to the north. When the Santa Fe engineers arrived in Brownwood in the early part of June, and began locating depot grounds, San Angelo's hopes fell.

As San Angelo's expectations sank, however, those of the towns to the northwest rose higher. It seemed certain to them

---

[31] Poor, *Manual of Railroads,* 1886, p. 722.
[32] *Albany News,* June 20, 1884.
[33] Poor, *Manual of Railroads,* 1886.
[34] *Taylor County News,* April 17, 1885.

that the general direction would be northwest. Big Spring for the first time began to push its claims vigorously. The idea became prevalent that the Santa Fe would cross the Texas and Pacific at some point west of Cisco. Baird, Abilene, Merkel, Sweetwater, Colorado, and Big Spring became active candidates for the coveted intersection. No one doubted that the successful town would have a marked advantage over all rival towns, and would probably become the great railroad center of West Texas.

A temporary setback occurred, however, when news came that a corps of Santa Fe engineers had surveyed a line from Brownwood by way of Coleman to San Angelo. The *Taylor County News* was the first to recover from the shock the news produced, and explain that "the San Angelo line is to be a branch of the main line which will intersect the T. & P. at Abilene."

A few days later Colonel M. L. Moody, vice-president of the Gulf, Colorado, and Santa Fe, with his brother, Major Leroy Moody, arrived in Abilene from a prospecting trip through Jones and Haskell counties. The appearance of these gentlemen at this particular time was the occasion for much excitement and speculation on the part of the citizens of the town. The account of their visit was published in the *Taylor County News* and republished in practically every newspaper in that section of the state. Every editor gave his opinion as to the significance of their visit.

Meanwhile, the company itself seemed to be undecided as to what its next move would be. In November, 1885, a survey was made from Coleman to Colorado. Another was being made from Coleman to Abilene. However, when the engineers were within a few miles of Abilene they were suddenly recalled, and the line abandoned. This caused considerable uneasiness for Abilene.[35]

[35] The editor of the *News* had been preparing against such an evil day for some time. On May 1, 1885, he had said,

"It will be a huge joke if the Santa Fe should give Abilene the 'go by' and find that they had missed one of the most valuable mining districts in the state."

On November 27, 1885, it became known that Coleman would be the terminus. This report seemed most unfavorable to any immediate extension to the north or northwest, but the agitation on the part of the towns in that direction went on with remarkable persistence. Baird became unusually active. Merkel, which heretofore had not been so energetic as some of her neighbors, made her position clearly understood.

During the first week in March, 1886, news came to the effect that the Gulf, Colorado, and Santa Fe had passed into the control of the Atchison, Topeka, and Santa Fe. The information was first received through a telegram from New York to the *Dallas News*. Within a week every newspaper in West Texas had republished the account. A wave of speculation swept across the country as to the effects of the consolidation on the various lines. For weeks editors indulged in editorials on the matter. Opinions were varied, but it was the general belief that the transaction would be followed by an immediate extension which would connect the two lines and give the Santa Fe system a connection with the Gulf of Mexico.[36]

A year passed and the Santa Fe had made no move towards an extension to the north or northwest of Coleman; but the towns in that direction had not lost hope. Shortly after New Year's, 1887, Abilene was thrown into a feverish state of excitement when news came that the engineers of the Gulf, Colorado, and Santa Fe had been locating the site for a town at Tebo switch, eight miles west of Abilene. Without waiting to ascertain the truth of the report, the citizens hurriedly set out to raise a big bonus to be used to induce the company to change its route and build to Abilene.[37] The rumor proved false, but the entire affair shows the state of mind of a railroad-hungry town of this period.

In February, 1887, the Gulf, Colorado, and Santa Fe started the extension of what everyone believed to be a branch from Coleman Junction, seven miles southeast of Coleman, west to

[36] *Albany News,* March 11, 1886.
[37] *Taylor County News,* January 7, 1887.

the Colorado River, in Runnels County.[38] The road reached the river in February, 1886, where the town site of Ballinger was laid out on land previously purchased by the railroad company.

Up to the time the road reached Ballinger, San Angelo had been highly hopeful that it would be extended on to that town before it stopped; but when January 1, 1888, came, and no move had been made towards extension, the citizens of San Angelo became exceedingly anxious. Several mass meetings were held, and the town offered to donate the right-of-way and grade the road from Ballinger. The company accepted this proposition, and by the middle of September the road was completed. September 17 was set as a day of celebration. San Angelo was at that time strictly a cattleman's town, and the affair was carried on in a typical cattleman's way.[39] A barbecue and ball were given and the "best of liquors were served."

In April, 1889, considerable excitement arose over a proposed extension of the San Angelo branch to El Paso. The occasion of this new interest was the fact that a number of the high officials of the company made a trip to El Paso to consider the project.[40] San Angelo and El Paso mutually rejoiced for a while, but their hopes were short-lived, as the extension was never made.

The San Antonio and Aransas Pass Railroad

From 1886 to 1890, the San Antonio and Aransas Pass caused among the people of central West Texas railroad excitement far out of proportion to the subsequent importance of the road. The reason seemed to lie in the fact that officials of the company had a considerable amount of frontier spirit themselves. They were inclined to be a bit talkative. The company was not wealthy, and it was much easier to make promises than to fulfill them. These promises were often the cause of the building

[38] *Austin Statesman*, February 25, 1886.

[39] *Taylor County News*, September 24, 1888.

[40] Exchange from the *El Paso Times* in the *Taylor County News*, April 12, 1889.

up of many false hopes on the part of the people to the north-west, and of periodical epidemics of intense excitement.

The company was chartered August 28, 1884, to build a road from San Antonio to Aransas Pass, a distance of 160 miles.[41] Track laying began in August, 1885, at Aransas Pass and was completed to San Antonio before the end of 1886.[42] The same year the charter was amended, increasing the capital from $2,000,000 to $5,000,000 and providing for an extension to the northwest. As soon as this was known every town from Kerr-ville to Vernon became interested.

In April, 1886, the editor of the *Mason News* went to San Antonio to interview Colonel Lott, the president of the road, in regard to the company's plan for extension. That officer was exceedingly communicative and enthusiastic. During the inter-view he drew a line on the map from San Antonio through Kerr, Gillespie, Mason, McCulloch, and Coleman counties, and through the Panhandle of Texas into western Kansas and thence to Denver, which he indicated would be the terminus. He stated that the work on the road would be begun at once and pushed rapidly, but that he expected the citizens along the route to donate liberally.[43]

Within three weeks the account of the interview had been published in practically every local newspaper in Texas along the proposed route, and the interest had grown into an intense excitement. Mass meetings were held at Comfort, Center Point, Boerne, Kerrville, and Fredericksburg during the latter part of May.[44] Permanent committees were appointed and delegates elected to attend a general mass meeting at San Antonio on June 11. On the evening of that date about two hundred citizens of San Antonio, including the officials of the road, met the com-mittees from the towns and counties at the courthouse, and the matter of an extension was freely discussed. The citizens of San Antonio were as desirous of getting the extension as were

[41] *Railroad Charters*, B, 94, office of Secretary of State.

[42] Poor, *Manual of Railroads*, 1886, p. 967.

[43] *Taylor County News*, April 30, 1886.

[44] *Kerrville Eye*, May 15, 1886.

the isolated inland towns to the northwest. These merchants had visions of a tremendous trade territory, permanently assured. During a recess of the meeting a subscription list was started among the San Antonio business men, and within fifteen minutes $50,000 had been subscribed by six citizens.[45] The account of this meeting soon reached even the remote towns in the northwestern part of the state. Enthusiasm begot enthusiasm. Before July 1, a number of new mass meetings had been held. Right-of-way from San Antonio to Albany and more than $200,000 in money was pledged by the towns along the route. At a second mass meeting in San Antonio $200,000 was pledged.[46]

Meanwhile, a bitter discussion was taking place between Kerrville and Fredericksburg as to which route the railroad should select. The *Kerrville Eye* accused the railroad committee of Fredericksburg of grossly misrepresenting the natural resources of Kerr County to the railroad officials.[47] The editor of the *Eye* said some disparaging things about the citizens of Fredericksburg. The Fredericksburg editor retaliated in kind; but his maledictions were in German, so the Kerrville townsmen were none the wiser for it.[48] Fredericksburg was extremely disappointed when the company decided to build by Kerrville.

General interest lagged for a few months, but in February, 1887, the discussion was taken up again with renewed energy.[49] New mass meetings were held in the towns to the north and northwest.[50] The *San Angelo Standard* got out a special edition on the strength of a rumor that the preliminary survey was to be run from Kerrville to San Angelo.[51]

[45] *Mason County News*, June 19, 1886.
[46] *Albany News*, July 15, 1886.
[47] *San Antonio Express*, July 7, 1886.
[48] *Mason News*, July 7, 1886.
[49] *Coleman Voice*, February 5, 1887.
[50] A mass meeting was held at Brady on February 12, a committee was appointed to collect data concerning the coal mine in the northern part of McCulloch County and submit the same to the railroad company as an extraordinary inducement.—*Taylor County News*, February 18, 1887.
[51] *Mason News*, June 25, 1887.

In the latter part of June, 1888, the people of Gillespie and Llano counties held mass meetings for the purpose of inducing the San Antonio and Aransas Pass to extend a branch from Comfort to Llano by way of Fredericksburg. Committees were appointed from both counties to go to San Antonio and confer with the officials of the company. The conference took place on July 3. The president, as usual, agreed to make the extension provided the citizens on the route would donate the right-of-way, depot grounds, and raise sufficient money bonuses. The committees went home, called mass meetings, and submitted the proposition.[52] A mass meeting, held about the same time in San Antonio, agreed to raise any deficit which Gillespie and Llano counties failed to raise.[53] The business men of San Antonio at this time shared in the popular belief that there were valuable coal and iron deposits in Llano and Mason counties, and they thought that, with the proper rail connections, their city might develop into an industrial center like Gary or Chattanooga. The branch was eventually completed as far as Fredericksburg, but no farther.

On April 12, 1889, someone in Ballinger received a letter from Colonel Lott, president of the San Antonio and Aransas Pass, which stated that the company would consider a proposition from the people of Ballinger in regard to an early extension of the road to that vicinity. The letter was turned over to the permanent railroad committee, which, in turn, called a mass meeting. At this meeting it was decided to invite delegates from other towns interested in the road to meet in Ballinger on April 19, 1889.[54] The general meeting was held on the designated date, but we have no account of what happened.

From this time on the San Antonio and Aransas Pass gradually dropped from the attention of the people of West Texas. There was a partial revival of interest in April, 1890, on the part of Ballinger and San Angelo. Mr. C. L. Houghton, a wealthy

[52] *Taylor County News,* July 6, 1888.
[53] *Mason County News,* March 30, 1889.
[54] *Ballinger Leader,* April 19, 1899.

cattleman of New Mexico, arrived in Ballinger the latter part of April. He claimed to be a member of a company of New Mexicans who had organized to promote a railroad from the coal regions southwest of Santa Fe to Aransas Pass. It was the plan of his company either to induce the San Antonio and Aransas Pass to build on to New Mexico, or to build a road themselves and connect with the San Antonio and Aransas Pass, at Kerrville or Fredericksburg. Mr. Houghton was on his way at that time to have an interview with Jay Gould, who was then making a tour of Texas. For the next few weeks Ballinger and San Angelo followed the movements of Mr. Houghton with great interest. As a result of his meeting with Mr. Gould, which took place in Dallas, it was reported that the magnate "was highly impressed with the project and promised to give the matter his earnest consideration."[55]

This ended the railroad excitement of West Texas so far as the San Antonio and Aransas Pass was concerned. The line was never extended from Kerrville or Fredericksburg. Perhaps more disappointment resulted from this railroad's failure to live up to expectations than from any other, unless it was the "Cattle Trail Route."

The Chicago, Rock Island, and Pacific Railroad

During the decade from 1883 to 1893, the Chicago, Rock Island, and Pacific was destined to produce widespread excitement in West Texas, and almost a corresponding amount of disappointment. The occasion for such an interest on the part of the people was not due to any promise or declaration by the officials of the railroad; those gentlemen were typically non-communicative. It was due rather to the railroad hunger of the people themselves. As early as March, 1883, it became known that the charter of the Rock Island called for Cisco, Texas, as one of the possible points of destination.[56] This information

[55] *Ballinger Leader,* April 30, 1890.
[56] *Albany News,* March 24, 1883.

was sufficient to put the towns from Fort Worth to Fort Stockton into a state of expectancy.

The Chicago, Rock Island, and Pacific had been chartered in 1851, and by January, 1883, a line had been extended almost to the southern boundary of Kansas, and the company was asking Congress for a right-of-way across Indian Territory to Red River. The *Albany News* was the first newspaper in West Texas to prophesy the outcome of these extensions and others soon took it up.

The matter rested there for more than three years. In December, 1886, a rumor was spread to the effect that the Rock Island was contemplating an extension from Wichita Falls to San Antonio, following the old cattle trail.[57] This put the people to talking and the local editors to writing again, and for the next six years the topic of the Rock Island was continually up for discussion and speculation. Two theories concerning the motives of the company became generally accepted: first, that the company intended to monopolize the cattle transportation of southwest Texas to the Kansas and Chicago markets; and, second, that the company wished to secure the same kind of advantage in regard to a route from the wheat regions of Missouri, Kansas, Indian Territory, and northwest Texas to a deep water outlet on the Gulf.[58] Just where this mythical line, which would serve for cattle movement in one direction and wheat in the other, should run was a question which provoked spirited rivalries, and in some cases, bad feelings between different sections. As is the case of most of the prospective railroad extensions, whether real or imaginary, the towns along the various proposed routes tended to form into groups so that they might more effectively advance their own claims and compete with all rivals.[59] Breckenridge, Cisco, Brownwood, Mason, and Fredericksburg formed one group, and Wichita Falls, Albany, Abilene, and San Angelo formed another.

[57] *Mason News,* December 18, 1886.
[58] *Taylor County News,* November 14, 1887.
[59] *Albany News,* January 2, 1887.

In September, 1887, the permanent railroad committee at Cisco sent Lieutenant Governor Wheeler to Kansas City to interview the railroad officials. As Mr. Wheeler traveled northward he met Mayor Freeman of Wichita Falls, who was going to the same place for the same purpose and the two traveled on together. They had several interviews with the officials, but, as Mr. Wheeler afterwards reported to his committee, every time they raised the question as to where the road would enter Texas, and what would be its route after entering the state "the officials played clam on us."

Abilene called a convention of delegates from San Angelo, Ballinger, Albany, and Wichita Falls to meet in Abilene, November 22, 1887. The representation was not as full as expected, so the convention adjourned to meet in Wichita Falls during the last week in December. The Wichita Falls meeting resolved to use every inducement to get the Rock Island Company to run a preliminary survey from Wichita Falls to San Angelo; and other committees were appointed from each county to have the surveys run at the expense of the various towns along the right-of-way, if the Rock Island refused.

During the first part of January, 1888, Lieutenant Governor Wheeler, acting on behalf of the railroad committee of Cisco, called a convention of delegates from the towns to the north and south to meet in Cisco on January 19. The delegation from each county had previously been informed by mass meetings at home what their county would offer to the Rock Island as an inducement to build over this route. A total of $170,000 and right-of-way over the entire route was pledged.[60]

During the months of January and February, 1888, the Abilene group was engaged in having a survey made from Abilene to Wichita. The engineer surveyed a line by way of Albany, Throckmorton, and Archer City, and reached Wichita Falls about February 15. His report showed what his employers wanted it to show; the route was an excellent one; the country was level; the grade was very slight; water was plentiful; there

[60] *Dallas News*, January 20, 1888.

would be few curves, very few cuts and fills, and no expensive bridging. After having rendered so excellent an account, the engineer was paid off and discharged; and his data, maps and field notes were sent to the officials of the Rock Island.[61]

Archer City, in Archer County, enjoyed a strategic position in the Rock Island controversy. The two proposed routes crossed there. Due to her pivotal position she could well claim to be on both sides. Her chances were so bright for securing the road that real estate in the town and surrounding country took a rapid rise in value during the winter of 1887-88, and the town experienced a considerable boom.

During February, 1888, the Rock Island engineers completed a preliminary survey from Red River to Cisco. When the party reached Cisco the citizens gave them a banquet. After the engineers had been "wined and dined," Captain Preston, the chief engineer, was called upon for a speech. The citizens leaned forward in their seats in their anticipation of hearing him say that he had found a splendid route, and was ready to make a most favorable report to his company. They were disappointed. According to the report given by the *Cisco Roundup*, the Captain "said but little"; that he found a "tol'able route only through the rugged hills of Stephens and Eastland counties," and "that it would be necessary to make other surveys." These statements threw a chill over the enthusiasm of the Cisco group and were received with a thrill of joy by the citizens of the Abilene route. The Abilenians thought their chances for the road better than ever before.[62]

In April, 1888, the Rock Island controversy took a slightly new angle. The company sent a corps of engineers to Albany, from which place they ran a preliminary survey to Coleman by way of Baird. This seemed to indicate that the company was seriously considering the cattle trail route. Some of these towns had previously been working enthusiastically with the Abilene group; and others, on the lower end of the trail, had been active

[61] *Albany News*, February 16, 1888.
[62] *Ibid.*, March 15, 1888.

in the Cisco group. Their situation now became embarrassing, but not for long; for after the survey was made, nothing more was heard of it so far as the Rock Island Company was concerned.

During the summer of 1888, various rumors were circulated to the effect that the Rock Island had purchased the Texas Central which then extended from Albany to Ross, a few miles north of Waco.[63] The reports were false, but no one took the trouble to produce proof; the people at large believed them. This was responsible for a widespread belief that the Rock Island would probably build to some connecting point on the Texas Central, and reach a deep water outlet on the Gulf by way of Waco, Houston and Galveston. It was also generally thought that the cattle region would be tapped by extending a branch from Albany to San Angelo by way of Abilene.[64] For many months to come this was the commonly accepted belief on the part of the people of West Texas.

Meanwhile, the Rock Island, apparently unconscious and unconcerned as to what the people in Texas were thinking, was busy extending its line across Indian Territory. In the spring of 1892, the road reached Red River some distance east of Wichita Falls. From that point it built down the old McCoy cattle trail to Fort Worth, missing Henrietta, Archer City, and all of the towns to the south and southwest which had been so sure of getting it. In April, 1893, the line reached Fort Worth. The *Fort Worth Gazette* got out an elaborate railroad edition, and the city held a celebration.[65]

The Fort Worth and Rio Grande Railroad

While the railroad fever in West Texas was at its apex, the Fort Worth and Rio Grande Railroad Company was organized and received a charter in May, 1885.[66] The primary purpose

---

[63] *Taylor County News*, June 14, 1889.
[64] *Albany News*, July 7, 1889.
[65] *Taylor County News*, April 21, 1893.
[66] *Railroad Records*, A, 422, office Secretary of State.

of the company was to extend a line to the cattle and sheep country in southwest Texas. The original plan was to build a road
from Fort Worth to San Angelo, and, eventually, on to some
point on the Rio Grande, but the company was forced to change
the route several times before the road was actually constructed.[67]
The indecision of the railroad officials caused considerable excitement and suspense on the part of the people along the various
proposed routes. The usual rivalries developed, but the towns
never organized into groups as in the case of the Cattle Trail
Route and the Rock Island. The principal rivals in 1886 were
Brownwood and Coleman.[68] The location of these two towns
made it possible for them both to be on the same line of the road
from Fort Worth to San Angelo, but after the Santa Fe
extended from Brownwood to Coleman in 1886, it was not likely
that the Fort Worth and Rio Grande would parallel the Santa Fe
for more than thirty miles; therefore, the two towns became
competitors. Several mass meetings were held at both places for
the purpose of trying to outbid each other.[69]

Construction was slow; it began at Forth Worth in November, 1886, and required two years to reach Dublin.[70] By this
time the extension of the Santa Fe from Coleman Junction to
San Angelo, caused the Fort Worth and Rio Grande Company
to amend its charter, providing for a line through Tarrant,
Parker, Johnson, Hood, Comanche, Brown, San Saba, McCulloch, Mason, Llano, Gillespie, and Kerr counties. The principal
towns in these counties became lively candidates for the road.
The people of San Saba, Llano, and Mason counties took special
pains to point out the vast amount of their undeveloped mineral
resources.[71]

Meanwhile, the company was uncertain what route to take.
In February, 1890, the officials announced they would complete
the line to Comanche, and make a survey from there to San

[67] *Taylor County News,* August 7, 1885.
[68] *Ballinger Bulletin,* November 25, 1886.
[69] *Taylor County News,* December 3, 1886.
[70] Poor, *Manual of Railroads,* 1890, p. 506.
[71] *Mason News,* February 16, 1889.

Saba, Llano, and Kerrville, and another survey from Comanche to Brady and Mason before determining a definite route. The road was completed to Comanche in October, 1890.[72] The proposed surveys were made, the offers considered, and Brownwood won. The road reached there in 1891. Brady and Mason were disappointed, for nothing further was done for twelve years. In 1903, an extension was made to Brady, which remained the terminus for eight years. The last extension reached Menard in 1911.

The Cattle Trail Route Railroad

The railroad project which provoked the greatest amount of interest, as well as the greatest amount of activity, on the part of the people of West Texas, was a proposed line north and south up the old Dodge Cattle Trail.[73] In spite of most valiant efforts of the citizens of the various towns along the proposed route, the road was never to be realized. The entire movement is an excellent example of the "paper railroads" which flourished during this period when the imagination was easily aroused.

By 1884, the enactments by the legislature of 1883 in regard to fencing were already curtailing the privileges of the drover in his annual drive up the established trail.[74] The rapid settlement of the country south of Dodge City threatened the existence of the cattle trade of that place. Consequently, a number of cattlemen of Dodge City and Saint Louis secured a charter for a railroad which was to extend from Dodge City to the boundary of the Indian Territory. The line was to be called the "Cattle King's Railroad." The *Taylor County News* announced that this was a wonderful opportunity for the Gulf, Colorado, and Santa Fe or the San Antonio and Aransas Pass to build by way of

[72] Poor, *Manual of Railroads*, 1890, p. 506.

[73] This trail extended from South Texas to Dodge City, Kansas via Mason, Brady, Fort Griffin and Doan's Crossing on Red River, about 12 miles north of Vernon. This trail was started about 1876, and was used almost exclusively by the southern drovers to Kansas from 1880 to 1886.— See files of the *Frontier Echo* from 1875 to 1886.

[74] *Albany News*, March 7, 1884.

Abilene and across the Indian Territory and connect with the
Cattle King's Railroad. The *News* further suggested, that if the
Gulf, Colorado, and Santa Fe failed to act, the San Antonio
and Aransas Pass could take advantage of the same opportunity
by extending its line from Boerne by way of Fredericksburg,
Mason, Brady, and Coleman. It pointed out that Northwest
Texas was being rapidly settled by small farmers and that the
overland cattle trail would soon be closed. The railroad which
took advantage of this fact would reap an immense harvest.[75]

The idea was taken up by the towns along the old trail,
Albany taking the lead by holding a mass meeting in February,
1886.[76] On March 4, the *Baird Clarion* published a stirring
article to interest the people of Callahan County in the matter.
Within the next few weeks mass meetings were held in every
town along the trail from Mason to Vernon. Permanent committees were appointed at each place to push the matter.

A heated dispute took place between Abilene on one hand
and the trail towns on the other. The arguments took an amus-
ing turn, although both factions were intensely serious. Abilene
was located on the old buffalo thoroughfare which led through
Buffalo Gap and to the winter grazing lands to the south. She
urged that the buffalo trail was the best route because the buffalo
had instinctively selected it, and that the cattle had been driven
up the old cattle trail thirty miles east, and had not been given
a chance to exercise this unfailing animal instinct in choosing
a route.[77] The trail towns retaliated with like arguments.
Meanwhile, the Gulf, Colorado, and Santa Fe set about extending its line to Coleman. The cattle trail towns received this
news with a shout of joy, for to them this was conclusive evidence that the extension up the cattle trail was a certainty. The

[75] *Taylor County News*, July 10, 1885.

[76] *Albany News*, February 25, 1886.

[77] "Coleman, Baird, Throckmorton, Albany, and other towns are urging
the Santa Fe to build up the old cattle trail for no other reason than that
in former times the Texans drove their bulls that way to the northern ranges.
The railroad officials must have a better reason or they will seek a better
route."—*Taylor County News*, December 2, 1886.

disappointment was great when the Santa Fe turned west to the Colorado River, in Runnels County, instead of continuing northward up the cattle trail.

This disappointment cast only a brief shadow over the aspiring towns, however; and mass meetings continued to flourish. Albany sent out a call for authorized delegates from all the towns along the trail to assemble in convention at Albany on December 15, 1886. The response was enthusiastic and unanimous. In every instance, except one, the delegates were elected by mass meetings. Those from Coleman were appointed by the permanent committee.[78] The convention met and with great solemnity a permanent organization was effected to promote the cause of the trail towns. A permanent central committee was to consist of the president, and one vice-president, and secretary from each of the six counties represented. The vice-president and secretary of each county were instructed "to prepare a map of the most feasible route through their respective counties and transmit the same with such data and statistics as possible to the secretary of Shackelford County, to be condensed by him and the president and vice-president of that county and put in proper shape to be presented to the railroad officials."

The delegates returned home to take up the railroad agitation with renewed vigor. Written agreements were circulated among the land owners of the various counties whereby the signers agreed to give a right-of-way across their lands, should the route be selected to run that way.

The activity of Abilene further aroused the vigilance of the "trail towns." During the week of December 16 to 23, several mass meetings had been held there; committees were appointed to take subscriptions and do whatever was necessary to secure the Santa Fe. The "trail town" newspapers published an account of what Abilene was dong to spur their own citizens to greater efforts.[79]

[78] *Albany News,* December 16, 1886.
[79] The *Albany News,* by way of reassuring her citizens, said, "The above from the *Abilene News* shows the urgent need on the part of the committee

At the same time the press along the cattle trail was trying
to arouse both the interest and fears of the prospective roads.
The most common method was playing one road against another,
and making it appear that the towns had a fine proposition to
offer, but at the same time assuming a very independent attitude,
telling the roads that the one that seized the opportunity first
would be indeed fortunate.[80]

Early in January, 1887, the central trail route committee sent
out circular letters to all the cattlemen in the state except those
in the extreme west, asking them to endorse the trail route.
Within three weeks over a hundred answers had been received,
and the opinion was unanimously favorable. One ranchman in
south Texas said he would ship 15,000 head over the route that
season if it could be finished. This man would require over
eight hundred cars.[81] The committee thought this kind of argument would be conclusive to any railroad company.

During February and March, 1887, the citizens and press of
the trail towns seemed to have almost completely dropped the
Santa Fe and turned their attention to the San Antonio and
Aransas Pass. A few mass meetings were held, and the news-

appointed along the old cattle route. Abilene will work, but she has 'to go
it alone,' as there are no other places along the route she proposes to assist
her, while along the old cattle trail route there are six towns, each one nearly
as able to do as much as Abilene. The Wind City of the West will hardly
get the Santa Fe, for that road will extend over the old cattle trail."

[80] The *Throckmorton Times* went so far as to reduce the benefits of the
proposed road to a matter of dollars and cents, specifically speaking,

"Reliable statistics show that the average cattle drive from Texas
alone for the last ten years has been 250,000 head per year, this of
itself will furnish a paying basis for the road for six months of the
year, to say nothing of the shipment of cereals and other products of
the great north and west to the south and east and the Gulf ports
for European exportation. It would pass through a vast undeveloped
country whose natural resources and advantages need only to be
made known and accessible to the world by railroad connection to
cause a rapidity of settlement and development such as has not yet
been seen on this continent." Quoted in *Albany News*, February 10,
1887.

[81] *Albany News*, January 20, 1887.

papers were filled with articles showing the advantages of the route and holding out inducements to the San Antonio road.

Even though the citizens and press of the trail towns had apparently forgotten the Santa Fe, the central committee had not. By the last of January the maps, statistics, and estimates which had been sent in by the various counties had been co-ordinated, and a meeting was arranged between the central committee and the directors of the Gulf, Colorado, and Santa Fe at Fort Worth on February 4. The delegates exhibited their maps and statistics, offered the road a free right-of-way, depot grounds in all the towns, and certain money bonuses, but neither the Santa Fe nor the Aransas Pass gave the cattle trail route any further encouragement. By November, 1877, the hopes of the trail people had sunk to a low ebb.

Another road appeared on the horizon, however. The Chicago, Rock Island, and Pacific was making preparations to extend its line from Kansas across the Indian Territory into Texas. The news of this came as a boon to the discouraged cattle trail towns. This time there was a new competitor in the field. Cisco, about thirty-five miles to the east of the old trail, bestirred herself with energy. A triangular dispute, therefore, was initiated between Cisco, the trail towns and Abilene.[82]

The Rock Island excitement was short-lived, and the Central Committee conjured its wits to find some new way of interesting a road. Resourcefulness was not lacking and a plan was soon devised.[83] It was proposed that a surveying corps be employed

[82] An example of the nature of the dispute entered into by the rival newspapers over the placement of the road may be seen in the following items taken from various papers:

Cisco Round-up to the *Albany News:* "Pucker to Whistle."

Albany News to *Cisco Round-up:* "A merry, merry tune it will be. The R. I. is not built to Cisco yet and it never will be. This is simply a prediction."

Round-up to the *Albany News:* "On with the boom. Cisco has condolence and tears for Albany and consolation for the numerous hamlets that blowed so much and got so little."

Albany News to the *Round-up:* "You had better 'can' your consolation, 'bottle' your tears, and 'preserve' your condolence for home consumption."

[83] *Mason News,* May 5, 1888.

by the various counties, to survey and tabulate the actual cost of a railroad from Mason to Doan's Store.[84] Each county was to pay the cost of the surveying in its borders. Mass meetings were held in different towns to endorse the plan, to raise money to pay the surveying cost, and to elect delegates to a second general convention to be held at Baird on May 25, 1888. The Baird Convention decided that the proposed survey would make a connection with the Fort Worth and Denver on the north and the San Antonio and Aransas Pass on the south, either at Boerne, Comfort, or Kerrville. Major Stanley M. Jones was employed as chief engineer, and instructed to survey the entire line.

Major Jones pushed the surveying work during the summer and fall of 1888. It was invigorating and encouraging to the people of the various communities along the old trail to have the engineers come into their midst, pitch camp, and spend days running lines and driving stakes. The people were paying the bill, but the activity helped to keep up their courage.

By January 12, 1889, the line had been surveyed, estimates of cost made from Mason to Vernon, and even twelve miles beyond Doan's Store. The engineer's report showed just what the central committee expected it to show,—that the entire road could be built at a surprisingly small cost, that it "could be graded, bridged, tied and ironed" for less than $10,000 per mile." [85]

The Central Committee had to decide upon their next step. It was suggested that they organize a company, build about twenty-five miles; then, bond the road for $15,000 a mile, and let the road build itself. This was easier said than done. In vain the Central Committee tried to interest capitalists of the north and east in the project.[86] The *Mason News* in desperation proposed that the people along the route grade the road by popu-

---

[84] Prior to this time Mason and Brady had not been so active; by May, 1888, they came to take the lead.

[85] *Albany News*, March 21, 1889.

[86] *Mason County News*, May 25, 1889.

lar subscription, and offer the enterprise to the Santa Fe, Aransas Pass or any railroad company which would accept it and agree to finish the project.

This plan was never carried out, but the idea of a north and south road which would carry the cattle of West Texas to northern markets lived on and was finally realized in the early 1900's in the Kansas City, Mexico, and Orient. By this time, however, conditions had changed and Fort Worth had become the cattle market for West Texas, and cattle movement was from west to east. This change in industrial conditions caused the Orient to be a failure from the beginning.

The Abilene, Wichita Falls and Kansas City Railroad

Another "paper railroad" was the Abilene, Wichita Falls, and Kansas City. The movement started, flourished, and died within a few months. It resulted from the general feeling that there should be a direct railroad connection between the cattle region of West Texas and Kansas City. In the fall of 1885 some newspaper editor suggested that a line should be built from San Angelo to Kansas City by way of Wichita Falls. Within the next few weeks the newspapers along the entire route began persistently to advocate the proposed road. The people in the various towns responded by holding mass meetings. Abilene sent all the Texas towns on the route invitations to send delegates to a general convention at that place on March 23, 1886. Representatives from Wichita Falls, Albany, Abilene, Runnels, and San Angelo assembled in the opera house. Although they had not been particularly invited, Jones and Haskell counties also sent delegates.[87] This fact eventually led to a dissension which was partly responsible for the disruption of the movement, for it was realized that if the proposed road were built through those two counties, it would miss Albany and Throckmorton and vice versa.

The convention resolved to organize a railroad corporation to be known as the Abilene, Wichita Falls, and Kansas City. To

[87] *Albany News,* March 23, 1886.

prevent antagonizing the Gulf, Colorado, and Santa Fe, then at Ballinger and contemplating an extension to San Angelo, it was decided to name Abilene as the southern terminus of the road, with the understanding that if the Santa Fe did not build to San Angelo the Abilene, Wichita Falls, and Kansas City would. A board of nine directors was elected, and immediately steps were taken to secure a charter. It was suggested that the capital stock be made $160,000, of which Wichita Falls should take $50,000, Abilene $50,000, and intermediate points, $60,000. A meeting of the directors was arranged to meet at Wichita Falls on April 15.

When these gentlemen assembled the two directors from Albany were not present. A committee had already framed a charter, and Albany was not designated as being on the route. The reason for the omission was to leave the route indefinite for a while and get Anson and Haskell to bid against Albany. Furthermore, the route through Jones and Haskell counties was through a much more fertile and level country. When the action of the Director's Committee became known in Albany, a storm of indignation swept over the town, a mass meeting was held, and the Albany directors were instructed to have nothing to do with the directory until the charter was changed to include Albany in the route. These proceedings became known to the other members of the directory when they met at Wichita Falls on April 15, and their first act was to change the charter in a way satisfactory to Albany.

The dissension was no sooner mended than another arose, which was to prove fatal to the entire movement. While the Abilene directors were attending the Wichita meeting, they heard a rumor that the Atchison, Topeka, and Santa Fe had determined to build a branch of their road to Fort Worth by way of Gainesville and another branch from Kiowa, Kansas, to Doan's Store, about eighty miles northwest of Wichita Falls. After hearing this report the Abilene directors became lukewarm in their interest in the Abilene, Wichita Falls, and Kansas City enterprise, and the meeting adjourned with nothing accomplished. When the

Abilene members returned home they called a mass meeting, and decided to return all money already subscribed on the Abilene, Wichita Falls, and Kansas City, and henceforth, to use all their means to encourage an extension of the Atchison, Topeka, and Santa Fe from Doan's Store, through Haskell and Jones counties. This action ended the Abilene, Wichita Falls, and Kansas City. For the next few weeks the press at Albany and Wichita Falls denounced Abilene as a "double dealer" and predicted she would "come to regret her mistake in the future." [88]

The Abilene and San Angelo Railroad

The idea of a railroad from Abilene to San Angelo was constantly in the minds of the people of both places for more than fifteen years. It originated in 1881, when San Angelo realized that the best chance to get a railroad was by means of an extension of a branch of the Texas and Pacific from Abilene. Abilene was quick to see the advantages of such a line, and united with San Angelo to secure it. All hopes of an immediate extension were killed in July, 1885, when the railroad committee at Abilene received a letter from J. C. Brown, receiver of the Texas and Pacific, which stated that if a railroad from Abilene to San Angelo were built the citizens of those two places would have to build it, since the drouth had curtailed the finances of his company and all he could give was advice.[89]

Some excitement occurred in Abilene on March 4, 1886, when a rumor was circulated that a number of wealthy business men of Dallas were talking of organizing a company to build the San Angelo and Abilene Railroad. A few days later two men, a Mr. Schneider and a Mr. Darris, claiming to represent the Dallas business men, arrived in Abilene to investigate the proposed route and ascertain how much Abilene and San Angelo would contribute. This seemed too good to be true, and a mass meeting was immediately called. It was decided to ask delegates from

[88] *Albany News,* May 6, 1886.
[89] *Taylor County News,* July 23, 1885.

Runnels City and San Angelo to meet a representative of Abilene at Runnels City on March 12. The latter places responded enthusiastically, and the meeting took place on the proposed date.

Messrs. Schneider and Darris were present. They asked that the people along the route donate the right-of-way, depot grounds, and certain bonuses, and raise money immediately to pay for the preliminary surveys. All these demands were promised, and the delegates returned home to raise money for the surveys.[90]

The surveying party, under the direction of Messrs. Schneider and Darris went to work at once. By April 28 they had reached San Angelo and started back to Abilene on a second route, which was completed on May 28. The people waited for further developments, but in vain. It came to light that Schneider and Darris had promoted the whole affair for the purpose of getting a surveying contract at a handsome price. Ballinger, who had been left out of the entire arrangement, laughed with glee at the way her neighbors had been duped out of their money.[91]

After the failure of the enterprise in the summer of 1886, Abilene and San Angelo revived their hopes of getting an extension of the Texas and Pacific.[92] In June, 1890, the Abilene Board of Trade resolved to raise $100,000 as Abilene's part as an inducement to the Texas and Pacific to make the extension.[93] The movement continued until it was superseded by another "paper railroad," the Red River and Southwestern, which was to include the same route from Abilene to San Angelo.

[90] *Ibid.,* March 19, 1896.
[91] This failure to get a railroad proved fatal to Runnels City. Within a few months her entire population had moved to Ballinger or elsewhere. Today the old town site is a farmer's field, and the crumbling walls of a single stone house mark the location of Runnels City.
[92] *San Angelo Standard,* September 21, 1888.
[93] *Taylor County News,* June 20, 1890.

The Red River and Southwestern Railroad

A sequel to the Abilene and San Angelo movement, and in part, to the Abilene, Wichita Falls, and Kansas City movement of 1886, was the Red River and Southwestern. On October 20, 1890, a convention of delegates from Henrietta, Archer City, Throckmorton, Albany, Abilene, Ballinger, and San Angelo met at Abilene to consider the building of a railroad from a junction with the Rock Island a few miles north of Henrietta to San Angelo. The movement started with a zest and momentum which made its success seem assured. A company was organized on the spot. Directors and officers were elected for twelve months.

A charter was applied for and secured, and some stock was sold.[94] By March 1, 1887, the company had surveying parties in the field. This was encouraging to the people along the route and more stock was bought.[95] By April 10 the contract for the first thirty miles of grading was let; and on April 17 the *Taylor County News* announced:

"It is now a settled fact that Henrietta and Abilene will be joined together by bands of steel by January 1, 1892."

But, before the first thirty miles were graded from Henrietta to Archer City, all the money was gone and no more stock could be sold. The directors soon found that it required more than enthusiasm to build a road. All efforts to interest men with capital failed. In 1895 the charter was amended to allow the road to be built through counties not mentioned in the original charter. The idea was to get the towns to compete with each other in offering immense bonuses. Had this plan been tried several years earlier it might have succeeded in part, but by 1895 the general railroad fever among the people of that section of the state had died down until such a scheme could not arouse much response. The Red River and Southwestern remained a "paper railroad."

[94] *Railroad Records*, C, 592, office of Secretary of State.
[95] *Taylor County News*, March 6, 1891.

The Texas Western and Circle Belt Railroad

The idea of a railroad from Gainesville to Abilene by way of Jacksboro, Graham, Crystal Falls, and Albany began in 1886. Its origin is not known, but by that year it was definitely established in the minds of the people in that section that a railroad should be built over such a route.[96] The idea was to be preserved for more than twelve years. Different railroad companies were to consider the route and reject it, but the idea lived on. The people would not let it die.

It was rumored by January, 1887, that the Missouri Pacific was interested in the route. Albany took the lead in proposing to the other towns along the route that they all cooperate to promote the movement. Local mass meetings were held from time to time in the various towns. No general convention was held, but each permanent railroad committee, through the newspapers, kept informed as to what the others were doing.

After several futile attempts were made to induce a number of railroad companies to take up the matter, general interest in the route lagged for a few years, but sprang up anew, when it was learned on October 4, 1898, that the Texas, Western, and Circle Belt Railroad Company had been organized, with its headquarters at Gainesville. The company proposed to build nine hundred miles of road, which would extend from Gainesville to Abilene, south to San Antonio, and back to the starting point.[97] The charter, which was filed with the Secretary of State at Austin, January 21, 1899, called for a capital stock of $5,000,000.

The company called on the towns along the proposed route for bonuses and right-of-way donations. By this time the more substantial class of people was losing its enthusiasm for railroads, and had begun to question whether they were worth securing at the cost of individual sacrifices. What took place in Abi-

---

[96] *Albany Star*, April 8, 1886.
[97] *Taylor County News*, October 14, 1898. *Railroad Records*, E, 151, office Secretary of State.

lene is typical of what happened in other towns. The committee there was asked to raise $50,000 in money and $15,000 in land. It was decided to secure the land first. A mass meeting was called February 3. The *Taylor County News* stated that, "although the room was pretty well filled, there was a marked absence of the wealthier property owners." The meeting was dominated by the local politicians and a few public-spirited men. In spite of stirring speeches and much forced enthusiasm, only $5,000 worth of land was promised. One speaker denounced the absent property owners in no uncertain terms. He insisted they should be marked and boycotted in their businesses by the rest of the citizens of the town. This statement was loudly applauded. A committee was appointed to canvass the town the next day in an effort to raise the remainder of the $15,000 land subscriptions. It met with very little success. Thus, the town which offered $100,000 and right-of-way across the county twelve years before would now raise but little over $5,000, notwithstanding the fact that population and wealth had increased considerably during that time. The Circle Belt Company, which had been depending on the generosity of the people along the route to a large degree, never did more than run a few surveys.[98]

One of the most noticeable effects of the building of the railroads was the large increase in the size and number of the towns in West Texas. Prior to 1879, with one or two possible exceptions, there was not a town between Fort Worth and El Paso with more than five hundred inhabitants. The average town had less than two hundred people. Furthermore, towns were extremely scarce. There was not an average of more than one town to a county west to the 100th meridian; and beyond that, one town to ten counties would be a conservative estimate.[99] The coming of the railroads caused the number of towns to treble within one decade, 1880-1890. It was a time when towns sprang up, like mushrooms, almost overnight. In the summer of 1880 the site of Abilene was a cow pasture. The railroad

[98] *Taylor County News,* February 10, 1899.
[99] See the *Federal Census Report* for 1890.

arrived in December, and by February, 1881, two thousand
people were there. A few wooden buildings had been erected,
but most of the people were living in tents. For a period
of two years the town was called the "Tent City." At
least three-fourths of the towns on the Texas and Pacific
west of Fort Worth had their origin in a like manner. Among
those which were especially spectacular in their development
were Baird, Merkel, Roscoe, Big Spring, Midland, and Pecos.

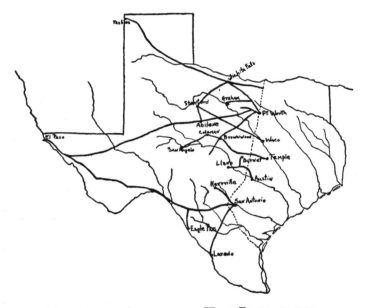

MAP SHOWING RAILROADS IN WEST TEXAS IN 1900.

The same thing happened with the building of other railroads.
The towns which were already in existence when the railroad
came increased threefold, fourfold, and sometimes tenfold, as
a result of the arrival of the road. The population of San
Angelo, for instance, in January, 1888, before the arrival of
the Santa Fe, was about 500. The Federal Census shows the
population in 1890 to be 2615. Albany had, before the coming
of the Texas Central in 1881, about 130 people and two years

later about 800.[100] Brownwood had a population of 725 in 1880. The size of the town increased but little until the arrival of the Santa Fe in 1885. The Federal Census of 1890 gives its population as 2176.

The coming of the railroads had a corresponding influence upon the population of the counties through which they built. Uvalde County, which had been settled for more than thirty years, had a population of 2541 in 1880. After the Southern Pacific had come through, the population in 1890 was 5457. This increase is typical of the counties which were already fairly well settled before 1880. Wichita County, which was sparsely settled when the railroad building began, had a population of 433 in 1880, and 4831 in 1890. The Fort Worth and Denver had arrived in 1883. The counties which did not get a railroad also showed an appreciable increase in population. The increase was generally in direct proportion to the proximity of the railroad. King County, which was about fifty miles from the railroad, had a population of 40 in 1880 and 173 in 1890, an increase of more than fourfold. Cottle County, which lies directly between King County and the Fort Worth and Denver, had 24 people in 1880 and 240 in 1890, an increase of tenfold.

During the decade, 1880-1890, eighty counties out of the 154 in West Texas had railroads built across them.[101] No county at the end of the decade was more than a hundred miles from a railroad; however, it was often much further to a trading point. Within twenty years after the first railroad entered West Texas, approximately 3300 miles of road had been built, the population had increased from 301,795 to 718,638, and land values had increased fourfold.[102]

As the railroad fever subsided about 1890, a reaction towards the roads started. Part of the very element which had clamored

[100] *Albany News,* March 24, 1883.

[101] It is to be remembered that at least a fourth of the total number counties of West Texas were unorganized at the end of the decade.

[102] Poor, *Manual of Railroads,* 1900; *Federal Census Reports* for 1880 and 1900; *The Almanac for 1873 and Emigrants Guide to Texas; Texas Almanac,* 1904.

loudest for railroads during the previous decade began to denounce the freight rates and demand governmental regulation.[103] The roads, without a doubt, needed regulating, but the people partially forgot what they had done for the settler and how materially they had contributed towards the development of the country.

[103] *Mason County News,* May 31, 1890; *Ballinger Banner,* June 11, 1890, July 2, 1890; *Taylor County News,* September 26, 1890; *Ballinger Leader,* August 27, 1891.

CHAPTER XI

FARMERS

THE development of agriculture was both a cause and a result of the railroad movement. West Texas was fairly well settled as far west as the 100th meridian when the railroad movement began.[1] It is problematical whether the fevered eagerness for railroads on the part of the people had much effect upon the larger companies, such as the Texas and Pacific, the Southern Pacific and the Santa Fe; but, there can be little doubt that it had a profound influence upon the small roads, such as the San Antonio and Aransas Pass, the Texas Central, and the Fort Worth and Rio Grande. Agriculture, as a major industry, could not develop until after a system of transportation was provided: The cattleman could make his herds walk to market, eat free grass, and thrive along the way; but the produce of the farmer was dead weight, and the expense of hauling it for great distances made farming unprofitable. Nothing was left for the settlers to do but raise a few cattle, hogs, some feedstuffs, a bale or two of cotton, and meanwhile live as economically as possible, and advocate the building of railroads. It was not until after the coming of the railroads that agriculture replaced cattle raising as the principal industry of the country. There were other handicaps, besides the lack of transportation, which had to be overcome before agricultural development could make much headway, such as the Indian menace, the idea that West Texas was not a farming country, the antipathy of the cattleman towards the settler, and the pests and drouths.

[1] Almost all of the public land and railroad land had been sold and nearly all the counties were organized, but with the exception of a dozen counties in the northeastern part of West Texas, the population could have increased tenfold and still not have been crowded. See map, p. 62.

227

So long as the Indians made their raids into the frontier settlements it was impossible for agriculture to make very extensive development, even if all the other obstacles had not existed. Figuratively speaking, the settler had to hold his rifle in one hand and his plow in the other. His eye shifted nervously from the

	Post Oak.
	Cedar, Oak, etc., of the Hills.

MAP OF WESTERN CROSS TIMBERS.
After Bray and Gannett.

furrow to the trees, bluffs, or ravines surrounding the field. He was in constant danger of having his work-stock driven away, his cattle and hogs butchered, his house burned, and his family scalped. Hired labor under such unsettled and unsafe conditions was unobtainable. Agriculture, except in the eastern edge of West Texas, which was far enough removed from the extreme frontier settlements in 1875 to feel some degree of security, had to wait until the Indian had departed.

The idea was generally prevalent, prior to 1885, that West Texas, especially west of the cross timbers,[2] was not an agricultural country. As early as 1865, Sam Newcomb, a school teacher at "Fort Davis,"[3] recorded in his diary, "Agriculture is not, and doubtless never will be, followed here, owing to the long and awful drouths."[4]

Numerous statements to the same effect are to be found in the newspapers, journals, reports, and correspondence from that region during the 60's and 70's, and, to a decreasing extent, during the 80's. The newspapers indulged in a lively and serious discussion in 1880 and 1881 over the question, "Is West Texas a farming country?"[5] As late as June 1, 1885, the *Taylor County News* emphatically declared, "The idea that this part of Texas will ever be an agricultural country is a great joke of huge proportions." The impression had been fast giving away since 1881, but the drouth of 1886 confirmed it anew. Although the prevailing belief that West Texas was not adapted to agriculture did not restrict immigration and settlement, it tended to make many settlers hesitate a bit before they abandoned stock raising for farming.

One of the most fruitful sources of the anti-agricultural propaganda was the cattleman. It was in the live stock journals that the strongest arguments appeared to discourage the farmer from going west.[6] The cattleman was one of the gravest obstacles to the settlement of Texas by farmers. Perhaps he was

[2] For location of the Western Cross Timbers see map, p. 228. From the standpoint of the development of agriculture the Western Cross Timbers would very conveniently be considered the eastern boundary of West Texas. The region west of the timbers in climate, soil and topograhy differed from that east of the timbers.

[3] A stockade in Shackelford County.

[4] "Newcomb's Diary" in *Shackelford County Sketches.*

[5] *Fort Griffin Echo,* September 17, 1881.

[6] The *Fort Worth Live Stock Journal,* edited by J. C. Loving, a secretary of the Northwest Texas Stock Raisers Association, never ceased to point out the folly of trying to farm in West Texas.

sincere in his contention that the region was intended by the Creator for a cattle country. Incidentally, as long as he could keep the settler back he could run his cattle on free grass. He wanted the free grass to last as long as it would, and, consequently, he threw every impediment possible before the advance of the settlers.[7] It was not uncommon for cattlemen to use severe methods to intimidate the earlier comers. When an adventurous frontier settler purchased a desirable tract of land located in a cattle baron's range and attempted to settle on it, notice was often served on him that he had better sell out (to the cattleman) and leave the country. If he disregarded the warning, there was a possibility of the affairs being settled permanently by a Winchester in the hands of one of the cattleman's trusted cowboys. This practice was not general enough to become the rule, but such things did happen. The cattle of the settlers would often become mixed on the range with those of the cattlemen. The farmer's cattle, often including the milk cows, would be gathered in the round-up and driven away. In some counties the farmers were compelled to organize stock associations of their own in order to resist the driving off of their cattle by the cattlemen. In spite of intimidations the settlers pushed on.

The cattlemen were forced to buy or lease and fence their pastures. This in turn led to the fence-cutting war. Fence-cutting was indulged in by both the cattlemen and the settlers. The settlers would often purchase small tracts of land along the water courses in a cattleman's range, and fence in the water holes at which the cattle were accustomed to water. The cowboys would then show their contempt for the detested "nester" by riddling the fence.[8] On the other hand, the cattlemen often

---

[7] For the attitude of a certain class of cattlemen during the drouth of 1886, see Chapter VII.

[8] Items like the following are numerous in the newspapers of the time:

"We are informed that Mr. Wise's fence was cut again last Friday night and a coffin nailed to one of the posts as a warning to Mr. Wise to keep quiet about it. It is also reported that a fence enclosing a pasture of 90 or 100 acres near Black Jack Grove has been cut." —*Albany Star*, December 12, 1882.

leased all the land surrounding a settler, or a community of settlers, fenced the entire tract, left but few gates, and put padlocks on them. The settlers would retaliate at the first opportunity by cutting miles of the ranchman's fence.[9]

The practice went on for more than 15 years.[10] Not infrequently, armed bodies of settlers clashed with armed bodies of cowboys. The death toll in the fence-cutting war has never been computed, but the number, if known, would doubtless be astounding. Laws were passed against the practice, but that did not end the trouble.[11] At last, the cattleman stubbornly gave way. His attitude and the impediments he improvised very effectively tended to retard agricultural development.

Various pests did their part to discredit West Texas as a farming region. The grasshoppers made periodical invasions. The destruction they occasioned was usually similar to that of a widespread hailstorm. They did unusual damage in 1876, 1884, and to a much lesser degree in 1891.[12] They came and

[9] *Albany Echo,* July 21, 1883; *Albany Star,* August 8, 1883; *Fort Griffin Echo,* August 18, 1883; *Albany News,* February 29, 1884; *Taylor County News,* December 25, 1885.

[10] Various plans were proposed to stop fence cutting. The following rather humorous suggestion was published in the *Albany Echo,* December 12, 1883:

"Nearly all the newspapers of the country have published plans for stopping the destruction of wire fences. The *Echo* now publishes a plan formed by one of our lawmakers. He thinks seriously of presenting a bill in the legislature, to build a Chinese wall around Coleman County, put all the fence-cutters inside it, furnish them with wire fence and nippers, and tell them to wade in. As the fence cutters prefer to do their cutting at night, the plan proposes stretching a great awning over the County, painting it black to represent night, probably cutting holes in it to represent stars, they would then be able to cut all the time, and they would abstain from sleeping so long that they would all die of sheer exhaustion. Our friend thought the free state of Brown or Hamilton would be the proper place but after careful study he has decided that Coleman County is the best locality."

[11] *Albany Echo,* February 8, 1884; *Ballinger Bulletin,* July 23, 1886.

[12] An idea of the numbers and appetite of the grasshoppers in 1876 may be had from the following item from the *Frontier Echo,* September 22, 1876:

"Those red-legged pests made their appearance in this county ten

went, but the prairie dog constituted a standing foe to the cattleman and farmer alike. It was estimated, in 1884, that the prairie
dog destroyed annually, grass and crops to the value of more
than $1,000,000.[13] Efforts were made to exterminate prairie
dogs by legislative aid, but to no avail.[14] The matter of
extermination was left to private enterprise. Anti-prairie dog
mass meetings were held. In some communities, it was agreed
at these gatherings, that each man should poison his own dogs;
thus, by concerted individual action the pest would be eliminated
in one season. In other communities the citizens would pool
their funds, assessing each man according to his acreage, and let
contracts to regular prairie dog exterminating companies. The
price varied from ten to fifty cents per acre, depending upon
degree of infestation. Contracts for blocks of land containing
from ten to fifty thousand acres were frequently let in this way.[15]
Both grasshoppers and prairie dogs tended to retard agricultural
development, just as wolves and other predatory animals
hindered the sheep industry.

No doubt, the greatest of all the obstacles, especially after
the Indians were permanently located on the reservations, were
the drouths. It was the extensive dry weather that caused the
prevalent idea that West Texas would never be a farming country. The farmers gradually learned by long, and sometimes
bitter, experience how to withstand the ordinary dry weather.
They discovered what to plant, when to plant, and how to till
the crops.[16]

The transition from cattle raising to agriculture as the pre-

days ago and the damage they have done to cotton is immense. Not
a leaf is to be seen on a cotton stalk in this county. A large portion
of the bolls, especially those not opened, have been eaten off. Trees
and weeds have been stripped of their foliage, dry corn stalks not
escaping the hungry pests. Tuesday last, they were moving north from
whence they came, flying in such myriads as to resemble white clouds
beneath the sun."

[13] *Albany News,* May 30, 1884.
[14] *Ballinger Bulletin,* November 21, 1887.
[15] *Taylor County News,* November 28, 1887.
[16] For the effects of the more serious drouths, see Chapter VII.

dominant industry was slow. The length of time necessary for a locality to pass from one stage to the other was from ten to twenty years. The settler, by buying the land in small tracts and fencing it, pushed the cattleman westward. He raised a few cattle, perhaps some sheep, planted a field of feedstuffs, corn, sorghum cane, and later, kaffir corn and milo maize. As the

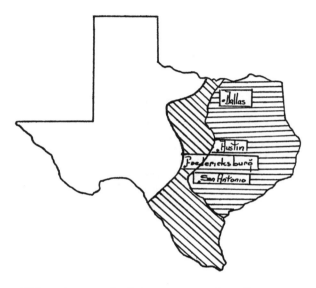

🌾 1 to 10,000 bushels per 1000 square miles.
🟰 More than 10,000 bushels per 1000 square miles.

DISTRIBUTION OF GRAIN FOR 1860.

(Based on Federal Census, 1860.)

years passed his fields tended to become larger and his herd of cattle and his flock of sheep smaller.

The advance of the grain (corn, wheat, and oats) frontier across West Texas is fairly indicative of the westward movement of the farmer. A small amount of grain was grown in the extreme eastern part of the area before 1850. During the next ten years the grain frontier moved from seventy-five to one hundred miles west. In 1870, it was practically where it was in

1860, but the intensity of production within the settlements had made a marked increase; 2,360,514 bushels were raised in 1870 compared with 343,621 bushels in 1860. In the decade, 1870-1880, the grain frontier underwent a tremendous change, especially in the southwest. The territorial expansion for the period was decidedly out of proportion to the intensity of the amount of

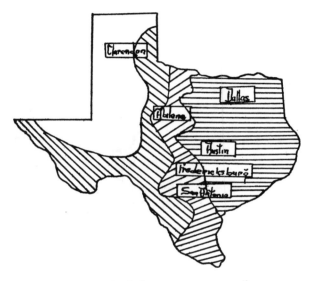

    1 to 10,000 bushels per 1000 square miles.

    10,000 to 100,000 bushels per 1000 square miles.

    More than 100,000 bushels per 1000 square miles.

DISTRIBUTION OF GRAIN FOR 1880.

(Based on Federal Census, 1880.)

grain raised. The production for the year 1880 was 6,205,344 bushles, an increase of less than threefold over 1870. During the next decade the grain frontier vanished. By 1890 some grain was being raised in all the arable sections of the state. Extensive cultivation had begun along the eastern edge of the plains. Notwithstanding the setback occasioned by the drouth of 1886, production increased fourfold during the ten years. The settlement

of the country and the opening of new farms continued steadily
through the decade, 1890-1900.   The production at the end of
the period was 40,238,000 bushels as compared with 28,465,534
bushels in 1880.

The one crop which marked the end of the period of transition and the beginning of the supremacy of agriculture was cotton.   It was the chief money crop, and after the cotton frontier

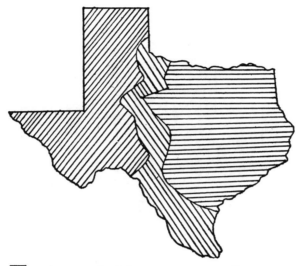

    1 to 10,000 bushels per 1000 square miles.

    10,000 to 100,000 bushels per 1000 square miles.

    More than 100,000 bushels per 1000 square miles.

DISTRIBUTION OF GRAIN FOR 1890.

(Based on Federal Census, 1890.)

had once reached a given point, the stock farmer, in the course of
a few years, became a cotton farmer, provided the vicinity was at
all adapted to the raising of cotton.

Prior to 1850, no cotton was raised in West Texas.   Between
1850 and 1860, the cotton frontier was pushed westward for a
distance varying from twenty-five miles west of San Antonio to
a hundred miles west of Fort Worth, but cotton raising within

this region was in the experimental stage. The yield did not
average more than fifty bales to the county in 1860. The Civil
War and the Indian depredations of 1866 and 1867 caused the
cotton frontier to loose ground during the next decade. In 1860
188 bales were raised west of the Western Cross timbers compared to eighty-seven bales in 1870. West Texas as a whole
made a gain during the decade; 879 bales were reported in 1860,

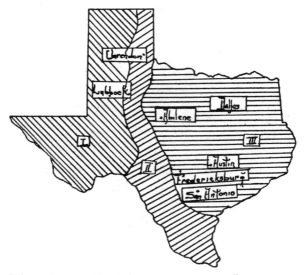

▨ 1 to 10,000 bushels per 1000 square miles.

▨ 10,000 to 100,000 bushels per 1000 square miles.

▤ More than 100,000 bushels per 1000 square miles.

DISTRIBUTION OF GRAIN FOR 1900.

(Based on Federal Census, 1900.)

and 6878 in 1870. The climatic conditions of the two years were
about the same. The increase was in the tier of counties between
Blanco and Denton counties. In these counties cotton had
become the predominant money crop.

The cotton frontier advanced slowly between 1870 and 1875,
but beginning in 1875 it gained a momentum which it never lost
until it had swept across the entire state. During the decade of

1870-1880, it moved about a hundred miles in the northwestern and about twenty-five miles in the southeastern parts of the state. By 1876, a few gins had been built in the tier of counties between Bandera and Clay Counties. The gins stimulated production. The cotton had to be hauled to the railroad points of Fort Worth, Austin, or San Antonio. A farmer could haul three bales of

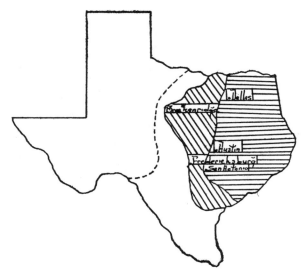

‒ ‒ ‒   Frontier of extreme settlements.

1 to 50 bales to 1000 square miles.

More than 50 bales to 1000 square miles.

DISTRIBUTION OF COTTON FOR 1860.

(Based on Federal Census, 1860.)

ginned cotton as easily as he could haul one bale of seed cotton.[17] Total production increased from 6878 in 1870 to 79,181 in 1880.

[17] Fort Worth was the biggest cotton market of West Texas between 1875 and 1878, when the Texas and Pacific extended to Weatherford; 18,201 bales were hauled there in 1877 and 44,004 in 1878.—*Frontier Echo*, September 13, 1878.

The decade, 1880-1890, witnessed a great advance of the
cotton frontier as well as increase in total production. The average
advance was about one hundred miles. The production in 1890 was
250,452 bales.[18]   The phenomenal increase was due to railroad
transportation.   With railroad facilities nearer at hand, the stock
farmers regarded cotton culture more seriously, notwithstanding

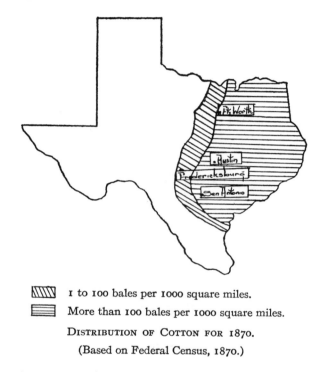

⫷⫷⫷⫷ 1 to 100 bales per 1000 square miles.
▤▤▤ More than 100 bales per 1000 square miles.

DISTRIBUTION OF COTTON FOR 1870.

(Based on Federal Census, 1870.)

the fact that many of them west of the Western Cross timbers
were still skeptical as to whether cotton could ever be grown
there profitably.[19]   The greater part of the development of the

[18] Both years were normal in respect to climatic conditions.

[19] The *Fort Griffin Echo*, February 21, 1880, expressed a majority opinion
in the following item:

"The subject of raising cotton is being agitated by a number of our
farmers who believe the staple has never been tried in this county

decade came in the last three years. Very little cotton was raised in 1885, practically none in 1886, and the yield was less than normal in 1887. Abilene shipped 2061 bales in 1888 and 10,000 bales the next year.[20] In September, 1888, the first bale ever ginned west of Abilene was sold at Sweetwater.[21] Two

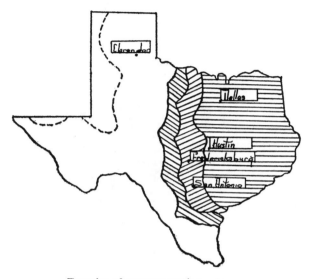

```
----    Frontier of extreme settlements.
▨▨▨     1 to 100 bales per 1000 square miles.
▨▨▨     100 to 1000 bales per 1000 square miles.
▤▤▤     More than 1000 bales per 1000 square miles.
```

DISTRIBUTION OF COTTON FOR 1880.

(Based on Federal Census, 1880.)

years later more than 5000 bales were shipped from the various railroad stations between Abilene and Big Spring.[22]

and it would be well for those who do engage in it to place their reliance on other crops until they can thoroughly test the adaptability of our soil for this crop."

[20] *Taylor County News,* May 17, 1889; *Ballinger Leader,* May 2, 1890.
[21] *Taylor County News,* September 28, 1888.
[22] *Ibid.,* January 23, 1891.

During the next decade, 1890-1900, the cotton frontier practically disappeared. By 1900 a little cotton was being raised everywhere that the soil and climate permitted. East of the caprock of the plains the farmers were relying on cotton as the main money crop. The plains region was still primarily a cattle country, but a few small patches of cotton were to be found, widely

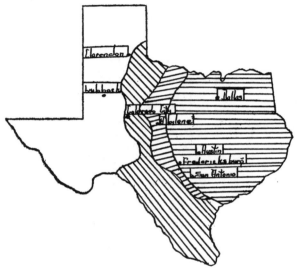

▨ 1 to 100 bales per 1000 square miles.

▨ 100 to 1000 bales per 1000 square miles.

▤ More than 1000 bales per 1000 square miles.

DISTRIBUTION OF COTTON FOR 1890.

(Based on Federal Census, 1890.)

scattered, over the entire area. The increase in production during the period was not as great as might be expected.[23] The year,

[23] The price of cotton may have had something to do with the greater proportional increase in cotton production for the decade, 1880-1890, than in the following decade. Between 1880 and 1890 the average price of cotton was about ten cents a pound; between 1890 and 1900, it was less than eight cents a pound.

1900, brought a production of 354,446 bales, which was an increase of 104,000 bales over 1880; whereas 1890 had an increase of 141,271. By 1900 agriculture may be said to have been paramount as far west as the 101st meridian.

Pecan raising received a marked stimulus as a result of the drouth of 1886. Pecan trees grew along the courses of practically all the streams east of the 100th meridian. No pecans were raised in 1886, but the following year there was an excellent pecan crop. The field crops were short that year. The pecans were gathered, and in some counties, brought more money than the cotton, wheat, and oats combined.[24] This fact made a profound impression on the people, since the crop came at a time when money was needed so badly. The idea became general that pecans had drouth-resisting qualities. For the next three years there was a great amount of agitation in the newspapers; the people were urged to care for, cultivate, and improve the trees they already had, and to plant pecan orchards.[25] One enthusiast, a citizen of Brown County, planted four hundred acres in pecans in 1890.[26] After a time, interest in the pecan business waned and no more was heard of it. Good pecan crops continued to be made every few years, but the people ceased to think of pecans as a substitute for cotton as a regular money crop.

When Hank Smith migrated to Blanco Canyon in 1878, he found hundreds of acres of a kind of wild currant growing there. The currants were blue-black in color and many of them were as large as small marbles. In 1880 Smith decided to commercialize the currant business. He sent a box of the fruit with his compliments to each of the several newspaper editors to the east. They gave the matter wide publicity, and for the next several months advertisements appeared saying that Smith would furnish roots of the vine in any quantity desired. After a few months the currant business dropped from sight.[27]

[24] *Albany News,* November 24, 1887.
[25] *Taylor County News,* November 22, 1889.
[26] *Ballinger Leader,* August 29, 1890.
[27] *Fort Griffin Echo,* September 11, 1880.

By 1889 considerable interest was being manifested in fruit trees.[28] The fruit tree agent was busy, visiting every farm house in the country, on horseback or in his buggy, and showing the farmer and his family large, wonderfully colored pictures of this juicy peach and that delicious apple. Almost every farmer, after he settled in West Texas, bought a number of trees and attempted to start an orchard. His efforts came to naught far oftener than they succeeded. The soil of the greater part of West Texas was not adapted to the raising of any kind of trees other than the native mesquite. Orchards could be successfully grown only in those communities which had a deep sandy soil.

The planting of Johnson grass became widespread during the 80's and 90's.[29] The plant was hardy and had excellent drouth-resisting qualities. It matured quickly and made good hay. Once started, it was next to impossible to get rid of it. The more one would plow, harrow, and break its roots, the thicker it would grow and the more it would spread. Although the farm journals warned the farmers not to plant it, the merchants continued to ship the seed in by the carload, and the farmers continued to sow it. The farmers of East Texas began petitioning the Legislature in the late 80's to pass a law making the sowing of Johnson grass illegal. Finally an act was passed in 1897 forbidding the sowing, selling, transportation,, or feeding of the grass. The press in West Texas vigorously denounced the measure. Local opinion was strongly against the law, and it could never be enforced.[30] The farmers kept on planting Johnson grass, much to their later chagrin.

The low price of cotton from 1890 to 1900 caused newspapers, farm journals, and public spirited persons to carry on a never-ending campaign for diversification. The farmers were urged to take up stock raising again as a complement to cotton raising, but cotton has always been truly "king." Once he invades a new country and becomes established, he will tolerate

[28] *Albany News,* February 21, 1889.
[29] *Albany News,* September 8, 1883.
[30] *Taylor County News,* March 19, 1897.

no rivals. A farmer who raises cotton is loath to give it up, even though he is aware that he is courting financial ruin.

An effort was made to get the people to take up bee tending. A number of farmers did try it half-heartedly. Several bee raisers' associations were organized. Their existence was brief; conditions for bees were generally unfavorable in West Texas with the exception of a district in the southwest in the vicinity of Uvalde County. The farmers' wives were urged, with appreciable results, to do extensive canning of fruits and vegetables. The culture of castor beans was recommended. In 1889 some authority on agricultural panaceas advanced the idea that broom corn would be the farmer's salvation. The newspapers took it up. Wonderful tales were related of its drouth-resisting qualities, of immense yields of broom straw as a money crop, how the plant produced as much forage as sorghum cane, and how from $20 to $40 worth of seed per acre could be threshed from the heads.[31] A few farmers tried a small patch of broom corn, but for various reasons found they had better stick to cotton. During the unusually favorable seasons of 1890 and 1891, a number of ingenious local editors advised their readers to plant tobacco as an experimental crop. A number did try it, but neither the soil nor the climate were adapted to its growth.[32]

A noticeable thing about the diversification campaigns of the decade, 1890-1900, was that no one suggested hog raising. People raised hogs for domestic purposes, but nobody advised hog raising as a source of money returns. The silence on this subject is problematical. Perhaps it was due to a general idea that hog raising belonged to a timbered country where a heavy mast was available. It is true that the price of hogs during the period was low, but, compared with cheap cotton, they might have been profitably raised, especially during years when a surplus feed crop was made.

The West Texas farmer had one trait which he usually acquired after his arrival in the country, and a trait which his

[31] *Wichita Falls Sentinel,* August 30, 1889.
[32] *Taylor County News,* August 7, 1891.

eastern brother did not have,—an aversion for all kinds of walking farm implements.   When he migrated to the west he
carried with him, as a rule, the farm tools he had previously
used, which consisted of a walking turning plow, a walking
planter, and a walking cultivator.   He had scarcely arrived when
he began to develop a strong dislike for walking.   The reasons
were twofold.   In the first place, an aversion for walking is an
indigenous trait of the country.   The plains Indians, especially
the Comanches, had a profound contempt for walking as a
means of locomotion.   A Comanche off of his horse was indeed
an awkward sight.   The cowboy had an uncanny endurance as
long as he was on horseback.   He could stay in the saddle for
days and nights at a time under the most strenuous circumstances, but to ask him to walk for an hour, even when he was
fresh and rested, was the surest way to break down his morale.
When the farmer arrived he found the same natural influences
silently working on him.   In the second place, the amount of
ground one man could cultivate in West Texas was so much
greater than that one man could till in a country where stumps,
rocks, and grass prevailed, that much more walking was necessary for the requisite amount of plowing and cultivation.   The
result was that the newcomer, as soon as possible, exchanged his
turning plow for a sulky plow, his walking planter for a riding
planter, and his walking cultivator for a riding cultivator.

A method of dry land farming gradually developed.   The
average settler had a profound contempt for scientific farming,
"book farming" as he called it; after experiencing a few dry
spells, he developed a system of his own.   He seldom deliberately
carried on experimentation; but he learned much from his neighbors, and made the most of his own successes and failures.   The
fundamental principles of dry land farming were simple.   It
stood to reason that if in an average year there would be a
limited amount of rainfall, two things must be done.   First, the
soil must be cultivated in such a way as to catch and retain the
greatest amount of moisture; second, crops must be planted
which had the most powerful drouth-resisting qualities.   Both

reason and experience taught that the land should be broken deep early in the season in order to catch the winter rains. If the crops were planted as early as possible in the spring, it would tend to enable the plants to mature before the extremely hot weather of mid-summer. It was possible to plant feed crops late in the summer. They could then get their growth in the cooler weather of early fall. In either case the fields had to be cultivated frequently in order to keep a loose mulch on the surface of the ground. The mulch broke up the capillary action in the ground, and made it possible to retain the greatest amount of moisture for the use of the plants. Milo maize and kaffir corn came in time to be recognized as having drouth-resisting qualities. In the later years they almost entirely replaced corn as a feed crop. Certain types of sorghum cane and cotton plants were found to be better adapted to dry weather than other types.

The settlers who migrated to West Texas during the period when agriculture was replacing cattle raising as the leading industry witnessed an exciting, colorful, picturesque, and, in earlier times, dangerous period of history. They saw the Indian sullenly retiring to his reservation, and the cattleman doggedly retreating to the arid region of extreme southwest Texas and New Mexico. They watched the last cattle drives go up the trail and endured with dull fortitude the blighting effects of the West Texas drouths. They awaited the coming of the railroads with fervent expectancy, and enthusiastically talked about imaginative mineral deposits. They danced, ran horse races, drank strong liquor, went to camp meetings, got religion, became prohibitionists, and were content with their home-made amusements. Meanwhile, agriculture was slowly becoming supreme.

AFTERWORD

William Curry Holden's view of his homeland, West Texas, brought to life in *Alkali Trails*, was a preview of its culture today, and the forerunner of a new concept in recording history. It focuses not on important people, but the activities and viewpoints of the immigrants to West Texas. This pattern set by Curry has been embraced by succeeding generations including his students and many other writers. What gives it authenticity is that it reflects the people he knew at that time and the tales they told him.

Anyone who looks at the holdings of the Southwest Collection of the Library of Texas Tech University will see an outgrowth of literature originating to a great extent from *Alkali Trails*. It all began in 1929 with the ranch records Curry hauled in the trunk of his old Model T Ford. Just glancing at the shelves of volumes, one finds extensive information on the cattle industry, immigration and settlement, mineral wealth, railroads, farming and the social interrelationships that built West Texas.

Footnotes in the volumes frequently reflect their origins from newspaper accounts. They undoubtedly came from the newspapers he asked his earliest college students to bring from their home towns. With these papers he created what he called the History Factory at McMurry College in Abilene, Texas. History was not just a vocation with Curry but an all consuming interest with family, friends, and colleagues—a part of his daily life.

Alkali Trails was an increasingly important account of early settlement, which was a part of Curry's own life. His family, parents, and grandparents were part of the

247

early migration from the older states to settle up the promised "free land" in Texas. With the approval of his doctoral dissertation in 1928, later published as *Alkali Trails*, Curry Holden earned his doctorate in History from the University of Texas at Austin, and also the respect of his professor and mentor, Eugene C. Barker, and of Professor J. Frank Dobie. His contemporary historians and authors took a fresh look at their characters and filled the pages of their historical novels and short stories with characters similar to Holden's. *Alkali Trails* and succeeding books written by William Curry Holden continue to be read not only by researchers and historians but by also those readers who love the "true stories" of the early West.

Frances M. Holden

INDEX

Abilene, the "Wind City," 140, 214
Adobe walls, 12
Advertising, newspaper, 92–96
Agriculture
  cattlemen's opposition to, 229–231
  climate unfavorable to, 229
  diversifications campaigns of the 90's, 242
  drouths delay advance of, 232
  dry-land farming, 244, 245
  grain frontier, 1850–1890, 233–235
  handicaps to agriculture in West Texas summarized, 227
  Indian menace, 228
  pests, 231–232
  transition from stock raising to farming, 233
  (*See also* names of special crops)
Albany, 60, 195
Almonte, 21
Amusements
  baseball clubs, 178
  bicycle clubs, 178
  brass bands, 179
  Christmas trees, 179
  churches as social centers, 175
  circuses, 184
  dramatic clubs, 182
  drinking, 173–174
  effects of religion on, 175
  fighting, 173–174
  fraternal orders, 176
  gun clubs, 178
  Lazy Man's Clubs, 176
  literary societies, 182
  military companies, 177
  parties, 179–180
  picnics, 184
  quilting bees, 180

Amusements
  raffles, 174
  road shows, 184
  school entertainments, 179
  singing classes, 181
  singing conventions, 181
  singing schools, 181
  volunteer fire companies, 177
Animals, predatory, 46
Anti-Texas Cattle Act, 27
Archaeological remains, 1
Archer City and the Rock Island controversy, 207, 208

Bands, *see* Amusements
Barbed wire, introduction of, 48
Barton, Miss Clara, reports to Red Cross on drouth relief, 1887, 145
Bee raisers' associations, 243
Bee-tending encouraged, 243
Belle Plains, 60, 187
Ben Ficklin, struggle of, with San Angelo, 69–70
Bison, *see* Buffalo
Blanco Canyon Quakers find well water, 49
Bounties, for predatory animals, 46
Boy Scout District, 33
Broom corn, 243
Brown, Rev. John, works for drouth relief, 142–143
Buffalo
  bone industry, 15–18
  characteristics of, 6
  dependence of Indian on, 5
  extent of area of, 5
  freighters, 14
  hides, 10, 12